War in
African Literature Today
26

African Literature Today

1-14 were published from London by Heinemann Educational Books and from New York by Africana Publishing Company

Backlist titles available in the US and Canada from Africa World Press and in the rest of the world from James Currey, an imprint of Boydell and Brewer

Note from the publisher on new and forthcoming titles

James Currey Publishers have now joined Boydell & Brewer Ltd. *African Literature Today* will continue to be published as an annual volume under the James Currey imprint. North and South American distribution will be available from The University of Rochester Press, 68 Mount Hope Avenue, Rochester, NY 14620-2731, USA, while UK and International distribution will be handled by Boydell & Brewer Ltd., PO Box 9, Woodbridge IP12, 3DF, UK.

Guidelines for Submission of Articles

The Editor invites submission of articles or proposals for articles on the announced themes of forthcoming issues:

Ernest N. Emenyonu, *African Literature Today*
Department of Africana Studies, University of Michigan-Flint
303 East Kearsley Street, Flint MI 48502, USA
email: eernest@umflint.edu
Fax: 001 810 766 6719

Submissions will be acknowledged promptly and decisions communicated within six months of the receipt of the paper. Your name and institutional affiliation (with full mailing address and email) should appear on a separate sheet, plus a brief biographical profile of not more than six lines. The editor cannot undertake to return material submitted and contributors are advised to keep a copy of all material sent. Please note that all articles outside the announced themes cannot be considered or acknowledged and that articles should not be submitted via email. Articles should be submitted in the English language.

Length: articles should not exceed 5,000 words

Format: two hard copies plus disk of all articles should be submitted, double-spaced, on one side only of A4 paper, with pages numbered consecutively. Disks may be formatted for PC or AppleMac but please label all files and disks clearly, and save files as Word for Windows or Word for Macintosh.

Style: UK or US spellings, but be consistent. Direct quotations should retain the spelling used in the original source. Check the accuracy of your citations and always give the source, date, and page number in the text and a full reference in the Works Cited at the end of the article. Italicise titles of books or plays. Use single inverted commas throughout except for quotes within quotes which are double. Avoid subtitles or subsection headings within the text.

References: to follow series style (Surname date: page number) in brackets in text. All references/works cited should be listed in full at the end of each article, in the following style:
Surname, name/initial. *title of work*. place, publisher, date
Surname, name/initial. 'title of article'. In surname, name/initial (ed.)
title of work. place of publication, publisher, date
or Surname, name/initial, 'title of article', *Journal*, vol. no.: page no.

Copyright: it is the responsibility of contributors to clear permissions

Reviewers should provide full bibliographic details, including the extent, ISBN and price, and submit to the reviews editor
James Gibbs, 8 Victoria Square, Bristol BS8 4ET
jamesgibbs@btinternet.com

War in
African Literature Today
26

A Review

Editor:	Ernest N. Emenyonu
Deputy Editor:	Nana Wilson-Tagoe
Assistant Editor:	Patricia T. Emenyonu

Associate Editors:	Francis Imbuga
	Emmanuel Ngara
	Charles E. Nnolim
	Ato Quayson
	Kwawisi Tekpetey
	Iniobong I. Uko

Reviews Editor:	James Gibbs

JAMES CURREY

HEBN

James Currey www.jamescurrey.co.uk
is an imprint of Boydell & Brewer Ltd
PO Box 9, Woodbridge, Suffolk, IP12 3DF, UK
www.boydell.co.uk
and of Boydell & Brewer Inc.
668 Mt Hope Avenue, Rochester, NY 14620, USA
www.boydellandbrewer.com

HEBN Publishers Plc
1 Ighodaro Rd, Jericho
P.M.B. 5205, Ibadan, Nigeria
www.hebnpublishers.com

1 2 3 4 5 12 11 10 09 08

British Library Cataloguing in Publication Data
War in African in literature today : a review. - (African
   literature today ; 26)
      1. African literature - 21st century - History and
      criticism 2. African literature - 20th century - History
      and criticism 3. War in literature
      I. Emenyonu, Ernest, 1939-
      809.8'896

ISBN: 978-0-85255-571-2 (James Currey paper)
ISBN 978-978-081-314-7 (HEBN paper)

Typeset in 9/11 pt Melior by Long House Publishing Services, Cumbria, UK
Printed and bound in Great Britain by CPI Antony Rowe, Chippenham, Wiltshire

Contents

Notes on Contributors

Isidore Diala is currently Head of the Department of English, Imo State University, Owerri, Nigeria. His articles on African Literature have appeared in journals and anthologies in Africa, Europe and the United States. He is the author of *The Responsible Critic: Essays on African Literature in Honor of Professor Ben Obumselu* (2006).

Oike Machiko is an Assistant Professor at Hiroshima University, Japan. She gained her PhD in comparative literature from Ochanomizu University in 1999, focusing on the works of Buchi Emecheta and Chinua Achebe.

Christine Matzke teaches African Literature and Theatre at the Institute of Asian and African Studies, Humboldt-University at Berlin. A graduate of the Workshop Theatre, University of Leeds, she specializes in Eritrean performing arts and has recently started to research African crime fiction.

Zoe Norridge is a PhD student currently researching pain narratives in contemporary African novels at the School of Oriental and African Studies, London University. She has published articles on Yvonne Vera's *The Stone Virgins* and Holocaust legacies in Southern African literature.

Chimalum Nwankwo is Professor and Chair, Department of English, North Carolina State University, Greensboro, North Carolina. USA. An award-winning poet, he has published several collections of poetry. He was the recipient of the Association of Nigerian Authors 2002 Poetry Prize.

Sophie Obiajulu Ogwude is a Professor of English in the General Studies Division, Federal University of Technology, Owerri, Nigeria. Her articles on African Literature have appeared in several journals in Africa, Europe and the United States.

Clement A. Okafor is a Professor of English at the University of Maryland Eastern Shore, USA. He has published widely in the area of African Literature in journals in Africa, Europe and the United States.

Ogaga Okuyade teaches in the Department of English, College of Education, Warri, Delta State, Nigeria.

Maurice Taonezvi Vambe is a Senior Lecturer at the University of South Africa in the Institute for Curriculum and Learning Development (ICLD). He is the author of *African Oral Story Telling Tradition and the Zimbabwean Novel in English* (2004), co-edited *Charles Mungoshi: A Critical Reader* (2006) and has written numerous articles on Zimbabwean Literature and African Literature. He has coedited and published with Abebe Zegeye a Special Issue on *Reimagining Africa* in *African Identities* (April 2007).

Iniobong I. Uko is currently the Head of the Department of English, University of Uyo, Nigeria. Her research interests are African and African American Literatures, and Women's Studies in which she has published several journal articles. She is the author of *Gender and Identity in the Works of Osonye Tess Onwueme* (2004).

Ernest N. Emenyonu

In an excellent introduction to his anthology, *A Harvest From Tragedy: Critical Perspectives on Nigerian Civil War Literature* (an important text which deserves more exposure and circulation than it has so far received), Chinyere Nwahunanya (1997), using the Nigerian civil war as premise, highlights the cumulative value of the corpus of literature inspired by war and its concomitant catastrophes on geo-political African realities. He states:

> In its re-creation and interpretation of history, Nigerian war literature has enriched the existing body of historical writing from Africa, especially historical fiction. In this way, the writers have made literature continue to function as the mirror of society. In the process of mirroring society and criticizing its pitfalls, the war literature also serves as a compass for social re-direction. A didactic function emerges in the process, especially in the portrayal of death, devastation, avoidable mistakes and sufferings engendered by the war. The ultimate intention of course is to see whether these records of a sour historical moment will enable the modern African to see the futility of wars as a solution to national problems which could be solved without a recourse to war, carnage and bloodshed. The suggested mistakes of the war initiators and administrators portrayed in these writings thus become invaluable guides to meaningful national growth and a stable and progressive society. If this lesson comes through, then African nations (and indeed the world) would have gained immensely from this harvest of tragedy. (14)

All through history, creative writers and historians have been known to bring their imaginative visions and critical skills to bear on the important events in the history of their people. Historians and literary artists of each era base their discourse and postulations on particular wars but their implicit philosophical inquiries point to a range of universal dilemmas – *Why are wars fought? Do wars achieve their declared initial objectives? Is war the ultimate solution to a human crisis at a point in time? Who benefits from war? Who are the toads of war? Who are the innocent victims of war? Is war inevitable in a human society?* Each writer approaches each of these questions from a chosen perspective and proffers answers intrinsically embedded in character types, narrative structures and patterns of conflict resolution. Seen from this angle, the discourse, whether histori-cal or imaginary, invariably translates into a didactic inquiry.

The creative writer – novelist, poet, playwright, or short story writer – who draws inspiration and themes from war situations, has other chal-lenges to confront. The imaginative work (a by-product of war), must still meet certain known aesthetic and critical standards by which it should be judged as a work of art. Its relevance, authenticity, integrity and accep-tance would ultimately depend not only on how convincingly the author has portrayed the unique human conditions brought about by war, but also on how the author handled the act of balancing emotional impulses and loyalty to art as a sacred entity. It is easy for a creative writer to stray away or be derailed from objective artistic visions because of partisan or passionate involvement in a *cause*. When this happens, the work could degenerate to running commentaries and propaganda. Artists do not create in a vacuum. They can, and do take positions on the serious political and social issues of their times, but this should be done in a manner that does not compromise the integrity of either the artist or the created piece. This is a challenge which some of the African writers must fully overcome in their sensitive war-inspired imaginative writings.

Chinua Achebe has defended in a compelling way, the desirability of contemporary African writers to be outspoken on the big political and social issues facing the continent, and share in the hopes and aspirations of their communities. In his classic article, 'The African Writer and the Biafran Cause' (1975), Achebe recaptures this theory of commitment with an enchanting imagery:

> It is clear to me that an African creative writer who tries to avoid the big social and political issues of contemporary Africa will end up being completely irrel-evant – like that absurd man in the proverb who leaves his burning house to pursue a rat fleeing from the flames. (78)

And on his active role on the secessionist Biafran side during the Nigerian civil war, he maintains:

> The involvement of the Biafran writer ... in the cause for which his people are fighting and dying is not different from the involvement of many African writers – past and present – in the big issues of Africa. The fact of the war merely puts the matter in sharper focus. (78)

This issue of *African Literature Today* on 'War in African Literature' embodies the findings of various studies on environments of war, the con-sequences of war, the role of the writer as a historical witness, the lessons that can be learned from the devastations of war (intended and unin-tended). It also includes discourses on how African writers have handled the recreation of war as a cataclysmic phenomenon in specific locations. *Have fictionalized representations demonstrated equitable balances between socio-political messages and the medium of conveyance?*

The authors of the ten articles in the volume have explored the subject of war in African literature from a variety of perspectives – panoramic, regional, individual case studies, and comparative analysis of identified artistic visions and literary techniques.

In the lead article, 'The Muted Index of War in African Literature and Society', Chimalum Nwankwo analyzes the handling of the theme of war across genres and geographical boundaries to show the monumental impact on both the human condition in Africa, and imaginative literature as an intellectual and cultural activity. He contends that the war literature deserves more serious attention than it has received so far. He argues that

> War is Africa's muted index ... The index could guide the insightful reader toward the foundations of Africa's numerous perennial or still unfolding tragedies. Clearly, the most quotidian of Africa's problems, ranging from human rights to various cultural, political, and socio-economic issues appear either related or traceable to a long and turbulent history of wars and their unsavory aftermath. (13)

Christine Matzke in her 'Life in the Camp of the Enemy: Alemseged Tesfai's Theatre of War', examines the use of drama and its performance (as propaganda) to boost the morale of people during the Eritrean liberation struggle against Ethiopia from 1961 to 1991. The focus is on the artistry, theatrical devices, and innovations of the premier playwright of the era Alemseged Tesfai, and analysis of relevant plays.

In her 'Of War and Madness: A Symbolic Transmutation of the Nigeria-Biafra War in Select Stories...' , Ini Uko studies the depictions of the war debacle in the short story genre using the first published work of fiction on the civil war, *The Insider: Stories of War and Peace from Nigeria* (1971). The focus is on the 'unraveling of the symbols in the relevant stories as a way of, first , explaining the relationship between the civil war in Nigeria and madness, and second, evolving a vision for the future of Nigeria.' She concludes,

> Technically, the kinetic imagery in this collection of stories ... translates symbolically into Nigeria's journey towards a true and authentic nationhood in spite of its diverse constituting ethnic groups and interests. The stories stress that as long as the Nigerian civil war remains a potent source of outrage, inter-ethnic hatred, discrimination, and intense nepotism, the bogey of insanity will remain among Nigerians, and the proper healing and development of the brutalized Nigerian mind and spirit, as well as the land, will continue to be an illusion.'

Oike Machiko in 'Becoming a Feminist Writer: Representation of the Subaltern in Buchi Emecheta's *Destination Biafra*', takes the position that 'studies of Biafran war literature have been male-focused .... works by women writers have not been paid serious critical attention ...' (60) She uses the novel, *Destination Biafra,* to demonstrate the dramatization of the complex problems of representing subaltern women in a war situation. Machiko perceives the novel as a serious feminist work (different from earlier works by women writers which were mere 'fictional autobiographical sketches'). She argues that fictionality distinguishes the text,

Destination Biafra, from others, and is doubly focused by its 'meta-fictional characteristics'.

Maurice Taonezvi Vambe, in his 'Problems of Representing the Zim-babwe War of Liberation in *The Contact, Pawns,* and *The Stone Virgins,* uses evidence from critical texts as well as imaginative fiction to discuss the complexities of fictionalizing the Zimbabwean war episodes and experiences.

Clement Okafor ('Sacrifice and the Contestation of Identity in Chukwuemeka Ike's *Sunset at Dawn'*), Sophie Ogwude ('Politics and Human Rights in Non-Fiction Prison Literature'), Zoe Norridge ('The Need to Go Further?: Dedication and Distance in the War Narratives of Alexandra Fuller and Alexander Kanengoni'), Isidore Diala ('History, Memoir and a Soldier's Conscience: Philip Efiong's *Nigeria and Biafra: My Story'*), and Ogaga Okuyade ('Of the Versification of Pain: Nigerian Civil War Poetry'), individually and collectively enrich the volume by the diversity and versatility of their explorations as well as the scope and vitality of their representative discourses and findings.

The literature of war has enriched contemporary African Literature both in the quantity and quality of output. Elsewhere (1995), I had discussed the findings of my studies on the vibrant and prolific represen-tations (in fiction and memoir), of the Nigerian Civil War and its aftermath, in the first two decades after the war. It was evident from those studies that

> where the commitment in political terms overwhelms the artistic vision, as has been the case with many of the novels so far produced on the Nigerian Civil War, the writer comes out with less than his/her artistic best. In the present cir-cumstances, the Nigerian writers on the war must allow a reasonable period of time to lapse before they can objectively write about the war, no longer as active combatants in the conflicts, but as writers who bring their imaginative vision to bear on the important events in the history of their people. Such works are likely to be more aesthetically pleasing and artistically rewarding than the skills demonstrated in the books examined in the study. *The great Nigerian war novel is yet to be written.'*(458)

This might prove to be as true about the war novel in Africa in general, as it is about the war novel in Nigeria in particular.

WORKS CITED

Achebe, Chinua. 'The African Writer and the Biafran Cause'. *Morning Yet on Creation Day: Essays.* London: Heinemann, 1975.

Emenyonu, Ernest. 'Visions of the Nigerian Writer on the Nigerian Civil War'. In Thumbo, Edwin & Kandiah, Thiru (eds) *The Writer as Historical Witness: Studies in Commonwealth Literature.* Singapore: Unit Press, 1995.

Nwahunanya, Chinyere (ed.) *A Harvest From Tragedy: Critical Perspectives on Nigerian Civil War Literature.* Owerri, Nigeria: Springfield Publishers, 1997.

The Muted Index of War in African Literature & Society

Chimalum Nwankwo

The impact of war on the human condition in African literature and society has not been taken as seriously as it deserves. It is now becoming, like the study of the colonial experience, a terribly repugnant exercise in which sometimes America is also studied and classified along with post-colonial Africa as a post-colonial subject. Thus, in contemplating Africa's wars, the cost of war in both impalpable and palpable human terms is wrapped in the wool of fanciful and fashionable paradigms, literary exercises better suited for the full-belly faddish reflections of blasé coteries of the metropolis. This attitude or inclination is responsible for the shoddy and haphazard diagnosis of the ills of the African continent. It blights the efforts of governments and distorts the projects of governance. No matter how well-meaning a rescue might be, certainly, it is clear in all circumstances that a problem must first be recognized and understood before one begins to proffer solutions. Many African poets and novelists are engaged in that enterprise.

The quiet agony of imperial humiliation left the new generation of African leaders and many new-breed post-colonial intellectuals who stepped into the master's shoes in a giddy Manichean desire to be like the master. It is there in the diffident preferences for all things foreign, from the character of infrastructural development to even the basic food the so-called educated Africans eat, from the most shameless malfeasance to the disgraceful gaps yawning between the African rich and poor, from the hunt for alien paradigms and hermeneutics by African scholars to the choice of sometimes unnecessary exile. This is colonialism still at work, expressed in what some Africans scornfully call 'colonial mentality', a confusion of abuse for a bullish ex-master and the disparaging of the befuddled indigenous replacement who disdains his own cultural base. To understand the gravity of this problem, it is necessary to classify the experience as part of the phenomenon called 'identity crisis'.

Most so-called educated Africans are still sorely afflicted with identity crises. One needs this kind of preparatory reflection and awareness to understand the impact of wars on the human condition in Africa. If colonialism was quiet, the wars which came at the heels of colonialism or in some cases with colonialism were not quiet and did more deleterious damage. African writers have followed the pulse of the continent and chronicled the historical event and upheaval simply and persistently, quite often with great candor, directness, simplicity, and in many cases an inventiveness which does not lose sight of the prize, to remain, as in much of traditional Africa, the last moral bastion of the people.

Contemplate this roll call. South Africa. Congo. Angola. Algeria. Rwanda. Mozambique. Uganda. Tanzania. Namibia. Kenya. Nigeria. Liberia. Sierra Leone. Chad. Zimbabwe. Liberia. Sudan. Eritrea. Ethiopia. Ivory Coast... The list of recent turbulent histories goes on with wars still raging in certain places as we read. Ostensibly, African history, if one may borrow the titles of works by two well-known writers, either trundles with *The Rhythms of Violence* (Lewis Nkosi) or appears perpetually *Bound to Violence* (Yambo Oulouguem). The kind of ethos needed to capture this undesirable index is what we find in the epic sweep of Syl Cheney-Coker's *The Last Harmattan of Alusine Dunbar* and Ben Okri's *The Famished Road*, though the magical and marvellous ambience of those works muffle and transform that ethos into fatalistic and nihilistic messages. *The Famished Road* salvages its own marred epical ethos though by anchoring the societal despair from an insidious and enervating politics in an ontological crisis where the nebulous and the concrete jostle for relevance in a world that has virtually become surreal because of the imponderable gulf between the rulers and the ruled.

There is still much work to be done by African writers for a needed harvest, however grim, which could serve as an index for a more comprehensive study and understanding of the nature of the crises bedeviling the African continent. Even though more specific references will be made to the situations in Zimbabwe and Nigeria for the examples in fiction in this paper, references to poets and poetry in this paper will cover a wider range. The African continent is a continent with a peculiar history and experience, and that peculiarity becomes more intriguing and sometimes almost perplexing as one moves from one region to the other. For instance, I believe that a more careful attention to South African history and politics draws attention to the fact that the country as we know it has been embroiled in one kind of war or the other, in high or low registers, from the arrival of Jan Van Reebek at the cape in 1652 to the final dismantling of apartheid in the early nineties. An understanding of the role of the Zulu nation in the South African space from as far back as Chaka enhances an understanding of South Africa and the volatile formations of its polity. And even after we have done understanding the South African picture, it remains imperative to extend attention to the impact of the dynamics of relationships between the British, the Dutch, the Asians and the various troubled black ethnicities of Southern Africa who constitute the majority population of that entire area. Can we also tell the story of

Southern Africa without extending our knowledge and understanding of the area to the relationship between that history and that of Zambia and Zimbabwe? If land hunger was the *casus belli* in the protracted rivalry between the Dutch and the British in South Africa, the imperial dreams of Cecil Rhodes complicates the history of the area and the consequent suffering of the black nations which continue to pay the price of aboriginality and of land ownership with a chequered history of instability and constant turmoil. Zimbabwe remains a product of the imperial adventurism and warped dream of Cecil Rhodes which began with his Cape to Cairo Pax Britannia project and only peaked with the treacherous deal between Rhodes' British South Africa Company and the Ndebele Chief Lobengula.

The wars which began with Ian Smith's Unilateral Declaration of Independence in 1965 when he wrested power from an equivocating British colonial administration to the present dark clouds of national doubt and questioning and even confusion are still the same war. We might even say that the ghosts of Cecil Rhodes and his diamond explorers and investors are still running crazily all over Zimbabwe in the light of the pretence of Western powers that the high-handed and untidy process of land redistribution by Zimbabwe's President Robert Mugabe has no history behind it. Zimbabwe's contemporary writers, who are amongst some of the world's best fiction writers, in freshness and innovative energy have in the last decade told and re-told these stories of concatenated wars with grace and eloquence and quite significantly in a poetry that frequently touches the sublime. Among these writers and their works, the following stand out: Chenjerai Hove in *Bones* and *Shadows*, and Alexander Kanengoni in *Echoing Silences* and *Effortless Tears*. For the peripatetic consequences of this bloody history, there is of course the moving testimony of Robert Zeleeza's *Exile*. Let me quibble awhile through the titles of the works of these writers and say that the silences of the history of Southern Africa and Zimbabwe are broken most thunderously by the old bones and shadows of a violent African history through the effortless tears of Yvonne Vera, particularly in *Stone Virgins*.

There are echoes of war and references to war in Vera's writings such as *Under the Tongue* and *Butterfly Burning*, but in *Stone Virgins*, she cracks the kernel of history, and the oblique rises to the harrowing in aftermaths that are as potent as the real experience. But this disgorged ugly blood of that history is not supposed to discourage but presumably to inspire. It is the kind of thesis one finds in Toni Morrison's vision. It is a vision which derogates and rejects fixation to past pain and the past itself in favour of the comprehensive and holistic. It is a vision which seeks for a teleological accounting of human action. Life and war become interchangeable analogues in *The Stone Virgins*. The poetry of the recapitulation skips nothing from memory. The villain is culpable but demands our sympathy in guilt, thereby increasing manifold our sympathy for the victim.

In that novel, the African dream is measured by war and conquest. New dreams from a present simultaneously benighted and full of promise search old agonies for light into the future. Human drama is set in times and places where a certain contemporaneity underscores the paradoxical nature of human destiny. A number of examples from the novel will affirm this point.

Opening the *The Stone Virgins* with the modern city of Bulawayo makes many points at once. The historical significance is unmistakable. It is an African city but the legacy and heritage of conquest and imperialism with stamps of a complex identity remain very clear. The streets are named after the master and obviously by the master. In case the issue of cultural supplantation is unclear, the names of poets from the imperial culture concretize that point. And of all the names and naming, Cecil Rhodes is of course included, along with his British South Africa Company. With such strokes we are reminded of the long arm of history. The descriptions also quickly tell the story of class oppression and discrimination. There are places where only the high and mighty enter. The poor can only peep in. And then, the beauty of the city is an exquisite tantalus with its blooming and radiant flowers speaking of all manners of hopes and dreams. The city of Bulawayo is the present, forbidden to some but accessible also to others, but certainly this access is limited. This is the African colony with the power of the colonial master evident in its eerie absence. The master is absent and gone but that absence is potent even without the master's physical presence. That is what makes it a defining paradox. Even though the cleverly historicized text conflates events in the opening portions of the story between 1950 and 1980, the long root of experience goes much further backward in time with echoes of the South African genesis.

When action shifts to Kezi, there is Kezi before the war for vengeance and cleansing. There is also Kezi after the war. Kezi before the war is the rural town of the Africans. These Africans had laboured together in battle to reclaim a heritage and a glory that was to be national independence. The drinking and gathering places are open to all, man and woman. Every spirit glows with the euphoria of victory. Kezi's nerve centre, Thandabantu store, and its proprietor, hold promises of a great future for man and woman.

Like the bridge between past and present, there is a bridge on the road between the city of Bulawayo and Kezi. Like the past and present, there is steady traffic between the city of Bulawayo and Kezi. And like the past and present, both feed from each other, with the present of course being less accessible than the past. Kezi is the point of transition, the crossroads. This is where the Africans have to redefine themselves. This is where they have to answer the questions of readiness for the present and the future. The polysemous symbolism of this section is simplified in the drama of love and by the drama of love between man and woman. The sweetness of love, between Thenjiwe and Cephas Dube will not endure, not yet. The sweetness of the relationship will endure when it is clearly understood by both parties; defined and named and nursed together. And so the seed given to Thenjiwe by Cephas Dube is spat away. Why not? It is as yet a seed named by man and known by man. Knowledge and experience are yet to be had and shared equally by man and woman in this telling reversal of the biblical sharing of the problematic apple in the garden of Eden. This unmediated gap becomes more obvious in the sights from the war when female veterans are in town to take the streets with the jaunty leisure of the men. There is clear evidence that the men of Kezi are uncomfortable with the liberated ease of the women. The men do not yet take into account that these women had also gone through the crucible of war, baptised into a new dispensation through bravery and sacrifice beside their men-folk. It seems that come cleansing time, women will be forced back into the hieroglyph of unfulfilled dreams depicted in the cave of Gulati, into a mythical African past of irrelevance and fruitless sacrifice, back into a virgin stone of silence! A new inter-ethnic war destroys Thandabantu store. It is that war which destroys the promise which placed Kezi and Thandabantu store at the crossroads. That is what is foreshadowed by the murder of Thenjiwe by a war-scarred insurgent. The same war-scarred man cuts off the lips of her sister, Nonceba, after raping her. It does not seem as if men are ready to share the same stage with women. Men still want women without their voices and speech. Kezi is not yet ready for the oblivious modernity which Bulawayo promises.

To understand the entire thesis upon which *The Stone Virgins* rests is understanding the third major setting of the novel: Gulati. Gulati, as the cave which houses the mythical hieroglyph defining the African women of Zimbabwe also carries in its echo the stones with which Zimbabwe as a reborn African republic is universally associated or identified. This is the setting which explains the relationship between myth and history and memory:

> Tall women bend like tightened bows beneath a stampede of buffalo, while the rest spread their legs outward toward the sun ... Disembodied beings ... They are the virgins who walk into their own graves before the burial of a king. They die untouched. Their ecstasy is in the afterlife. Is this a suicide or a sacrifice or both? ... everything in Gulati rots except the rocks, history is steady; it cannot be tilted forward or backward ... In Gulati, I travel four hundred years, twenty more ... (103–4)

The warped consciousness of a warped and insensitive body reflects on the past, on the role of women in Zimbabwe history. It is a muddled history of pain and futility and empty strife. A man who finds solace in a ritualistic visitation of that cave cannot be normal. He is in need of salvation. It is Sibaso, who killed Thengiwe and raped her sister. He is a symbol of the blighted male spirit needing salvation from ancient ways and habits locked in the rocks and myths of history. He is man caught in the dichotomy of attraction and resistance to the female maternal essence. We will need another kind of man, who is both comfortable and at ease with what womanhood means, to advance the cause of national justice and liberation for man and woman. We will need all hands involved in a true national reconstruction as the extended family network in that section indicates. We will need man and woman to explore each other slowly and understand the necessity of accepting each other despite difference/s. That is what the relationship between Cephas Dube and Nonceba artistically proposes. When they feel each other out, it is a slow and methodical intellectual thing which tries to affirm that the head matters as much as the heart. It is different from the earlier sensual and sexual relationship in the first part of the novel between Cephas and Thenjiwe. Inchoate in resolve and mutual respect, they are also symbols of man and woman in Zimbabwe at a stage in life or national history in which their strivings are unlikely to either endure or fructify. Foundations come first before edifices.

To read *The Stone Virgins* and open the layers or whorls of the mythopoeia of its construction is to read the sad story of Zimbabwe from its pre-colonial and colonial history and understand the roots of its present post-colonial crises. It is an evocative story not just of the war of liberation or of ethnic cleansing but of the older wars going back to the basal wars driven by land hunger among the European colonists of Southern Africa and the dreams of mercantile and imperial adventurers like Cecil J. Rhodes. Thoughtful readers must see these wars as veritable indices for the reading and understanding of the instability and volatility of the polity in that part of Africa.

The Nigerian civil war, 1967–70, tells its own story, too, of the Nigerian tragedy or probably of a tragedy that is still unfolding. During a military coup in January 1966, many Northern Nigerian military officers were killed. Officers of Igbo extraction were blamed for the ethnically lopsided deaths. A retaliatory counter coup was conducted in July of the same year which went beyond the military echelons and into the civilian Eastern Nigerian population all over Nigeria, and especially in Northern Nigeria. Less than ten years after independence from British colonial rule, the Eastern Region of Nigeria sought secession from an ill-brokered federation to form a Republic of Biafra. The roots of the war are as deep as the history of the country. This motley assemblage of incompatibly endowed ethnicities is another British imperial dream forced into painful reality by wars. 'Though tribe and tongue may differ/In brotherhood we stand' runs the lines of Nigeria's first, but now repudiated, national anthem written quite significantly for the Nigerians by a British subject. To create by war has not turned out well anywhere in Africa. The bitterness remains. The civil war itself remains stolidly in the nation's psychic albumen from where the politics of the new Nigerian dispensation is driven. And quite often today, Nigeria moves from the smoulder of old pains to brief and bloody orgiastic re-enactments. Many of such have been untidily garbed in the euphemism of 'religious riots'. It has been indeed for the Nigerian nation, since its creation, a tragically perpetual *Dance of the Forests*.

Unlike Zimbabwe, whose agonies run like fresh springs in the fictions of its authors, Nigerian writers are, creatively, still in the shallows and margins of that bloody experience. There are war stories like Eddie Iroh's *Forty-eight Guns for the General*, and Ossie Enekwe's *Come, Thunder*. They are racy accounts which do not probe. There are harrowing private stories like Wole Soyinka's *The Man Died*, a good psychological excursion which is not a confrontation of the war but of the callous excesses of its chief executor, General Yakubu Gowon. None of such writings respond to/in the gravitas of Christopher Okigbo's heraldry of gore and of massive injustice demanding the apocalyptic denouement projected in the 'Paths of Thunder' movement of *Labyrinths*. There has been more robust attention to an unsettling aftermath than to tragic incidence as is clear in works like Elechi Amadi's *Estrangement* or Cyprian Ekwensi's *Survive the Peace*. Perhaps one should simply say that the Nigerian creative psyche is still afraid of the war. Certainly, Chinua Achebe and Flora Nwapa's short stories, *Girls at War* and *Wives at War* offer a few memorable cameos of the war. Some of the war stories included in the collections of stories by Festus Iyayi, especially in *Awaiting Court Martial* are also effective. The angst from Nigeria's wars has not fully plumbed the depths of political dysfunctionality and national malaise with the same consistency and intensity or on the scale that the Zimbabweans are doing with their war/s. What Nigerians have produced in relation to its teeming and turbulent and volatile population is still disproportionately inadequate. One hopes and wishes for more exploratory works. For the purposes of this essay, Nathan Nkala's *Drums and the Voice of Death* (1996) is a rather unique novel in the manner in which it attempts to capture the unravelling of a national psyche and its physical bolsters. What happens in the novel is the prosaic equivalent of what we find in the poetic fiction of Yvonne Vera. In Vera's vision, a cleansing, in line with a mythicized experience follows the incidence of war. In Nkala's vision, it is not so. The culture of the Igbo world, with its famously fierce republicanism is totally defanged. War produces a pathetically lame and rudderless polity in which all manners of shameless treachery and scams and skullduggery become a way of life. The whole moral landscape in its deracination and its encouragement of whole scale subversion of justice anticipates the present national circumstances of Nigeria in its amorality and aconscient insensitivity.

In that novel, even though the theatre is still too narrow, the tale still too racy, and the level of creative flight not as high as such a disturbing novel ought to be, it plumbs quite a bit with its numerous flashes of wit and conflicting human motives, of lyricism, and a wistfulness and nostalgia for peace and harmony in society. We feel in this novel the spirit of the fun-loving Nigerian. We sense the sundering of life and the help-lessness of the people. The war is there as a sudden catastrophe which tears friends and families and consequently the entire nation apart. The novel, however, is not clear about the ethnic fault lines of a quake that is clearly deeply seated in the foundations of the country and its polity:

> Terrible things were beginning to happen to the elephant of a country. It was as if some superman had tripped the elephant flat on its side. Lilliputian creatures were scurrying all over its hulk, wielding axes and matchets, spears and arrows. Sizeable chunks of its meat were already sizzling in small fires all over the land. (22)

That is the surface picture of a frenetic Nigeria after the second military coup which sets the stage for the civil war in the first section of *Drums and the Voice of Death*. The rest of the book follows historical events very closely. The Igbo retreat to their Eastern enclave. War begins, and pro-tracts into Igbo suffering and eventually, defeat.

What this book reveals is the peculiar suffering of the Igbo people which indeed is parallel in the politics of the author to the larger Nigerian nation's crisis. The root cause of the crisis is probably for artistic purposes left deliberately unclear, but what is clear is that the upheaval will also leave long-term consequences for all. In its social analysis, this novel echoes a paradigm ubiquitous in Ngugi wa Thiong'o's Afro-Marxist thesis. When things go awry in society, the establishment finds its scape-goats from the powerless masses of the population. The powerful who perpetrate much of the crises and disarray are ignored or avoided when solutions or answers are being sought. The suggestion by Nkala in *Drums and the Voice of Death* is that sooner or later what is bound to develop is anarchy, a situation in which the oppressed have terror as their only recourse. But even as that, terror in every form, whether it is civil unrest or rioting or even as the familiar African military putsch of recent years, has to be sponsored by somebody. Inevitably, it is still the rich who have the money, and it is the rich who occupy the so-called seats of justice. That is how this story works itself out.

The prologue of the novel has a member of a new generation of young dreamers under arrest for armed robbery awaiting execution by a firing squad. The body of the novel retroactively tells the entire story of the nation. The war through which the nation unravelled was a war whose causes go back to the faulty foundations upon which the nation was built. The sectional and ethnic rivalries and differences are also the products of the same faulty foundations. The individuals are what they are, whether they are swindlers, gold-diggers, corrupt civil servants or armed robbers, because of the national circumstances and not necessarily because of their ethnicities. At the end of the novel, the story offers the shocking revelation that the armed robbers were merely scapegoats of bigger men in society who are able to get away with one form of proxy participation or the other in crime. The suggestion of the author is that a systemic crisis requires a deep probing of the roots and foundation and not a cosmetic redressing or hasty finger-pointing which only amounts to a mere nipping of the branches of the crisis. The disarray in the Igbo world, with the same criminal or general human propensities as in Nigeria before the war and the creation of Biafra, places everybody in Nigeria and Biafra, or in Igbo land on the same fallible human frame. In other words, the country needs more than fractional campaigns of cleansing for a renaissance to take place.

What are the general implications of all this? Power bases need to be revisited comprehensively in order to establish the roots of national crises. War is only a symptom of a general malaise with roots that are most times deeper than the adventitious eruptions associated with ethnic differences. War is a useful index because it highlights other problems. In Vera's *The Stone Virgins*, the problems of gender become clearer when they are linked to myth or historical events, and in Nkala's *Drums and the Voice of Death*, ethnic problems lead us far back into the shoddy foundations of colonial nation-building.

African poets and poetry, in engaging war as a subject, also provide a very good index for those watching Africa. We may again look at a few countries and note how they stand out as examples of cases where national development has a lot to do with how peaceful or turbulent a nation is. Rwanda is in that regard a pre-eminent example. Rwanda came under German colonial rule in 1885. It slipped into Belgian hands during World War I. With its history read carefully, one does not know what to call the recent pre-debacle regime of Juvenal Habyarimana and indeed the regime of its precursor, Gregoire Kayibanda which began in 1961. What is clear in such phenomena of national growth is that wars create fertile grounds for all sorts of instabilities and political apostacies. If we do not yet find in the fiction or poetry of Rwanda what we might call some sort of guiding index, earlier African poets like Nigeria's Christopher Okigbo or Congolese Tchicaya U Tam'si provide in the eschatological and apocalyptic sweep of their poems representative disillusionment and gloom and the incipient anarchy presaging all wars. Okigbo's 'Path of Thunder' is a prophecy and a definition of a debacle in the making with its anticipated gory consequences. U Tam'si's 'Epitome' holds up for clear view the spirit of a people battered and mangled by the chicanery of international politics. It is for U Tam'si, a world in which the tragedy of nation is a badge from which nobody can successfully hide, whether it is the betrayal of Patrice Lumumba or the psychological implications of the helplessness of the Congolese or indeed Africans in general. Thus he writes in 'Viaticum':

You must be from my country
I see it by the tick
Of your soul around the eyelashes
And besides you dance when you are sad
You must be from my country (60)

When there is war, what follows involves mutating interests in evolving national structures and spaces. Hope is spectral in such circumstances and processes. Why not? How does one begin to make sense out of the recent eruptions in the Ivory Coast, or the perplexing limb-hacking horrors of Sierra Leone? Such phenomena indicate that a final formation of Africa in terms of fixed and stable nations appears still a dream in many places. Global market forces and ethnic interests, mostly driven by greed appear still to rule the shape or structures of present formations. The courageous and confident patriotism that drove the nationalistic spirit of older nations are yet to be found since the first African intellectuals battled colonial forces from one united front. Perhaps all the present volatility is because ideological monoliths are difficult to come by and the cultural or philosophical commonalities are too tenuous to bond warring entities in a continent of arbitrarily conglomerated nations.

You may superimpose Europe's Cold War, the ideological lunacies of Soviet Marxism-Leninism and Western capitalism over all Africa's wars, and you will begin to understand and appreciate the nature of the quandary Africa has been in. The Cold War became in Africa a hot and sweltering fratricide of intra-national waste and destruction. Nascent post-colonial African polities became a smoulder of wars in layers, translating into enduring psychological injury and protracted political hostility leaving economies in shambles and all hope hobbled by incalculable human disasters. Let us take again a few African poets and see how they respond to these circumstances. Gabriel Okara, a premier post-independence Nigerian poet takes up the issue of war head-on when he writes these words in the height of the Nigerian civil war:

The noon sun
shrivels tender buds
today's wanton massacre
burns up tender words
and from the ashes
hate is growing, forcing its way
like mushroom through yielding soil
but its an alien growth
a cancer that destroys its host. (41)

And with Africa's multiplex cultures and ethnicities, we have a truly desperate ailment in our hands. Okara calls his poem 'Cancerous Growth'. Like a cancer indeed, our discovery and realization come with some despondency; the complexity of the continent's insidious crises becomes

much clearer, and clarity magnifies the enormity of the morass and inten-
sifies its insuperable character. But all these are needed if we are to understand Africa's chroniclers of Africa's wars and how understanding those
various wars might be of use to those who really care about Africa and the
imponderable human condition in the continent.

The voices of many other African poets clearly register the pain and
impatience and hopelessness and anger that we hear in the voice of
Angola's poet-beaureaucrat, Jofre Rocha in his poem 'Guerilla Fighter':

> I knew a guerilla fighter
> Small but courageous
> Who challenged death to combat
> and won.
> He was small but in his veins
> howitzers of fury
> and fire
> and his blood was a river
> flowing with the salt and honey of victory (81)

But not everybody is as measured and as forgiving as Rocha. Reactions are
sometimes peculiar to the conditions and circumstances of specific
countries. Angola tottered from a creaking Portuguese colonial rule into a
long and brutal tragic civil war fueled by the characteristic African mix of
old and confusing ethnic rivalries; mindless, treacherous, and starry-eyed
Cold War politics, with a bizarre dash of piratical diamond-trading. Of
course, compatriots were mutual agents of Death. Today, the Angolan
nation is temporarily on its feet with the blood of erstwhile combatants
'flowing with the salt and honey of victory'. How much more chilling can
anybody describe victory? See how despair over a similar unfortunate
legacy drives Zimbabwe's nimble-witted but fragile-spirited Dambudzo
Marechera into ripping existential anguish in a poem most aptly titled
'Desert Crossing':

> Sharp howling winds scattering grit
> Crack and roar like creatures of the pit
> The heart is a desert place, an earth of piercing heat
>
> The burning sky above is fixed,
> The consuming grave at our feet baffles the priest;
> Day after day the sand-dunes of living shift about,
> Creeping forever across the desert's immense minute (112)

In Africa, the only thing fixed is its desert of pain and despair. And
measured by that index, the continent is indeed very small and experien-
tially uniformed. War and the threat of war is one thing the huge
continent shares without quibble. By and large, the voices of poets from
each country eerily echo the cries of pain or the crises in a neighbouring
country. A voice-driven panoramic view of the continent's throes indicate
that in a country like Malawi through the voices of its leading poets, Jack
Mapanje, Frank Chipasula and Steve Chimombo, the dictatorship of their

time harks of unease and explosive danger in the wings. For the spirit of past wars with an ominous moan of fear for the future and fear of past ghosts, unmollified, Uganda and Zimbabwe provide big windows into Africa's soul and its unpredictable and precarious condition. For Uganda's Acam-Oturu, 'An Agony ... A Resurrection' defines the fall and a yet processual resurrection. But now, even that resurrection is being threatened once more by the quixotic horde which calls itself the Lord's Resistance Army. In Zimbabwe's Musaemura Zimunya, there is a warning in 'Arrivants' for the need for deeper self-examination, for cautious pre-scription of solutions, for chances to heal. This is something, we see, insistently repeated by Zimbabwe's novelists. Between Nigeria's post-independence triumvirate, Achebe, Soyinka and Clark-Bekederemo, there is a conflict between a posture of censure and exhortation for the privileged and powerful adopted by the former two, with the latter in his collection, *Casualties*, attempting establishmentarian exoneration and a rather quirky distributive justice. The feelings of African poets cover a full gamut in the nature of their reactions to war or impending war, the havoc of war in the continent. Two other poets, one from Tunisia, and the other from Sierra Leone define the problems and the necessary task of rehabilitation. For Syl Cheney-Coker, enamoured of a Latin-American hyperbolic realism ubiquitous in his art, an African silence deceives with its stillness because 'the graveyard also has teeth'. Some supernatural attrition appears at work in the fabric of things. Buffeted by the pessimism of African life, the sensitive individual always harbours this nameless fear. The heart senses something that ought to be palpable but is not. Long before there is any conflict in Sierra Leone, Cheney-Coker captures this edginess in the deracinating pessimism of 'When the Revolution is Near at Hand' :

> ... thus do I deceive them listening with my mortal soul
> until these bombs in my heart detonate themselves
> echoing the ghosts of the generation demanding at the eclipse
> why they sacrificed the bones in that graveyard which has teeth
> spraying their mummies with blood
> without their knowing my volatile madness (61)

And in another poem, 'Analysis', we feel directly the flames of the poet's 'volatile madness':

> Ah taste the vinegar
> In the air it has more sweetness than my joy
> My rage my tears, my groaning, my raving
> to whom? For whom? To whom I ask?
> To Africa for permitting a perpetual butchery of her womb
> To those who barter her on Wall Street and the World Market
> Muckrackers, smugglers, politicians and the like
> To know them by their smiles Wall Street buys your heart
> Think of your agony Africa your capitalist war-mongers ... (11)

It is a double entendre in which Africa knows and does not know the roots of her crises. There is enough blame for the culpable and complicitous, local or foreign.

In the delicate brush strokes of Tunisian poet, Amina Said, there is a poignant call for Africa to come to terms with the reality of her beautiful nature and sad destiny. As she writes in 'The Africa of the Statue', the despoliation of war or violence is clear but so also is the task of the artist, the inevitable picking up of the pieces:

> The Africa of the statue
> Flows out in a sawdust of blood
> ...
> griots discover
> that they are the stuff of memory
> ...
> the dream of the past
> is as a future (76)

African writers have been able to keep virtually in lockstep with the fortunes and misfortunes of the continent, particularly on the subject of war. Many writers are either products of the wars which they write about or produce works about Africa's wars which keep the subject in clear view of those who care to see. Careful studies of works from Africa's familiar hotbeds of crises reveal this important relationship. While novelists have the advantage of fuller representations of Africa's wars because of the spatial advantages of fiction, poets capture in precision the feelings and moods of the people. Between those two genres, we find a reliable index for reading the impact of war in numerous African societies, and how all those wars affect both the human condition and destiny in the continent. War is Africa's muted index but muted as it is, one could read beyond simply trying to capture the regular zeitgeist which good national literatures capture. The index could guide the insightful reader toward the foundations of Africa's numerous perennial or still unfolding tragedies. Clearly, the most quotidian of Africa's problems, ranging from human rights to various cultural, political, and socio-economic issues appear either related or traceable to a long and turbulent history of wars and their unsavoury aftermath.

NOTE

Most of the poets referred to in this paper are represented in Tanure Ojaide and Tijan Sallah's comprehensive anthology *The New African Poetry* (1999). Otherwise, references are to the single volumes of the poets identified in these notes and references.

WORKS CITED

Achebe, Chinua. *Girls at War*. New York: Ballantine Books. 1972.

Amadi, Elechi. *Estrangement*. London: Heinemann Educational Publishers, 1986.

Cheney-Coker, Syl. *The Graveyard Also Has Teeth with Concerto for Exile*. London, Heinemann Educational Books, 1973 & 1980.

—— *The Last Harmattan of Alusine Dunbar*. London: Heinemann Educational Publishers, 1990.

Clark-Bekederemo, John Pepper. *Casualties*. Teaneck: Holmes and Meier Publishers, 1970.

Ekwensi, Cyprian. *Survive the Peace*. London: Heinemann Educational Publishers, 1976.

Enekwe, Ossie. *Came Thunder*. Enugu: Fourth Dimension Publishers, 1972.

Hove, Chenjerai. *Shadows*. Harare: Baobab Books, 1991.

—— *Bones*. Harare: Baobab Books, 1998.

Iroh, Eddie. *Forty-Eight Guns for the General*. London: Heinemann Educational Publishers, 1986.

Iyayi, Festus. *Awaiting Court Martial*. Lagos: Malthouse Press, 1996.

Kanengoni, Alex. *Effortless Tears*. Harare: Baobab Books, 1993.

—— *Echoing Silences*. Oxford: Heinemann Educational Publishers, 1997.

Nkala, Nathan. *Drums and the Voice of Death*. Enugu: Fourth Dimension Publishing Company Ltd, 1996.

Nkosi, Lewis. *The Rhythm of Violence*. London: Oxford University Press, 1964.

Nwapa, Flora. *Wives at War and Other Stories*. Trenton, NJ: Africa World Press, 1992.

Ojaide, Tanure and Tijan Sallah. *The New African Poetry*. Boulder, Lynn Rienner Publishers, 1999.

Okara, Gabriel. *The Fisherman's Invocation*. London, Heinemann Educational Books. 1978.

Okigbo, Christopher. *Labyrinths*. London: Heinemann Educational Publishers, 1971.

Okri, Ben. *The Famished Road*. London: Jonathan Cape, 1991.

Oulouguem, Yambo. *Bound to Violence*. London: Heinemann Educational Publishers, 1971.

Soyinka, Wole. *The Man Died*. London: Rex Collings, 1972.

—— *Dance of the Forests* in *Collected Plays*, Vol. 1. Oxford: Oxford University Press, 1973.

UTams'i, Tchicaya. *Selected Poems*. London, Heinemann Educational Books,1970.

Vera, Yvonne. *Under the Tongue*. New York: Farrar, Straus and Giroux, 1996.

—— *Butterfly Burning*. New York: Farrar, Straus and Giroux, 1998.

—— *The Stone Virgins*. New York, Farrar, Straus, and Giroux, 2004.

Nkosi, Lewis. *The Rhythm of Violence*. London: Oxford University Press, 1964.

Zaleeza, Paul. *The Joys of Exile*. Toronto: Anansi Books, 1994.

'Life in the Camp of the Enemy'
Alemseged Tesfai's
Theatre of War

Christine Matzke

During the Eritrean liberation struggle against Ethiopia from 1961 to 1991 culture played a prominent role as a medium of self-definition, entertainment and education. Both liberation movements, the Eritrean Liberation Front (ELF) and its challenger, the finally dominant Eritrean People's Liberation Front (EPLF), featured cultural troupes which mounted variety shows comprising songs, music and ancestral dances as well as the occasional dramatic sketch for propaganda purposes and recreation. Full-length plays were also produced, but rather sporadically, often lengthy enactments of Eritrean history or allegorical plays which referred to Ethiopia's annexation of Eritrea. While the ELF can be credited with the establishment of the earliest cultural troupe in the late 1960s, it was the EPLF that encouraged cultural activities on a much broader base and facilitated artistic specialisation. In this article, I will take a closer look at the development of written drama and its performance in the EPLF after the strategic retreat of 1978.[1] The focus will be on the theatre of Alemseged Tesfai who can be considered not only as the premier playwright of the liberation struggle, but also as one of its main cultural theorists.

Historical Backdrop:
Revolutionary Culture on all (Front) Lines

While in 1977 both fronts had controlled most of the Eritrean countryside and a number of towns, the following year began a period of trials and tribulations. From 1978 to mid-1979 the Eritrean resistance suffered a succession of offensives by the Ethiopian Derg regime and had to abandon most of the liberated territories. While the ELF was harder hit and eventually ceased to operate as a fighting force in Eritrea, the EPLF managed an orderly strategic withdrawal into the mountainous northern highlands of the Sahel. The retreat called for a reconsideration of military tactics and organizational structures. For 'culture' in general, it was certainly a watershed since the central cultural troupe (CCT) was temporarily disbanded and cultural activities were encouraged at all levels of the EPLF. 'Culture' also began to be more aggressively promoted as 'revolutionary culture' in the field.[2] Influenced by the socialist realism of the communist world and embracing all art forms practised in the liberation struggle, revolutionary culture hoped to further the national project more efficiently than previous cultural work, and help to boost the morale of the people.

At first, cultural ventures were decentralized and performance groups established in virtually all sectors and departments, military and non-military alike. This led to an upsurge of cultural activities on different levels, from the so-called 'recreational groups' (A. Tesfai [1983]) whose work was an amateurish ad-hoc affair, to groups on Brigade or Army Division levels which were given more time, space and resources to develop their talents. While most continued their work until de-facto independence, the CCT was revived in 1981 and the Division of Culture split into two separate subdivisions: the Music Section and the Section of Literature and Drama, with Drama being directed by Alemseged Tesfai.

Until then Alemseged Tesfai, a qualified lawyer who had abandoned his doctoral studies in the US to join the liberation struggle, had worked in the educational sector of the EPLF. In 1981 he was appointed to advance drama though he had virtually no theatre experience.[3] The new base where he and other cultural officers were to take up their work, known by the code name Arag was located in the inaccessible highlands of the northern Sahel. A permanent, subterranean base was built which featured offices, shelters, galleries and a rehearsal hall, all underground to protect the fighters from Ethiopian air raids.

When the CCT was reconstituted, it was on the premise of its being at 'a higher level of thinking and organisation' (interview with Solomon Tsehaye, 4 August 2000) than its predecessors. The new CCT had to complement the existing entertainment groups and function as the official cultural representative of the EPLF, and had thus to include the best singers, dancers and writers. Specialization was now greatly encouraged, as was the study of different cultural disciplines. While written works had been previously credited to the front, not an individual person, this began to change in the 1980s. Alemseged Tesfai was among the first to be acknowledged as a playwright when, in the mid-1980s, one of his works, *'Eti Kale' K^winat* (*The Other War*), was documented on video film. More individually known authors followed with the promotion of literary competitions in the field.[4] Research into long-established performance forms was also strongly encouraged, mostly by way of participatory methodology. Alemseged Tesfai was not engaged in field research, but was adamant that only by delving into local performative expressions could a truly Eritrean theatre emerge (cf. Plastow 1999: 57). Focusing on the development of written drama, he spent his days reading, and partially translating, the few books available on theatre arts. The choice was limited and mostly related to European drama – Shakespeare, Molière, Ibsen and Gogol – but he also covered selected African plays and theories, above all works of the Kenyan writer Ngugi wa Thiong'o. Between 1982 and 1984, Alemseged[5] wrote and directed three plays – *Le'ul* (written in 1982, performed in 1983), *Anqetsi* (*Meningitis*, 1983)[6] and *'Eti Kale' K^winat* (*The Other War*, 1984) – and published a novel in 1983, *Wedi Hadera* (*The Son of Hadera*). He also produced the first two full-length studies on Eritrean literature and theatre respectively, *Literature, Its Development, and Its Role in Revolution* (1982) as well as *Drama* (1983).[7] Obviously, he was not the only one to start writing seriously, but given his prominent position became one of the most influential intellectuals in the cultural field. 'We in the Literature and Drama section began to understand what literature meant to the author and drama to the actors,' Weyni Tewolde, an actress with the reconstituted CCT, recalled.

> The work we started now was different to the work we had done previously. Then we didn't have any idea about drama. Now, Alemseged taught us what drama meant and how it had developed historically, for example among the ancient Greeks or about Ngugi's drama. We became totally absorbed. Thanks to Alemseged, we were getting to know fundamental ideas about drama. (interview, 29 February 2000)

Engendering Drama in the EPLF

At this time of war, the early 1980s, theatre work was hampered by many obstacles: the constant threat of military attacks, especially air raids; the dearth of materials and rehearsal time, but also the lack of training, experience and performative skills. Even the designated professionals in Arag were unsure of how to mount certain performance forms. Drama in particular was not well established. Only a minority of fighters were familiar with its urban Eritrean form; and only a tiny fraction of those who had spent time abroad had been involved in theatre. 'In connection with this', Ghirmai Negash in his study on Tigrinya literature in Eritrea remarks:

> it is perhaps relevant to mention that play writing is not a developed craft in Tigrinya. True, plays have been staged by students and by professional music & [sic] theatre groups such as 'Asmara Theatre Association' [...]. Moreover, (touring) cultural and musical troupes of the liberation organisations have regularly shown theatre performances in the liberated zones of Eritrea as well as for Eritrean expatriate communities during the liberation time. Nevertheless, actors have almost always relied on provisory [sic] sketches, and printed versions of the texts are seldom found. (G. Negash 1999: 181)

With the few exceptions of earlier local theatre associations, drama had indeed been the prerogative of the various colonizing powers in Eritrea; the Italians, the British and the Ethiopian forces. Europeans had introduced neoclassicist ideas of drama, especially nineteenth-century realism and naturalism, into modern Eritrean theatre arts; they had also popularized buffoonery of the Chaplin and Laurel-and-Hardy type via the cinema. Modern Ethiopian theatre forms, on the other hand (with their roots in classical Western tragedies, ecclesiastical symbolism and *qene*, double-entendre poetry (cf. Plastow 2004: 192–202) had begotten a predilection for iconic, not individual, characterization (as seen in the production of allegorical plays) and a tendency to dichotomous, polarized presentations. The absence of mythological themes, such as found in West African theatre, for example, was striking.[8] Now, the EPLF set about appropriating and advancing the genre for their 'revolutionary' ends. This had substantial political import as developing drama in a local language was part of the larger internal and external decolonization process of the EPLF in line with ideas of decolonizing the mind advocated by Ngugi.[9] The written word had always also been associated with the church and the landed gentry in Eritrea which together had constituted an oppressive feudal system over many centuries. Extensive literary campaigns in the EPLF – to which scripted drama might be seen as a creative extension – were thus a means to claim control over the written word. Writing plays and attempting to develop a 'revolutionary' form of theatre moreover served purposes linked with the internal dynamics of the EPLF; it was not, however, intended to establish an elitist form of 'art' or 'elite' theatre as happened in various other African countries during the period of decolonisation.[10] Writing drama became a means of gauging and controlling the 'revolutionary' merit of theatre in the field; it also became a means of improving its dramaturgical standards.

Alemseged Tesfai's Critique of Drama & Drama Performance in the EPLF

In the virtual absence of a critical discourse on theatre in the liberation war and a larger body of creative writing,[11] I will utilize Alemseged Tesfai's insightful drama critique of 1983 to highlight some of the limitations of scripted drama work in the field. According to Alemseged, drama in the EPLF had passed through two distinct stages by 1983. Phase one covered the period from 1979 to the early 1980s in which 'long serious dramas, mostly tragedies, and some short educational comic sketches' were performed; phase two continued from 1980 to 1983 and was characterized by 'message-carrying comical sketches and short, serious symbolic [meaning: allegorical] dramas' (A. Tesfai [1983]).[12] At the time of writing, a third stage was said to be underway on which the author felt not yet ready to comment but which, in retrospect, was clearly influenced by his own theatre work.

While I cannot necessarily confirm the first couple of phases for lack of dated material, it can be safely assumed that from the mid-1980s drama by individually recognized playwrights was steadily on the rise (cf. E.

Tseggai 2002: 13). As much as possible, dramas were produced in neo-naturalistic, illusionistic mode; representational acting was aspired to, though presentational performance (with its focus on display rather than verisimilitude) often made up for lack of means to produce a 'life-like' portrayal on stage. 'Abstract' scenery was unheard of in the field. Non-figurative art works were rejected for being incapable of projecting the Front's revolutionary agenda, while orthodox Christian symbolism was abolished because of its link to religious dogmatism and the old feudal order. Equally uncommon was experimental dramatization of whichever kind, for the simple reason that ideas of avant-garde theatre had not reached the liberation movement. Over-acted slapstick and buffoonery, on the other hand, remained very popular in the field, and was often the only form of theatre audiences recognized as 'drama'.

The reason behind the desire to improve the standard of dramatic per-formances appears to have been a general discontent with the quality of theatre. At times plays were too long and too didactic to be enjoyable. Combatants got bored and started to dub drama 'political education' (M. Zerai 2001: 30). Though Alemseged believed in the creative potential of 'the people', he soon realized that without clear guidance the project of 'revolutionary culture' would fail. Criticism of cultural works was tenta-tive and sporadic, mainly for fear that it would discourage budding, but inexpert, artists. Now and then plays were so crude that performances were effectively counter-productive to the objectives of the organization. Alemseged observes that in non-scripted pieces actors often lost a sense of direction in terms of plot, character building or overall meaning of the play, resulting in 'muddled' messages or incoherent 'rambling' on stage (A. Tesfai [1983]). Then there was the tendency to overload the plays the-matically. 'Although drama is a reflection of reality', Alemseged explains, 'it cannot hold all of its aspects' (A. Tesfai [1983]).

Stereotypes were also a problem for non-scripted and early scripted works, as were overacted stock characters. The bespectacled, serious-looking bearded young man reading a newspaper – a representation of the 'learned revolutionary'– was just one example of modern typecasting, as was the greedy licentious barmaid, *barista*. The ignorant old peasant, on the other hand, constituted a typical 'traditional' image. It was, of course, problematic to confront rural spectators with images of stupid fellow peasants as opposed to 'learned (urban) intellectuals' (cf. Rohmer 1999: 211). As an educational concept, it was certainly dubious; as entertain-ment, however, it was immensely successful. Alemseged concedes that 'comedies are captivating, but the harmful views they covertly slip in are not easily overcome. This is true whether it is done on purpose or inad-vertently. In our and many other societies, for example, jokes and proverbs exist which belittle women [or] cheapen the relationship between husband and wife' (A. Tesfai [1983]). Time and again, these attitudes were utilized to engender laughter among the spectators, for mirth was believed to be the ultimate measure for the success of a show:

> Actors go to great length to use abusive language for comic effect. In plays
> against feudalism women are beaten just to make people laugh, not because of
> the logical development of the drama. Sometimes the audience demands an
> *encore* of such things. [...]. Even if it makes people laugh, such things should
> not be encouraged through crude drama. If women are to be slapped on stage, if
> it makes people laugh, there has to be an accompanying message telling that
> such practices as beating women should be abolished. Laughter should be a
> form of objection, not derision. The spectator should say: 'We cannot help
> laughing, but the matter is burning in our hearts'. Otherwise our laughter will
> be at the expense of the oppressed and will be counterproductive to the objec-
> tives of revolutionary culture. (A. Tesfai [1983])

Indeed, Alemseged feared that such tendencies would hamper 'the development of writers, directors and actors' (A. Tesfai [1983]). Devising
comical sketches was not a laughing matter; it had to be taken as seriously
as writing a full-length play.

The above examples indicate that Alemseged was also concerned
about the theatrical representation of women, in both his critical and his
creative works. He especially objected to the persistent usage of women as
national allegories, mainly the woman-forced-to-marry-cruel-husband
type of drama which referred to Eritrea's annexation by Ethiopia. 'Such
plays', he writes, 'have been performed so many times that no aspect of it
is new and appropriate for dramatic utilization' (A. Tesfai [1983]).

On closer scrutiny, however, the reason behind the censure was not
only limited to the stereotypical casting of women into the passive role of
sexual object and patriotic symbol. Rather, it was connected to the unpredictable nature of allegorical plays. 'Symbolic drama' had always been
appreciated in Eritrea for carrying clandestine meanings, similar to
double-entendre local orature. It also complied with the 'culture of
secrecy' (cf. A. Tesfai 2000: 28) cultivated in the field which was rooted in
the ancient practice of withholding one's deeper thoughts and feelings.
Allegorical plays, so it seems, would have been an ideal theatrical
medium had they not been open to a multiplicity of interpretations.

> If unsophisticated plays can look as if carrying a political message, there will be
> no limit for symbolic drama [i.e. allegorical plays]. As meaning is indistinct,
> different interpretations are encouraged which will serve different interests.
> This violates one of the basic principles of social realism. [...] It is for such
> views that symbolic drama should not be mounted too frequently. (A. Tesfai
> [1983])

These ideas, reminiscent of Bolshevik theatre criticism, illuminate why
modes and forms in Eritrean fighter theatre have continued to be inclined
towards farcical sketches, moral fables, campaign theatre and other
straightforward realistic plays, often in hyperbolic exaltations of Eritrean
strength and ethics. Plays that could potentially criticize the official view
of things had to be curbed and contained. No matter how much the
'masses' were invoked in the struggle, drama in Eritrea was, and has

continued to be, a theatre for, not of, the 'people'. To my knowledge, theatre never criticized the elite sector of the EPLF, and much drama was characterized by a benevolent top-down approach to enlighten the semi-literate 'masses', without engaging them in a participatory way. Despite adhering to the tenets of 'revolutionary culture', however, Alemseged also wrote plays which, on the whole, avoided rigid polarized representations, but were multi-layered and critically engaged.

In the following section I will analyse two of his dramatic works, *Le'ul* (1983) and *The Other War* (1984), to illustrate how the author realized 'revolutionary culture' in his own theatre practice, with regard to both text and context. Each section will comprise an introduction to the background and production of the respective play, a summary, and a first critical reading. Interestingly, in both pieces Alemseged focuses on civilian, rather than combatant, life to portray the trials and tribulations of people at a time of war. References to the constant fighting are oblique, if present at all, thus alluding to the complexities of armed conflict rather than reducing them to a one-dimensional hagiography of the battlefield. Set in areas under Ethiopian control, they portray 'Life in the Camp of the Enemy' (A. Tesfai 2002: 137) in which battles of very different kinds were fought.

Le'ul

Le'ul was Alemseged Tesfai's first play as Head of Drama in the Division of Culture. Written in 1982 and performed for the Workers' Congress at Arag in 1983, it went on tour throughout the field, including parts of Sudan, until succeeded by the production of *The Other War* (1984). With *Le'ul*, the author explains, 'theatre controlled by a script took shape in the field' (A. Tesfai, email, 28 August 2002). From its very inception, *Le'ul* was intended to be more than a mere agit-prop piece mounted on the occasion of an important labour convention. 'I did not want it to be a one-show affair', Alemseged continues:

> The intention was to celebrate the role of women factory workers in Asmara who were very active in the clandestine cells within the city. Before I wrote it, I talked at length with a former woman worker who had to leave Asmara because her cell had been broken or discovered by the Ethiopian security. From the insight that she gave me, I tried to give as realistic a picture as I could of a woman squeezed between harassment at work, the anxieties of a clandestine and closely watched and suspected fighter and a good husband who vents his political and financial frustrations on a wife who loves him and who he loves. (A. Tesfai, email, 28 August 2002)

As with all of his plays, *Le'ul* was written with particular actors in mind. Though they were household names in Eritrean fighter theatre, it was a rather challenging undertaking for the author-cum-director to get the performers to learn their lines. 'I remember having a hard time trying

to convince the actors that they should stay true to the dialogue as originally written. We had some big fights' (A. Tesfai, email, 28 August 2002).
In the end, however, the artists rose to the challenge and began to appreciate working with scripted drama. Alemseged writes that some of the play's
lines even ended up as quips and common sayings among the fighters.

Outline
Le'ul is a realist one-act play in five scenes which alternate between an
Asmara factory, Le'ul's home and a bar in the streets. Le'ul, the eponymous heroine, her older colleague, Kidisti, and Letergergish, the youngest
and most ambitious of the three, are workers in a textile sweatshop. Le'ul
is still mourning the death of her infant son, angry at having been denied
three days leave to receive condolences. There are great tensions within
the team: Kidisti and Le'ul deeply frustrated by the unjust conditions and
the constant pay cuts as a form of punishment, Letergergish creaming up
to the Ethiopian Cadre in order to rise in the current scheme. Le'ul, as we
soon find out, is a member of a clandestine resistant cell led by Mussie, a
colleague and trusted friend. Problems are mounting, at home and at
work. Since the death of their child, Weldu, Le'ul's husband, has spent his
time going out drinking and abusing her. After a violent showdown in
their modest room, Le'ul cannot bear it any longer and begs Mussie to
send her to the field. Mussie, however, tracks Weldu down in a bar and
talks sense into him. The couple finally make peace. The concluding
scene brings us back to the factory, a few days later. Kidisti approaches a
much happier Le'ul, hoping her friend will help her join the EPLF mass
organizations. In the meantime, Letegergish is promoted to *maestra*,
forewoman. After work, Le'ul lingers as usual to meet comrade Mussie.
With Kidisti, Mussie is guarded as he considers her temper a potential
cause for problems. For Le'ul, however, home has become a much happier
place, and Mussie assures her that this is only the beginning. Weldu will
grow into someone stronger; all it needs is patience, courage and
fortitude.

Reading Le'ul
Following the normative ideal of the nineteenth-century drama, the clear,
pyramid-like structure of *Le'ul* helps highlight the 'revolutionary' contribution of the working class to the struggle for independence. The drama
follows a cyclical pattern, beginning and ending with a factory scene
which embraces a domestic setting, with the bar as the *cul de sac*
midpoint of the play, denoting a crisis. *Le'ul* is cast in a framework of
Marxist ideology where oppressive modes of production and the sufferings of the working class mirror the dealings of the authoritarian regime.
The 'linear, goal-oriented, single-stranded plot' (Pfister 1993: 241)
indicates that socio-economic conditions have enormous bearing on
people's private life, and that it is from there that challenge and change

must begin. Unlike previous plays, *Le'ul* does without hidden motifs or national allegories; it equally forgoes melodramatic love scenes or moments of Ethiopian mayhem. *Le'ul* operates with subtlety rather than spectacle, and succeeds in creating an atmosphere of the trying everyday suffering of Eritreans. It succeeds also in ending on a hopeful note by expressing people's commitment to the liberation struggle and suggesting 'revolutionary' strategies. Even the marriage between Le'ul and Weldu serves this purpose by anticipating what the author would eventually formulate in his later drama study:

> To secure its revolutionary form, love has to thrive from the love of society. [...] When an individual relationship breaks up, it can be replaced by a new love; but when society disintegrates it cannot be replaced by personal love. Therefore personal love should promote the safety of society and should support individuals in fulfilling their revolutionary duties. (A. Tesfai [1983])

In four of the five women characters the author explores the allegiances with either the 'people's' struggle or the capitalist system which, in a twist of irony, is represented by the purportedly socialist Derg regime. The female Cadre (most likely an Ethiopian) is seen as committed to an exploitative ideology that trusts in production increase and profit rather than human potential. Letegergish represents that part of the population for whom immediate material gratification is more important than long-term nationalist goals. Indeed, having seen her flirting with an Ethiopian technician, Kidisti accuses her of sleeping with the enemy. There are other signifiers which mark Letegergish as unpatriotic by linking the current rulers with the whole lineage of colonizing powers in Eritrea. Letegergish's promotion to *maestra* (Italian for forewoman) is one such example, as is her preference for European names. What had signified a break with confining norms among urban performers in the 1950s and 1960s when it had linked them to other modernities (Matzke 2002: 36), is now seen as a betrayal of the nationalistic cause: foreign identification suggests the foregoing of one's Eritrean identity. Among Letegergish's co-workers her new names thus result in derision, not status, and make her an object of contempt and ridicule.

Kidisti, on the other hand, is a character with 'revolutionary' potential; good-natured and diligent, with a strong sense of right and wrong. However, her unseemly emotional outbursts prevent her joining the urban underground movement. This indicates that a person engaged in revolutionary duties needs to be not only passionate, but also trustworthy and mature. Le'ul, the eponymous heroine, is such a character; committed, fearless, and obedient. Though never clearly spelt out, it is obvious that the struggle for independence is essentially based on a strict hierarchy, those who give orders and those who follow them. Mussie, the omniscient underground leader, is of course a most exemplary character in the play; astute, prudent and personally concerned about the comrades under his care. Yet Mussie is almost too good to be true. It is noteworthy that it is not Le'ul, the protagonist, but a male character who controls the happenings on stage. One word from Mussie, and Weldu miraculously transforms from abusive husband to caring partner. One word from Mussie, and Kidisti is not yet to be admitted to their inner circle. There is an element of wishful thinking reminiscent of melodrama in the play, above all Weldu's astonishing metamorphosis from drunkard to committed revolutionary. Weldu initially serves as foil to the over-large figure of the underground leader, but also as a symbol for what the revolution can achieve.

In sum, Le'ul is an open-ended propaganda play which, unlike most pieces in the genre, offers neither prescriptions nor neat solutions. It does, however, emphasize the continuation of the struggle for independence by affirming that accord, vigilance and solidarity are the true weapons against the oppressive Ethiopian regime. With men and women working together, the play suggests, Eritrea will finally overcome its subjugation.

'Eti Kale' K^winat – The Other War

'Eti Kale' K^winat or The Other War was premiered in 1984 and confirmed Alemseged Tesfai's position as leading playwright of the liberation struggle. The last play in a series of three, it has to date remained his final drama. During 1985–6, The Other War toured the frontline; later it was video-filmed and distributed among exile and diaspora Eritreans. It was also the first Eritrean play to be translated, published, and staged in English abroad, and the first to receive international critical attention.[13]

The idea to write The Other War came as early as 1970 when Alemseged, then a junior legal assistant to the Ethiopian Ministry of Finance, was taken on a trip to the Ogaden in southern Ethiopia where the authorities had been trying to suppress a long irredentist war with ethnic Somalis. As the military conflict was impossible to contain, Amhara soldiers, then the leading ethnic group in Ethiopia, were encouraged to have children with local women, by consent or by force, in order to 'breed out' Somali identity. Such concepts struck a cord with the playwright. In a recent afterword to his play, Alemseged notes that

> the Colonel's 'policy' settled into the depths of my thinking, my consciousness. I could neither forget nor forgive it. It became a permanent fixture, a grudge-generating fixture in my psyche. In 1981, when I moved to the EPLF's Cultural Division to help develop drama, the urge to portray such a 'policy' in a play became an obsession. (A.Tesfai 2002: 215)

Alemseged however insists that he never objected to inter-ethnic marriage as a rule. The play had 'and still has everything to do with governments and colonizers that use sex and marriage as instruments of ethnic cleansing. It has nothing to do with love and lovers, no matter their origin' (A. Tesfai 2002: 216).

The second incident on which *The Other War* draws was an anecdote about an Eritrean mother whose daughter had divorced her Eritrean husband to live with an Ethiopian cadre. Alemseged managed to track down the woman in a refugee camp and learnt how she had found living with the new couple intolerable and had left for the field, taking with her the 'three purely Eritrean grandchildren from her daughter's earlier marriage, and leaving the children of the Ethiopian' (Plastow 1999: 58). Both sexual and ethnic 'purity' are central themes in *The Other War*, and are critically scrutinized in the course of the action. Ultimately in the play, unlike reality, both grandchildren are taken to the liberated areas, the Eritrean granddaughter, Solomie, and the baby boy, offspring of an Amharic father. For the most part, however, the focus is on the female characters in the play who 'are not mere sexual or maternal objects, but active, politically, socially and domestically engaged subjects of the drama' (Plastow 1999: 57).

In my reading of *The Other War*, I will refer not only to its authorized English translation, but also to the 1980s video film to help highlight some of my arguments.

Outline
The Other War is again divided into five acts with no further subdivisions; all are set in the protagonist's living room. The play runs for just under an hour with no interval.

Letiyesus, a woman of around fifty, returns home after a trip to her village to find her house invaded by her daughter, Astier, and her new husband, Assefa, an Ethiopian cadre. Astier has a teenage daughter, Solomie, from a previous marriage to an Eritrean, and an infant son, Kitaw, whose name means 'punish them'. Letiyesus's own son, Miki-el, a liberation fighter, is an acknowledged presence in the house, whom the audience never sees.

Astier soon becomes the chairwoman of the local *kebele* (urban dwellers' association, the Derg's administrative units, usually a means of government control) and thus an outcast to the local community. While initially all family members try to keep up a minimum of social appearance, the situation at home quickly disintegrates with the deteriorating political situation. Two factions become apparent: Letiyesus and her granddaughter Solomie (together with Letiyesus's friend, Hiwot) who secretly support the liberation fighters; and the younger couple, Assefa and Astier, as representatives of the Ethiopian regime. The situation hits a crisis point in Acts 3 and 4 when Assefa demands to know Miki-el's whereabouts at gunpoint and Solomie deliberately scalds her stepfather while preparing his footbath. The violent encounter prompts Letiyesus to leave for the field, together with Solomie, her friend, Hiwot, and the baby boy, now renamed Awet – Tigrinya for 'victory'.

Reading The Other War

On the surface, *The Other War* is a drama about civilian life under the Derg. Set in the intimate space of a home, however, it replicates the larger conflict in the divided loyalties of the family members. As in *Le'ul*, but more dramatically, the personal and political are intertwined. As the title suggests, *The Other War* is as much about conventional warfare as it is about another site of conflict, the bodies of women, on which a different kind of battle is fought. Alemseged takes up the well-worn motifs of Mother Eritrea and woman as national allegory, only to defy their one-dimensional interpretation. Instead, he demolishes theatrical clichés and translates them into a more self-directed system. While (re-)negotiating questions of gender, belonging and identity, the author does not however do entirely away with assumptions of masculine authority, even though he challenges the historical agency of men.

The Other War is naturalistic in form, the set showing a typical Eritrean living room of an average, better-off highland family; a chest of drawers, a table and some chairs, with one door back centre stage as the only exit. While this is the more representative part of the room, some stools and a *forniello*, a portable charcoal stove, indicate the 'women's corner' on the lower floor. It is here that Letiyesus and Hiwot have their heart-to-heart talks, and the grandmother comforts and confides in her granddaughter, Solomie. Significantly, Astier never ventures into that part of the room except once, when her husband orders her to see to his footbath herself. Astier and Assefa usually occupy the 'representative' area of the living room which the other family members only use in their absence. Their action establishes a spatial hierarchy, which resembles the then current political power structures in the country. At first sight, Ethiopia is represented as the more powerful force, further indicated by the banners high up on the wall, by Astier's frequent changes of clothes which are expensive and fashionable, by the radio and the telephone they have installed. These are imposing status symbols which contrast starkly with Letiyesus's modest frocks and her ordinary kitchen equipment. However, it is from her viewpoint that the spectator experiences the events and learns to see through the hollow façade of Ethiopian pretensions.

House and body – often related concepts in Eritrea – are the main symbols in Alemseged's play. Letiyesus returns from the village to find her home invaded by Astier and her Amhara husband. Earlier on, she had been subjected to a crude physical inspection:

> **Letiyesus** Mbwa! I left this morning but because of all these checkpoints it took all day. Oh, what a terrible life … and those men at the checkpoints! Tell me, are they human beings, or animals? Shameless people! (Grabbing her breasts and imitating their voices and gestures.) What have we got here … huh? What have you hidden here? They wouldn't spare anyone, even old women.[14]

The incursion into the domestic and corporeal terrain immediately translates into the occupation of the national territory. For Letiyesus, the idea of her daughter willingly sleeping with 'the enemy' – a voluntary, perhaps even pleasurable, incursion – is therefore the ultimate form of treason. 'We had no idea she would be driven to this, no idea whatever that someday she would betray her own country and people' (p. 280). Alemseged first feeds, then cleverly discards this notion by portraying a more complex picture than the usual Manichean allegory. As the embodiment of the traditional mother figure, and an icon of national values, Letiyesus does not quite fit into the stereotype of the gentle self-sacrificing carer. Letiyesus is tough, headstrong and sometimes narrow-minded; she also comes across as aloof, even if dignified.[15] More importantly, the tense relationship with her daughter is partly Letiyesus's own doing.

> Astier [...] remember when you married me off to Zecharias? That's when you lost me. Yes, Mother, you and father gave me to a drunkard, just because his parents had money and some fancy titles. You didn't even notice that I was only half his age. Now, who are you to give me any advice? (p. 275)

For Astier, we learn, this was only the beginning of a torturous ordeal. Beaten and sexually abused, she could only survive by cutting the bond between herself and her Eritrean heritage which she experienced as far more oppressive than Ethiopian colonization.

> Astier [...] I was beaten up, trodden on by Zecharias so much that I thought it would never end. My face was constantly swollen. Look at the marks under my eyes. I spent my youth, lying in bed, crying endlessly, waiting for him to come back drunk and use or misuse me, as he saw fit. Now, Mother you are asking me why I am so enthusiastic about these people here? And why shouldn't I be? Zecharias locked me behind bars, Assefa opened the door and my eyes to the world. My heart was full of hatred, Assefa filled it with love. I was ignorant, today I am a chairwoman. [...] Now, what do you have to say? Who are my people? You or them? (p. 275)

The daughter's explicit rejection of her ancestry, and her proactive embracing of an identity associated with the enemy forces, leaves Letiyesus speechless and on the verge of tears. Initially, this was criticized as an 'unrevolutionary' weakness by cultural cadres who had been invited to comment on the play (Plastow and S. Tsehaye 1998: 47). Yet, the strength of the drama lies in the fact that it does not reduce the story to a single propagandist dimension, even if ultimately adhering to the official line. Sympathies between Letiyesus and her daughter are divided, and this caused considerable controversy. Plastow and Solomon Tsehaye write that 'it was argued that Astier's strength overwhelmed that of her mother and that it was not good to show any sympathy for her' (1998: 47–8). Yet, Astier's change of heart is comprehensible and demonstrates that 'there is bad in the good, and, even more difficult, that there can be elements of good in the bad' (Sachs 1990: 20), as the South African lawyer and senior ANC member, Albie Sachs, once put it. After all, Assefa is quite a sympathetic figure initially, polite and considerate and trying to mediate between the household members. At one point he even invites

Letiyesus to sit on a proper chair, thus trying to lift her 'up' symbolically to his own level. Letiyesus, however, adamantly refuses to be drawn into the world of powermongers and traitors. Throughout the video performance of the play, the gap between the two factions is mapped out spatially, not only in terms of the layout of the room, but also corporeally. Except for the brief welcome in the opening scene, there are no affectionate exchanges between the two parties; Letiyesus and Solomie on the one hand, Astier and Assefa on the other. If two members of each group happen to be close physically, distance is immediately created by avoiding eye contact. Astier and Solomie have their own cheerless history. In her previous marriage Astier had taken out her frustration on the girl, thus perpetuating the vicious circle of abuse and aggression. And since, for Letiyesus, Solomie is the only family member 'purely' Eritrean in body and soul, she lavishes her affection on her. Scenes between Letiyesus and Solomie are the most demonstrative in the play, an interplay between loving hugs and caresses that contrasts starkly with the otherwise frosty atmosphere. Usually, 'they immediately separate' (p. 287) when someone else enters the room; yet, when Assefa threatens Letiyesus with a pistol, Solomie clutches her grandmother with one hand from behind, with the other holding her baby brother, Kitaw. (The formation is significant in several ways, for Solomie will indeed become the key mediator between age and ethnic schisms). Determined, and with his son on their side, the women are too strong a force for Assefa to dominate. His menace with the phallic pistol shrivels into a sign of impotence, and so he exits the room. However, when Assefa uses the same hand gun in the final scene to terrorize Astier, there is no one to give support to his wife. Broken, she is left lying in the floor, imprisoned in the very house she had helped to occupy.

The true 'object of contention' (Plastow 1999: 58) in the play is of course the baby boy, the offspring of an Eritrean woman and her Amhara husband. For Alemseged he constitutes 'a symbol of either oppression or freedom' (Plastow 1999: 58). Like Miki-el, he is a mute and (semi-)absent character throughout, but one who literally embodies the conflicting positions. Having been told that his name means 'punish them [him]' (p. 268) – i.e. the liberation fighters – Letiyesus never touches the boy, even if partly responsible for his care.[16]

> [...] **Letiyesus** (*looks at* Kitaw *in disgust*) Ouff, what a nose. I hate noses like that.
> **Solomie** No, he's handsome, Grandma.
> **Letiyesus** (*going to her fornello* [sic]) He doesn't look like us. He is not one of us. (p. 285)

Letiyesus still believes in the ultimately racist conception of ethnic 'purity', which goes in line with the sexual 'purity' so important for Eritrean women. Both are equally repressive and misused instruments of control. Initially, the play seems to validate these beliefs, only to deconstruct them in the penultimate scene. For Assefa, his son is a means of penalizing and subverting this secessionist nation; Solomie, Hiwot and Letiyesus, however, turn the tables on him by giving the boy a new identity and thus 'appropriating' the child as a symbol for national liberation.

> **Assefa** [...] Your daughter, Astier, comes from that Eritrean womb you are so proud of. I, Assefa, planted my seed in your own daughter's womb. Kitaw was born. Kitaw walks on this earth, just like your Mika-el [sic]. My roots are firmly planted in Eritrea and no power can ever pull them up. So, get this straight. Eritrea no longer belongs to the Mika-els [sic], it belongs to us, (*Pointing at* Kitaw) to the Kitaws. (p. 291)

It is initially Solomie who deflates this idea. The girl is adamant that the infant must come with them to the field, because he is her brother and only a child, guiltless of political scheming. Hiwot reinforces her view for different reasons, urging her friend not to be governed by the same bigoted opinions, but to twist them around in self-defence: 'Take the child away from them. Snatch him, Letiyesus. He is your flesh and blood too. [...] Don't let them use our own wombs to rule us!' (p. 294).

Thus Kitaw becomes Awet – 'victory' – and the sexual manipulation of women is shattered. Together, the three women take down the myth of ethnic purity, demoting the power of Amhara 'blood' to a fancy of the imagination. By 'appropriating' Kitaw/Awet for the liberation struggle, they draw attention to the construction, not innate essence, of social and cultural identities. Astier betrays her country not necessarily by giving her body to the nation's enemy – there are enough examples of female underground agents using sexual favours to trap and betray their Ethiopian suitors (cf. Wilson 1991: 84–6) – but by a change of heart. This, however, the play reveals, was brought about by a repressive social order in Eritrea which the EPLF proposes to eradicate.

While women are finally portrayed as agents of historical events, masculine authority is still unquestioned. According to custom, it is Assefa who rules the family. Together they live in a house which is not Letiyesus's, but Miki-el's (p. 265). The absent fighter becomes the ultimate reference point for the nationalist faction in the play, while Kitaw heralds an 'Ethiopian' Eritrea for his parents. Yet again, Alemseged manages to diffuse these symbols by reducing them to cherished, but mute and silent emblems. It is Solomie who is the true heroine of the play, defying both old and new(ly imposed) authorities. That she looks for guidance to the liberation movement is the logical conclusion for a play set against, and emerging from a struggle for independence. Solomie (in the video) marks this change by replacing her childish braids with an unruly Afro in the course of the action.

Ultimately, *The Other War* continues to be a piece of EPLF propaganda, but the most subtle I have been able to trace. It demonstrates the immense development of writing and performing drama in the field, also with regard to the portrayal of women. Yet, it would also remain an exception rather than the rule whose common denominator was still a preference for simplified morals and one-dimensional representations.

Acknowledgements

The author gratefully acknowledges the financial support of the DAAD and the *Cusanuswerk, Bischöfliche Studienstiftung*. For administrative and office support I am indebted to Solomon Tsehaye, formerly Director of the Bureau of Cultural Affairs, Ministry of Education, Asmara, and The British Council, Eritrea, under its Director Negusse Araya. Thanks also to my Eritrean colleagues, Mussie Tesfagiorgis, Tekeste Yonas and Tesfazghi Ukubazghi, for their invaluable help.

NOTES

1 In the context of this essay, 'drama' is used when referring to the largely dialogic form such as is prevalent in the West, in both scripted (written) form and in performance. 'Theatre' embraces the wider range of performing arts, including drama, music and dance. 'Performance' relates to the public presentation of a creative, artistic act before an audience. Cf. Plastow (1996: 1), Kennedy (2003).

2 Fighters of the liberation struggle refer to those areas in which they operated as 'the field'.

3 For further biographical details see Plastow (1999: 54–60).

4 For *The Other War* see *Music and Drama of the EPLF* [video mid-1980s]; cf. (Plastow and S. Tsehaye 1998: 51). From the mid-1980s to independence, three literary competitions took place in the field. For further details see G. Negash (1999: 187–92).

5 Note that Eritreans are usually addressed by their first name, the second being the forename of the father rather than a 'surname' as in western usage.

6 Until recently, the manuscript of *Anqetsi* was considered lost in the field. In January 2003, however, while reading a draft chapter of my research, Solomon Tsehaye, a senior cultural officer and then Head of Literature, was convinced that I had somehow unearthed the play. Questioning the playwright confirmed the find. Renamed as *Tsälot Nedhmet Hezbi Ertrea (Pray for the Safety of the Eritrean People)* by an apparently unknown author, the play had been in the Asmara Research and Documentation Centre (RDC) all along, just one floor below Alemseged's own spacious office. *Anqetsi* is a developmental play on meningitis written for a medical congress in 1983 and cannot be dealt with here.

7 The publication of *Drama* is dated '1986 (?)' on the Tigrinya manuscript; cf. G. Negash (1999: 181). Solomon Tsehaye however insists that the study was written in 1983, prior to Alemseged's theatrical masterpiece, *The Other War*, in which he tried to realize his own critical suggestions. Solomon's argument seems convincing, especially since Alemseged had already been moved to a different department in 1986. The author himself was unable to remember the exact date.

8 In February 2000 Alemseged Tesfai noted that West African plays were not appreciated in Eritrea: 'Too many images, too much mythology. We are not very strong on mythology in Eritrea. [...] Our mythology is about saints – Gabriel, Michael, and so on. We are very old Christian and Muslim societies' (interview, 22 February 2000).

9 All plays were written in Tigrinya, the dominant of the nine official languages of Eritrea: Tigrinya, Tigre, Bilen, Saho, Afar, Hedareb, Kunama, Nara and Arabic. While long-

established performance forms and musical numbers catered for virtually all linguistic communities, Tigre-language plays were only introduced in the late 1980s; other-language drama still remains an exception.

10 For examples see Kerr (1995: 105–32), Mda (1993: 47), Rohmer (1999: 39). Jane Plastow related that during her first meeting with Alemseged Tesfai in the early 1990s, the latter had never heard of the distinction between 'art'/'elite' and 'popular'/'people's' theatre.

11 Altogether I was able to trace 16 scripts from the field, some providing a mere plot summary, others being fully scripted. Most scholarly writings on EPLF theatre so far draw attention to the enormous theatrical achievement in the liberation struggle, rather than viewing matters more critically.

12 It should be noted that neither theatre practitioners nor spectators were particularly familiar with Western theatre jargon on which EPLF drama work ostensibly drew. Hence theatrical terms were sometimes confused, or words were imbued with atypical meanings.

13 *The Other War* saw a short run at the West Yorkshire Playhouse in Leeds in 1997, and again in 2001 at Barnsley College, UK. For coverage of *The Other War*, see Banham and Plastow (1999: xxi–xxiv), Plastow (1999: 57–8), Plastow and S. Tsehaye (1998: 42–53), Warwick (1997: 229–30).

14 (A. Tesfai 1999: 263). All further references in the play follow the 1999 edition.

15 Indeed, when the video version had reached Eritrean diaspora communities, the figure of Letiyesus was criticized 'for being too cold, especially towards the small boy whom she effectively stole from her daughter' (Plastow and S. Tsehaye 1998: 48).

16 In the video, Letiyesus gives the boy an unfriendly rap on the nose.

WORKS CITED

Eritrean authors are listed with their father's name ('surname') first to comply with international citation systems. Sources originally published in Tigrinya are quoted in the English translation available to the author.

Banham, Martin and Jane Plastow (eds). *Contemporary African Plays*. London: Methuen, 1999.

Kennedy, Dennis (ed.). *The Oxford Encyclopedia of Theatre and Performance*. 2 vols. Oxford: Oxford University Press, 2003.

Kerr, David. *African Popular Theatre: From Pre-Colonial Times to the Present Day*. London: James Currey, 1995.

Matzke, Christine. 'Of *Suwa* Houses and Singing Contests: Early Urban Women Performers in Asmara, Eritrea'. In Jane Plastow (guest ed.). *African Theatre: Women*. Martin Banham, James Gibbs and Femi Osofisan (eds). Oxford: James Currey, 2002: 29–46.

Music and Drama of the EPLF. Video. EPLF Cine-Section. [mid-1980s].

Negash, Ghirmai. *A History of Tigrinya Literature in Eritrea: The Oral and the Written, 1890–1991*. Leiden: Research School of Asian, African, and Amerindian Studies, University of Leiden, 1999.

Pfister, Manfred. *The Theory and Analysis of Drama*. Transl. John Halliday. Cambridge: Cambridge University Press, 1993 [1988].

Plastow, Jane. *African Theatre and Politics: The Evolution of Theatre in Ethiopia, Tanzania and Zimbabwe: A Comparative Study*. Amsterdam: Rodopi, 1996.

—— and Solomon Tsehaye. 'Making Theatre for a Change: Two Plays of the Eritrean Liberation Struggle'. In Richard Boon and Jane Plastow (eds). *Theatre Matters: Performance and Culture on the World Stage*. Cambridge: Cambridge University Press, 1998: 36–54.

—— 'Alemseged Tesfai: A Playwright in Service to Eritrean Liberation'. In Martin Banham, James Gibbs and Femi Osofisan (eds). *African Theatre in Development*. Oxford: James Currey, 1999: 54–60.

—— 'Ethiopia and Eritrea'. In Martin Banham (ed.). *A History of African Theatre*. Cambridge:

Cambridge University Press, 2004: 192–205.

Rohmer, Martin. *Theatre and Performance in Zimbabwe*. Bayreuth: Eckhard Breitinger, 1999.

Sachs, Albie. 'Preparing Ourselves for Freedom'. In Ingrid de Kok and Karen Press (eds). *Spring is Rebellious: Arguments about Cultural Freedom by Albie Sachs and Respondents*. Cape Town: Buchu Books, 1990: 19–29.

Tesfai, Alemseged. *Literature, Its Development, and Its Role in Revolution*. Mimeograph. Transl. Mussie Tesfagiorgis. N.p.: EPLF, 1982.

—— *Drama*. Mimeograph. Transl. Tekeste Yonas. N.p.: EPLF, [1983].

—— *Wedi Hadera (The Song of Hadera)*, 1983.

—— 'Not By Guns Alone: The Pen and the Eritrean Struggle for Independence'. Unpublished paper presented at the international conference 'Against All Odds: African Languages and Literatures into the 21st Century', Asmara, Eritrea, 11–17 January 2000.

—— *Two Weeks in the Trenches: Reminiscences of Childhood and War in Eritrea*. Transl. Alemseged Tesfai. Asmara: Red Sea Press, 2002.

—— Unpublished email to the author. 28 August 2002.

—— 'The Other War'. Transl. Paul Warwick, Samson Gebregzhier and Alemseged Tesfai. In Martin Banham and Jane Plastow (eds). *Contemporary African Plays*. London: Methuen, 1999: 261-301. (Repr. and with an 'Afterword' in Alemseged Tesfai. *Two Weeks in the Trenches: Reminiscences of Childhood and War in Eritrea*. Transl. Alemseged Tesfai. Asmara: Red Sea Press, 2002: 167–216).

—— 'Le'ul'. In Alemseged Tesfai. *Two Weeks in the Trenches: Reminiscences of Childhood and War in Eritrea*. Transl. Alemseged Tesfai. Asmara: Red Sea Press, 2002: 139–65.

Tseggai Tesfazghi, Esaias. 'Theatre During the Long Struggle for Eritrean Independence'. Unpublished MA dissertation. University of Leeds, 2002.

Warwick, Paul. 'Theatre and the Eritrean Struggle for Freedom: The Cultural Troupes of the People's Liberation Front', *New Theatre Quarterly*, 13.51 (1997): 221–30.

Wilson, Amrit. *The Challenge Road: Women and the Eritrean Revolution*. Trenton, NJ: Red Sea Press, 1991.

Zerai Asghedom, Misgun. 'The Theatre Experience in Eritrea'. Unpublished MA dissertation. University of Leeds, 2001.

Interviews

Alemseged Tesfai, playwright, lawyer, historian. Rec. interview in English, 22 February 2000, Asmara, Eritrea. Interviewer: Christine Matzke (CM), transcript: Mussie Tesfagiorgis (MT).

Solomon Tsehaye, Head of Cultural Affairs Bureau, Ministry of Education. Rec. interview in English, 4 August 2000, Asmara, Eritrea. Interviewer/transcript: CM.

Weyni Tewolde, actress, PFDJ Cultural Affairs. Rec. interview in English/Tigrinya, 29 February 2000, Asmara, Eritrea. Interviewer: CM, translator: Tesfazghi Ukubazghi, transcript: MT.

Sacrifice & the Contestation of Identity in Chukwuemeka Ike's *Sunset at Dawn*

Clement A. Okafor

Nation states are analogous to human beings; they are conceived and are born after an appropriate gestation period. Thereafter, their parents and well-wishers watch them with keen interest as they grow from infancy to adolescence in the hope that the young nations will survive to mature old age. Unfortunately, sometimes tragedy befalls the nations and they teeter on the brink of collapse. Such is the misfortune of the nation, which is portrayed in *Sunset at Dawn*,[1] a historical novel that is based on the Nigeria/Biafra civil war.

Like a human being, the nation state of Nigeria was conceived during the Berlin conference of 1884/85. It was at this meeting that various European states allocated to themselves portions of the continent of Africa as their colonies. In this manner, Britain was allotted the territory that she later named Nigeria. The gestation period lasted 29 years, that is, from 1885 to 1914, during which time Britain ruled the Northern and Southern sections (protectorates) of Nigeria as separate entities. The date of birth of Nigeria as a nation state was 1914, since that was the year when the British colonial government amalgamated the two protectorates into one entity. Yet, the colonial government did not institute one administrative system for the entire nation. Rather, it administered the two units differently. In the South, it encouraged Christian missionaries to establish churches and schools as Westernizing influences, while in the North it established a system of indirect rule that operated through the existing feudal organization. Besides, the British recognized the North as the domain of Islam. Consequently, the new Nigerian state was nurtured and grew up with two distinct identities: one Western-oriented, the other Islamic-oriented. Furthermore, the Nigerian nation was encouraged to grow up with this split personality until independence in 1960. Then, Britain withdrew its colonial administration and left the Nigerians brought up under the two different mind-sets to work together in a lop-sided federation in which the Northern Region was much bigger and more populous than the Western and Eastern Regions combined. This was obviously not an arrangement that made for a harmonious relationship among the federating units.

Like a young adult, the newly independent state of Nigeria experienced many growing pains, principal of which was the military *coup d'état* that overthrew the corrupt and Northern-dominated post-independence government. The genesis of the unravelling of the Nigerian post-colonial state is traceable to the revisionist interpretation of this regime change, which was initially perceived as nationalistic, but was later viewed as a strategy for Igbo domination of the newly independent Nigerian state. Since the new order that resulted from the change of government was viewed, especially in the North, as inimical to its interest, it launched a revanchist coup d'etat that ousted the first military administration in Nigeria. In the ensuing genocide, the Northerners slaughtered approximately fifty thousand Easterners living in their midst.[2] These were the dark clouds that eventually exploded into a storm: the Nigeria/ Biafra civil war – the historical event that has informed Chukwuemeka Ike's *Sunset at Dawn*.

In his portrait of the Nigeria/Biafra conflict, the overarching concept is the ambivalent gaze of a mother on her unwanted child. Here, the attitude of Nigeria to Biafra is an example of that ambivalent gaze. In real life a mother, who is faced with such a predicament, often experiences conflicting attitude swings towards the infant. Sometimes, her maternal instinct makes her wish to retain and nurture her baby. Yet, at other times, she hates the child and may either wish to kill the baby or abandon it at a site where someone else may find and rescue it. As Chinua Achebe has argued quite convincingly, one of the major issues that confront the real Nigeria is its ambivalent attitude towards the Igbo people.[3] On the one hand, most of the other ethnic nationalities in Nigeria are envious of the spectacular advances made by the Igbo people in all fields of human endeavour and, consequently, would love to be rid of them. On the other hand, these same ethnic groups want to preserve the territorial integrity of Nigeria; hence, they do not want the Igbo people to secede from Nigeria and become an independent state.

In *Sunset at Dawn*, the ambivalent gaze of the mother – symbolized by the vicious hen that devours its young ones – results in child endangerment, which is the metaphor for the genocide of the Igbo people resident in Northern Nigeria. Furthermore, in this work, Chukwuemeka Ike explores the implications of the mother's ambivalent gaze on her unwanted child through three major narrative strands. The first chronicles the contestation of identity, while the second interrogates the meaning of sacrifice and patriotism. The third, on the other hand, is a love story that examines the outcome of the interethnic marriage between the protagonist, Dr. Amilo Kanu, an Eastern Nigerian and his wife, Fatima, from the North, with the birthplace of each spouse representing one of the two antagonistic identities that are chronicled in the novel.

The author introduces his readers to the issue of the contestation of identity right from the very opening pages of the novel in the parade of the enthusiastic volunteers from the 20 provinces of Biafra. The assembling of these young warriors here is reminiscent of the gathering and naming of heroes before major battles in traditional epics the world over. In this assembly, although the contingents sing different songs, all are united in the belief that their cause is just and that they will prevail in the end; hence, their new identity as Biafrans will endure:

> We are Biafrans
> Fighting for our freedom;
> In the name of Jesus
> We shall conquer (p. 1)

However, their identity is bitterly contested by Nigeria – the entity from which they have broken away. More importantly, the Nigerian riposte is swift and is delivered by means of a jet bomber that scatters the gathering, as everyone scrambles for safety under the nearest available shelter:

> '*Ewo*! shouted a driver outside the hall. 'It's a plane!
> Everyone in the hall reacted as if he had a split second to escape from the vicinity of the examination hall before Kill-We (the Biafran Superman) smashed the building, roof, wall and all. Chairs and volunteers were trampled upon in the stampede to take cover outside. One volunteer made for the glass panels on the folding door with the speed of a ram and the blindness of a millipede. He did not notice that he had any cuts until he was a safe distance from the building, squatting inside a cassava farm whose leaves offered him the protection he badly needed from the enemy plane. (p. 12)

This incident establishes the tone and tempo of the unequal contest that pits Nigeria and its supporters: the British, the Russians and the Islamic world on the one side and isolated Biafra on the other. (It is remarkable that Britain and the Soviet Union make common cause against Biafra on this occasion, given that the events are set in the Cold War era.) The Biafrans realize that the odds are against them, but they are not disheartened, since they see the war as a re-enactment of the biblical contest between David and Goliath, the giant.[4] They regard themselves as David, and Nigeria and her supporters as Goliath, and this further convinces them that they will prevail in the end.

Since the genocide of the Igbo people in Northern Nigeria, the Nigerian emblem, the eagle, has become synonymous in the minds of the Biafrans with the legendary vicious hen that devours its offspring. With the outbreak of war and the Nigerian indiscriminate bombing and shelling of Biafran markets and churches, the eagle further symbolizes in Biafran eyes the quintessence of evil. The rising sun, the emblem of Biafra, on the other hand, represents rays of hope to these beleaguered people. Thus, on the symbolic level, the war is a combat between the eagle and the rising sun. The Biafrans, the people of the rising sun, know that the road to their new identity is strewn with monumental obstacles, but they are confident of eventual victory:

> 'We are fighting what people who speak the English language call a war of survi-'
> ' –val!' echoed the gathering
> 'War of survi-'!'
> ' –val!'
> Our sons who studied history assure us that no nation fighting a war of survival as we are now fighting has ever been defeated. As the Big Man says, by the grace of God we shall van-'
> '-quish!' echoed the audience. (p. 63)

In addition to the reassurance from history cited above, Biafrans also have a traditional belief that no misadventure can ever uproot someone permanently from his home.

In *Sunset at Dawn*, one of the events that has helped to unite all Biafrans in their new identity as the people of the rising sun is the genocide of approximately 50,000 Easterners in the Northern Region. Given the vibrant extended family system portrayed in the novel, it means that there is hardly anyone in Biafra who does not have a kinsman who was murdered in the genocide that was perpetrated in the North. What has helped to unite the Biafrans further in their revulsion over these incidents is the gruesome manner in which these people were killed. The butchery of Mr Uche, the railway clerk, merely serves as an example:

> We could not have reached my sister's house in the city before a group of armed soldiers and civilians, carrying a list of Eastern Nigerians they were assigned to kill, rushed into the quarters shouting 'Where is Mr. Uche?' 'Mr. Uche, tally clerk, come out at once!' ... Without knowing it, my husband ran into another group of murderers who were searching for their own marked men. A shot got him in the stomach and he fell. To punish him for resisting capture, the soldiers who had failed to catch him plucked out his two eyes, ripped open his stomach and then left him in the open air to die painfully (pp. 93–4)

This horrendous massacre of 50,000 unarmed men, women, and children was an affront to the conscience of the world and has been immortalized in the Hollywood movie *Tears of the Sun*[5] featuring Bruce Willis as the Navy S.E.A.L. lieutenant, who rescues an American lady doctor endangered by the Nigerian army's wholesale slaughter of the Igbo inhabitants of her medical outpost. Furthermore, this pogrom of the Easterners in the North is reminiscent of the mass murder of the Jews by the Nazis during the Second World War. As has been indicated earlier, the nature of the Igbo extended family ensures that there is hardly a family in Biafra that does not share a sense of bereavement on account of the genocide.

Another factor that helps to consolidate the new Biafran identity is the experience of having to flee one's home and sometimes having to abandon all one's possessions as one joins the exodus of thousands of terrified people fleeing the onslaught of the advancing and menacing Nigerian army, as is exemplified in the following account of the exodus from Onitsha:

> The traders in the all-engulfing Onitsha Market fled, abandoning thousands of pounds' worth of wares. It was more chaotic than the stampede which followed the unannounced total eclipse of the sun in Eastern Nigeria in 1947. There was no question of running to the house to look for your family or to collect your personal effects. Every child in Biafra had of course been drilled in what action to take in such a situation – to move with the crowd rather than to roam about looking for the parents or next of kin. (pp.104–5)

This scene is repeated whenever a Biafran town or village falls to the Nigerians. Sadly, the plight of the Biafrans at such moments parallels the agony of the Israelites as they crossed the Red Sea, with the Pharaoh and the Egyptian army in hot pursuit.[6] When these uprooted Biafrans get to a safe distance, they go their separate ways in search of refuge among their kinsmen who live in other more secure parts of their new nation. Unfortunately, those who cannot find accommodation in this manner are housed in refugee camps. At the initial stages of the war, the refugees in the camps were well fed, but as food became scarce due to the Nigerian policy of using starvation as a weapon of war, the refugees had little or nothing to eat and slowly starved to death. The pathetic situation in the refugee camps is exemplified in the following description of the inmates of one such camp:

> You could not tell the colour of the skin from the colour of the rags they had on – those of them who still had rags. Their bones could be seen under their skin, more clearly than on an X-ray film. Most of the children had no energy left even to cry: they crouched on the floor at a corner of the transit camp, looking like deceased chimps. The only two people who looked normal were the two children who still suckled their mothers. Their mothers, however, were so shriveled and weak that it was difficult to imagine how anything could have trickled into the mouths of their robust babies from those flabby, lifeless breasts... (p. 174)

Losing one's entire material possessions is very traumatic. However, the ritual implications of flight from one's homeland are even more devastating. Flight from one's homeland would ritually be tantamount to the abandonment of one's ancestors, since there would be no one left behind to pour libations to them. Such a calamity is the antithesis of the aspirations of every Igbo *pater familias*, namely, that his lineage should not perish, as is reflected in such popular names as *Obiechina* (May my household never perish), and *Amaefuna* (May the entrance to my home never disappear).

The loss of towns and surrounding farmlands discussed above resulted in food deficiency in Biafra, which, in turn, created 'Harold Wilson's children', named after the then British prime minister who supplied vital intelligence, weaponry and diplomatic support to the Nigerian side. The Biafrans attribute their losses in the battle field to Harold Wilson's ardent support of the Nigerian war effort; hence, they also blame him for creating the situation that led to the malnourishment of these children, who are afflicted with kwashiorkor – a protein deficiency disease. Initially, the disease is limited to the most vulnerable in society, namely the children and the very old. However, as the war continues and as Biafra loses more arable land and other sources of protein the disease spreads to able-bodied men all over the new nation. In this manner, scarcity of food becomes another unifying common denominator for Biafrans.

Yet another factor that has helped to unite Biafrans in their new identity is Nigeria's indiscriminate bombing of Biafran civilian targets like churches and markets. This is exemplified in the following account of the bombardment of Obodo, an ordinary Biafran town:

> Prophet James' thriving church was at one side of the circle and all that remained of it was the red laterite which previously constituted its walls. The thatched roof simply disappeared; nobody could say whether it had ascended into heaven with the prophet or had been burnt without leaving behind any ashes. It was impossible to identify the prophet's remains, or to tell from the ruins how many worshippers perished in the disaster. Bits of human flesh and fleshless bones were strewn over the entire area. (pp. 137–8)

The bombing of the Red Cross office in Umuahia that kills six Biafran Red Cross workers and totally destroys a nearby typing school and dismembers its students also bears eloquent testimony to the Nigerian disregard for the lives of non-combatant civilians:

> Five Biafran Red Cross workers were killed; one of them who had been standing beside a pillar was neatly chopped into two. A woman caught running down the external stair case had been disemboweled, and fell with her intestines spread over the stair case. ... At the typing school across the road, items of clothing turned out to be the only clue for assembling the different portions of the students' disemboweled bodies. (p. 180)

The bombing of such obviously non-military targets is probably aimed at terrorizing the Biafrans into surrendering. However, the outcome is totally different; it convinces the Biafrans that the Nigerians want to exterminate them and that the war is merely an amplification of the earlier genocide committed against them in Northern Nigeria. This conviction strengthens them in their resolve to fight in order to preserve the Biafran identity. Their resolve is expressed in the following song:

> Armour'd-u car
> Shelling machine
> Fighter and bomber – kpom!
> Ha enwegh ike imeri Biafra
> Biafra win the war! (p. 142)

> Armoured car
> Shelling machine
> Fighter and bomber – kpom!
> Even these cannot defeat Biafra
> Biafra [will] win the war! (my translation)

Another unifying factor in the Biafra portrayed in *Sunset at Dawn* is the hardship occasioned by the change of currency from the Nigerian to the Biafran notes. Since Biafra has not minted enough notes, it directs all its citizens to deposit their Nigerian notes in banks with a view to redeeming them later with Biafran notes. As it turns out, however, the exercise results in interminable queues outside every bank. The unintended outcome is that some people even faint while waiting in line to deposit their money. Worse still, the exercise drastically curtails the money available to the populace and introduces another kind of suffering to the list of hardships that mould the Biafran identity. It also introduces 'moneyokor' (lack of money) into the Biafran lexicon. Nevertheless, the Biafrans remain convinced that with God on their side they will surmount all these difficulties. Their song below is not only a plea for God's assistance; it is also an affirmation of the faith in their ultimate victory:

> Nuru olu anyi, nna, nuru olu anyi,
> Nuru olu anyi, nna, nuru olu anyi.
> Odigh mgbe ike Gowon gakari ike Ojukwu.
> Odigh mgbe ike Gowon gakari ike Ojukwu
> Nna nuru, Chukwu kere uwa nuru olu anyi (pp.122–3)

> Listen to our petition, Father, listen to our petition,
> Listen to our petition, Father, listen to our petition.
> Gowon's power will never prevail against Ojukwu's
> Gowon's power will never prevail against Ojukwu's
> Father, listen, God who created the world, listen to our petition.
>   (My translation)

The belief of the Biafrans in their ultimate victory is also strengthened by the recognition of the independence of Biafra by the African nations of Tanzania, Gabon, and Ivory Coast in quick succession. The Biafrans are convinced that the recognition of the sovereignty of their new state by these countries will guarantee the survival of their new identity. However, it produces the very opposite effect. It makes their Nigerian adversaries desperate to capture even more Biafran towns, especially Port Harcourt, which is the only remaining sea-port in Biafra:

> Port Harcourt was a different story. The Nigerian Navy came with all it had, the way the motorized column of the Nigerian Second Division had been equipped to bulldoze its way into Onitsha. Biafra had no warships, no submarines ... It was an unequal combat. The Nigerians had the 'right of weight,' and once again God sided with the bigger battalions. The Nigerians successfully landed troops in Port Harcourt. (p. 164)

Despite the Nigerian successes in the battlefield, however, the Biafrans are not intimidated; an aspect of the emerging Biafran identity is a total contempt for Nigerians, especially the Northern Nigerians, whom they regard as intellectually inferior and lacking in basic personal hygiene. Thus, they constantly refer to the Northern Nigerians by such derogatory expressions as 'sho-sho', and 'jigger-infested vandals'. Consequently, the Biafrans believe that the Nigerian charlatans cannot prevail in the end, their momentary victories notwithstanding. More importantly, the Nigerians, too, believe in the innate superiority of the Biafrans; hence, the Nigerians find it necessary to recruit the military collaboration of other nations in their own war effort, particularly the Egyptian pilots, who undertake much of the Nigerian bombing missions against Biafra:

> And even the Nigerians will admit that if the two sides were left alone, they would be no match for us. The big snag is that the world has not left us alone to slug it out. The British are vying for the first place with the Russians as Nigeria's backers. It's the first time I have seen Britain and the Soviet Union backing the same side ... (p. 190)

In addition to their contempt for the Nigerians, the Biafrans are justifiably proud of the ingenuity of their scientists, who within the short span of the war have built mobile petroleum refineries, new international airports, distilleries, and a broadcasting network that the Nigerian jet bombers and fighters have not been able to silence. In the sphere of weaponry, the Biafran scientists have not only manufactured guns and grenades but also rockets and amoured cars:

> 'Some foreign journalists visiting Biafra had the surprise of their lives two days ago. The D.H.Q. took them over to one of our workshops to show them some of the things our scientists have produced. They admired the different types of grenades and locally-made guns. Then an armoured car drove towards them, stopped opposite them, and out jumped a Biafran girl smartly dressed in army uniform and gave the salute to the officer accompanying the journalists. They could not believe it when they were told the armoured car was made in Biafra.'
> 'Stories like that make me proud to be a Biafran,' Barrister Ifeji announced. (pp. 39–40)

Even in the field of battle, the Biafrans fight very gallantly too. The spectacular heroism of Biafran warriors is exemplified by the exploits of Corporal Nwafo, who captures a Nigerian tank although he is armed merely with a rifle. Equally impressive is the deadly accuracy of the Biafran shore batteries that sink so many Nigerian warships that the Nigerians eventually give up their effort to go across the River Niger from Asaba to Onitsha – a short distance of only one mile. This is the reason the Biafrans gladly refer to Onitsha as *odi nso elu aka* (near, but beyond reach):

> The Nigerians kept shelling Onitsha and trying to pour in troops. Every evening, Biafrans tuned their radios to find out from the 'War Report' how many vandal boats had been sunk by Biafran shore batteries. Soon Biafra faced serious danger of an epidemic, unless the thousands of bodies of Nigerian soldiers scattered along the bank of the Niger were buried. (p. 110)

Yet more spectacular is the Biafran annihilation at Abagana of the motorized column of the Second Division of the Nigerian army. The feat is so awesome that people regard it as miraculous:

> The advancing column, more than a hundred vehicles strong, carried more
> military hardware than Nigeria required to capture every inch of Biafran soil,
> and estimated at more than three times the armament stocked by the entire
> Nigerian army before the blackout. A BBC commentator who had waited a
> lifetime for this final act in the Nigeria-Biafra drama, was unequivocal in his
> prediction that the end of Biafra was in sight. Africa's largest army, Africa's
> deadliest weapons, were on the march to Onitsha and Biafra lacked the capabil-
> ity and the ingenuity to delay the advance. (p. 111)

Contrary to the prognosis of the journalist, Biafra does not only have the
capability to delay the advance but the ingenuity to destroy the formida-
ble Nigerian force in its track. By firing a bullet into one of the fuel
tankers, the Biafrans incinerate the miles of tankers, armoured cars,
military supplies and accompanying troops.

Still, by far the most strategic Biafran success in the battle field is the
conquest of the Midwest Region. This is such a brilliant manoeuvre that
had the spearhead of the Biafran advance maintained its momentum,
Biafra would have captured Lagos and won the war:

> While Nigerian troops were gaining ground slowly in Biafra, Biafran forces
> sprung a surprise on them by taking the war onto Nigerians. The success of the
> lightning operation stunned even Biafrans, most of whom had no inkling that
> any such invasion was contemplated. It was one of the few secrets which
> remained secret inside Biafra. An unbelieving world woke up one morning to
> hear that gallant Biafran forces had captured Mid-Western Nigeria. The
> commander of the invading force proclaimed Mid-Western Nigeria an indepen-
> dent state under the new name of the republic of Benin. A BBC reporter
> announced that the advancing Biafran forces had already reached Ore, some
> seventy miles beyond Benin on the way to Lagos. (p.18)

Unfortunately for Biafra, their forces are betrayed by their commanders as
part of a failed coup d'etat that not only demoralizes the Biafran armed
forces but drives a wedge between them and the civilians. This singular act
of treachery sets Biafra on a slippery slope from which it never recovers;
thereafter, it experiences one setback after another until finally the entire
state is overwhelmed by its bigger adversary. When Nigeria wins the war,
the Biafrans lose the contest to maintain a separate, independent identity
that has emerged through the exigencies of war and privation. In terms of
icons, this also means that the eagle eventually prevails over the rising
sun.

In addition to portraying the contestation of identities, *Sunset at Dawn*
is also a chronicle of the monumental sacrifice made by the Biafrans on
both the individual and the communal planes. The very opening pages of
the novel also introduce the reader to this with the parade of the 10,000
enthusiastic volunteers from the twenty provinces of the new nation.
These youngsters constitute the machete brigade that is willing to make
the ultimate sacrifice for Biafra. They volunteer to defend their nation's
capital, Enugu, with their lives even though they are armed merely with
matchetes and dummy guns, while the enemies they face are armed with

armoured cars and heavy artillery. Amazingly, their commitment does not waver even after their parade has been bombed by a Nigerian war plane. Rather, in the following song these brave Biafrans profess their readiness to die for their new homeland:

> Oh my father, don't you worry;
> Oh my mother, don't you worry;
> If I happen to die in the battle field
> Never mind, we shall meet in heaven... (15)

Another form of communal sacrifice discernible in *Sunset at Dawn* is *igba ndu*. In reality this is the Igbo blood oath that binds the participants to one another in a solemn covenant. In the novel, this covenant serves as a ritual by means of which an entire town swears allegiance to their new nation, Biafra:

> *Igba ndu* won unanimous support as the answer. The next *Nkwo* market day was chosen for the solemn ceremony. Every Christian would swear by the Holy Bible, and every non-Christian by the *Ofo* that he would never assist any enemy to attack or enter Obodo nor sell his town or fellow townsman in any other way; if he did, the Bible or the *Ofo* should kill him outright. (pp. 60–1)

Communal sacrifice is also evident in the novel in the manner of implementing the contingency plan to disperse the various government agencies from Enugu in the event of the fall of the capital city. As planned, most of the war directorates move to Umuahia, which is the unofficial capital of Biafra, while many Government ministries move to Owerri and Aba. Some of the banks also move to the three big cities, while others relocate to the villages adjudged safe from enemy attack. Meanwhile, the Posts and Telegraphs department ingeniously matches the Enugu addresses to the war locations of these agencies. Above all, Radio Biafra, Enugu – on account of the inventiveness of the Biafran telecommunication engineers – continues to transmit from its new locations in different towns. By so doing, the Biafrans ensure that the fall of Enugu, their administrative capital, to the Nigerians turns out ultimately to be a pyrrhic victory; it does not cripple the new nation's ability to continue to wage its war of self-defence.

Further evidence of such sacrifice is in the portrayal of the communal feeding of Biafran soldiers. Acting on an announcement made by the town crier, each town levies all its adult members various food items and in this manner generates ample food supply for the Biafran fighting men and women. In Obodo, for example, every adult male contributes one big yam every day, while every woman donates five tubers of cassava, which is the equivalent of one cup of garri. Meanwhile, every village contributes one tin of palm oil daily towards the feeding of the troops.

The novel also describes the sacrifices made in the accommodation of the refugees. As has been stated earlier, whenever a Biafran town or village is about to fall to the enemy, its inhabitants move out en masse to nearby towns and villages that are considered safe from imminent danger. On arrival, the refugees seek shelter among whichever member of their extended family they can locate, even if they have not been in contact with them for years. Indeed, many latch on in this manner to the most tenuous of relationships in order to find shelter. However, those who cannot claim affinity to any member of the host community are accommodated in the refugee camps set up in every Biafran town and village. The host communities often have an ambivalent attitude towards the refugees, though. On the one hand, they wish to help them, as fellow Biafrans. On the other hand, they are very suspicious of these strangers. The townspeople fear that the refugees are jealous of them for continuing to live in their own homes and they also suspect that the refugees may not be averse to betraying their homeland to the enemy infiltrators. Still, the town leaders know that permitting the construction of refugee camps in their midst is the right thing to do. Hence, they tolerate the refugee camps that enable Biafra to accommodate its teeming population even as its territory continues to shrink.

Although the novel shows that communal sacrifice is a salient factor in the Biafran struggle, it also demonstrates that individual sacrifice is equally critical to Biafra's effort to survive. Specifically, it shows that the foundation which sustains the superstructure of communal sacrifice in Biafra is built on the solid bedrock of individual sacrifices made each day by most of its citizens. Such selfless sacrifice is seen in the patriotic action of parents, who willingly send their sons to fight in the Biafran army and their daughters to work in the Biafran Red Cross. These parents know quite well that their offspring may die on the war front, but they are undeterred. Similarly, the tireless action of the voluntary vigilante groups who work tirelessly to prevent enemy infiltration of their communities at the numerous checkpoints in the villages is a manifestation of personal sacrifice, as is the dedicated service of Biafran scientists and technologists, such as Dr Osita, who toil day and night to invent Biafran weapons of war.

The war is also being fought on the spiritual plane, and Prophet James is an embodiment of the spiritual sacrifice made by many Biafrans. His seven-day fast prior to the 'Abagana miracle' is viewed by his people as an offering for the welfare of his nation. Consequently, many of the inhabitants of his hometown, Obodo, attribute the awesome events in Abagana to the efficacy of his prayer and fasting.

Bassey Duke, also known as Indigenous, is not expected to support the new state wholeheartedly, his home is in Ikot Ekpene – a non-Igbo part of Biafra, yet he identifies himself totally with the aspirations of the nation and donates most generously to its welfare. At the outbreak of the war, he donates the considerable sum of five hundred pounds sterling in foreign exchange towards the Biafran effort to purchase a war plane. In addition, he donates two station wagon vehicles to the government. He is indeed so dedicated to the cause that he does not evacuate his supermarket in

Enugu till the very last minute so as not to cause panic among the city dwellers. Most of his trusted friends are Igbo Biafrans and they stand by him through all his tribulations, but what almost breaks his heart is the perfidy of Chief Inyang, from his hometown, who plans with the Nigerians to entrap and kill him.

Mrs Halima Uche dedicates her entire life to the new state, even though she was not born within its territory. On the contrary, she is a Northerner by birth, but marries an Igbo who works in the North. During the pogrom, her husband is brutally murdered and although she had never previously visited his home, she flees the North and endangers her life in order to save the two sons she has with her husband. When she finally gets to Biafra, she identifies so completely with her husband's kinsmen and adapts so well to their way of life that they give her the honorific title of '*nwanne di na mba*' (a close relation can be found among the strange people in a strange land) (p. 95). Sadly, this exemplary model of personal sacrifice pays the ultimate price for her dedication to Biafra. First, one of her two sons dies of kwashiorkor and finally she and her remaining son are killed by a Nigerian jet bomber.

However, it is the protagonist of the novel, Dr Amilo Kanu, a one-time director of mobilization of Biafra. He is an unlikely candidate for a Biafran patriot, since he is in many ways an ideal Nigerian, having been married to a Northerner, and is working at the University of Ibadan in Western Nigeria as a young medical officer, with a brilliant academic career ahead of him in the faculty of medicine. Not surprisingly, therefore, he is initially reluctant to leave Ibadan when the other Easterners return home in the wake of the genocide in the North, especially as he is genuinely committed to the concept of Nigeria:

> 'Disintegration or regionalization or secession,' he had argued on one occasion, 'is the short-cut adopted by people who are not men enough to face up to the challenge of group living.' He had regarded it as a short-cut that would ulti-mately lead to the creation of one state for one person, if carried to its logical conclusion. He firmly believed the Federation of Nigeria could stay together if only every Nigerian would be man enough to face up to the challenge. (p. 31)

Indeed, it is the fake telegram announcing his father's death that eventu-ally makes him travel to the East in the first place. Once he gets there, however, he begins to view the unfolding events differently. Realizing that Nigeria is about to splinter anyway, he wishes to be with his people in their time of need. In addition, he is persuaded to bring his wife, Fatima, home because he is assured of her safety in the first instance. He is persuaded that on account of their contacts in Nigeria, he and his wife can become useful intermediaries between his people and the Nigerians at the appropriate time. Indeed, at the inception of the war, he is appointed a member of Biafra's negotiating team and in no time becomes the new nation's Director of mobilization. All the same, perhaps, because he knows that other people suspect that he has divided loyalty to Biafra on account of his marriage and his friendship with the leaders of the abortive coup d'etat, Dr Kanu strives to demonstrate his total fidelity to the new nation at all times. Soon his actions make it clear that his devotion is a matter of conviction rather than convenience. His readiness to lead a machete brigade group in its dangerous plan to attack heavily armed Nigerian troops, especially after the death of his first son, proves beyond any doubt that his loyalty to Biafra is without blemish. Even so, he feels that he is not doing enough for Biafra by merely recruiting soldiers to fight for its defence in his capacity as Director of mobilization. Consequently, he offers to join the Biafran army:

> All our achievements on all other fronts are of no avail unless we also achieve victory on the war front,' Dr. Kanu went on. 'I have great faith in Biafra. Our scientific and technological achievements in less than two years as a nation, and a nation at war, the unprecedented involvement in and commitment to the national cause, and the high degree of self-reliance and self-confidence which our people have manifested, prove beyond any doubt that we have the makings of a great nation. I have come to the conclusion that many more of us must join the Armed Forces if our dreams for Biafra are to be realized. Accordingly I hereby offer my services to the Biafran Army in whatever capacity I am considered fit. (p. 210)

In the light of the genuine conviction expressed above, not even the Biafran Head of State can dissuade this courageous Biafran patriot from his chosen act of self immolation on behalf of his new nation. Indeed, the events that are portrayed in *Sunset at Dawn* show without any doubt whatsoever that the countless acts of sacrifice of individual Biafran citizens, like Dr Kanu and others, are what makes it possible for Biafra to remain one entity throughout the war, even as its population is being subjected to horrendous danger and monumental deprivation.

Thus far, we have demonstrated that *Sunset at Dawn* is a portrait not only of sacrifice but also of the contestation of identities. Nevertheless, the novel is a love story, too; it is a portrait of the transformational power of love between the protagonist, Dr Amilo Kanu, a medical doctor and his wife, Fatima, a radiographer. Amilo is an abbreviation for *Amam ilo?* (Do I know the enemy?) Indeed Dr Kanu does not know the enemy, for he marries a woman whose uncle later becomes one of the organizers of the genocide of his people, but fortunately for him, his wife loves him and has no hand in her uncle's perfidy. They are married in England, where the ethnic differences between Nigerians do not seem to matter, and on their return to Nigeria, they reside in a university which is located in the cosmopolitan city of Ibadan and plan to visit Dr Kanu's hometown briefly only once in a while. Thus, their interethnic marriage, they imagine, will not be problematic. However, events do not work out as planned: the genocide of Dr Amilo's people and the impending break up of Nigeria propel them to relocate to the Eastern Region. Initially, they live in Enugu, another cosmopolitan city, where their marriage does not generate many problems.

Sadly, their love for each other is later sorely tested in Enugu. The death of their first son, Amilo Jr, severely tests their relationship, for while Fatima is devastated by their son's death, her husband is preoccupied with the preparations for the imminent machete operation. Fortunately for their marriage, the operation is cancelled on the orders of the Biafran Head of State; hence, Fatima does not get to know about this very dangerous undertaking.

The next important test of their love comes after the fall of Enugu when Dr. Kanu decides that Fatima and their only surviving son, Emeka, should relocate to Dr Kanu's hometown, Obodo, while he lives in Umuahia, Biafra's new administrative capital. His major concern is the safety of his family, but his wife does not like rural life, especially as she does not speak Igbo, the language of the villagers. Worse still, although her husband has been building her a house and has done everything possible to make her comfortable, Fatima suspects that the real reason her husband does not want her to live with him in Umuahia has something to do with her Northern origin. Indeed, she imagines that her husband considers her ethnic background embarrassing. However, her acquaintance with Mrs Halima Uche, another Northerner, makes her begin to see things differently; it makes her begin to appreciate and treasure her marital life:

> Mrs Halima Uche had taken away the blinkers which had narrowed her horizon. Halima's account of her wretched experience highlighted some of the noblest ideals of marital life which Fatima suddenly recognized were woefully deficient in her own. Halima had sacrificed personal comfort and risked her very life in her determination to identify herself with her husband. She had demonstrated that Mrs Uche could remain Mrs Uche even when the outlook was bleak. (p. 99)

Unfortunately, the composure that Fatima has learned with Halima as her role model is shattered by the sudden and tragic death of Halima and her son in a Nigerian bombing raid. In the wake of this personal calamity, Fatima is unnerved by the nightmare in which Aliyu, Fatima's former suitor, threatens to kill her, her son and her husband. In her frantic search for solace, Fatima visits her husband in Umuahia without any prior warning, only to find him with another woman in the house. This is undoubtedly another major test of their relationship, but their love for one another enables them to overcome this trial.

Their relationship is tested again when Fatima is close to having a nervous breakdown and cannot withstand the pressure of living in Biafra any more. She is so paranoid on account of the constant danger of Nigerian air raids that she spends all day in the bunker and comes out only at night. Consequently, the Biafran authorities grant her a special favor by authorizing her and her son, Emeka, to travel to Libreville, the capital of Gabon – one of the countries that earlier recognized the independence of Biafra. There, she works in the children's centre, caring for malnourished Biafran children. Surprisingly, it is also while Fatima is in

Libreville that she experiences her epiphany and realizes for the first time that she has been completely transformed into a Biafran patriot. It is for this reason that she rejects her parent's offer to return to Nigeria:

> She was amazed at herself, after despatching that letter to her parents; amazed that she should reject the offer to return to Nigeria at a time when she was at liberty to go back home without hindrance. (p. 230)

More importantly, the parcel of scarce commodities that Fatima sends to her husband from Libreville, shows that she has not only been trans- formed into a patriotic Biafran but has also metamorphosed into a very loving and compassionate wife; the gifts are not for Dr Kanu alone but also for the people who are very dear to him: a packet of razor blades for her husband's best friend Akwaelumuo, a reel of hair thread plus two cakes of Lux soap for Akwaelumuo's wife Rose, and an entire head of tobacco for her own father-in-law. Of special significance is her gift to her husband of packets of condoms; it shows that she has finally become not just mature but very realistic too.

When Dr Kanu is killed, surprisingly, Fatima is not dispirited despite having already lost her first son who was killed by a Nigerian mortar shell in Enugu. On the contrary, the tragic event transforms her into a fearless warrior. Thereafter, she refuses to return to the safety of Libreville. Rather, she wishes to bring back her second and only surviving son, Emeka, from the Gabonese capital so that they can both of live in Biafra. Indeed, it takes the wisdom of her father-in-law, Mazi Kanu, to convince her that the only way she can make the sacrifice of her first son and her husband meaning- ful is by preserving the life of her lone surviving son. This is how the revered old man persuades Fatima to elevate her commitment and dedi- cation to Biafra to a higher level by returning to Libreville and thus, by tactically withdrawing from the war front, this born again Biafran warrior places herself in a position to prepare her son to re-contest the future.

The subsequent war that pits Nigeria – whose emblem is the eagle – against Biafra – whose emblem is the rising sun – is a contestation of antagonistic identities. Hence, on the symbolic level the contestation is between the eagle (the incarnation of the vicious hen that devours her young ones) and the rising sun (the rays of hope for an endangered people). The title of *Sunset at Dawn* is also an allusion to the total eclipse of the sun that occurred one afternoon in Eastern Nigeria in 1947. Since the populace was not forewarned before the event, many people were petrified and believed that the cosmic phenomenon was indeed a prelude to the end of the world. Consequently, they were relieved when the eclipse cleared and daylight returned to the territory. Although the event was frightful, it was short-lived. Unlike the eclipse that lasted a short time, however, the effect of the victory of the eagle over the rising sun has long lasting and dire consequences for the Biafran people and the identity for which they have sacrificed everything dear to them. Hence, the premature sunset that is dramatized in the novel symbolizes not just a transient phenomenon but the cataclysmic collapse of a people's dreams and aspirations.

Above all, in *Sunset at Dawn*, Chukwuemeka Ike deftly portrays Biafra as a comet that for 30 months blazed through the firmament, revealing the potentialities of an African nation that has purposeful and innovative leadership. The Biafran image that is discernible in the novel shows that an African nation can carve out a niche for itself even in this modern, scientific world. The transformational power of love and sacrifice has turned the character Fatima into a valiant proxy for the new nation that has been engaged in a life and death struggle for its independence and identity.

NOTES

1   Chukwuemeka Ike, *Sunset at Dawn*. Glasgow: Fontana Books, 1981. All references are to this edition.

2   *The Violations of Human and Civil Rights of Ndigbo in the Federation of Nigeria (1966 – 1999): A Petition to the Human Rights Violations Investigating Committee by Oha-Na-Eze Ndi Igbo (The Apex Organization of the Entire Igbo People of Nigeria) for and on Behalf of the Entire Ndi Igbo*. October, 1999: 16.

3   Chinua Achebe, *The Trouble with Nigeria*. London: Heinemann, 1984, 45–60.

4   *The Holy Bible. Authorized King James Version. Giant Print*. Grand Rapids, MI: Zondervan, 1994: 438–42.

5   *Tears of the Sun*. Culver City, California: Revolution Studios, 2003.

6   *The Holy Bible. Authorized King James Version. Giant Print*. Grand Rapids, MI: Zondervan, 1994: 102.

Of War & Madness: A Symbolic Transmutation of
the Nigeria–Biafra War in Select Stories from
The Insider: Stories of War & Peace from Nigeria

Iniobong I. Uko

It is around 40 years now since the civil war in Nigeria ended, yet its ugly
scars on the Nigerian mind and soul remain visible and glaring. The
defective healing process of the wounds on the Nigerian psyche from the
war has resulted in an extensive gulf between the people of the defunct
Biafra and Nigeria, the two parties in the war that lasted from 1967 to
1970 and the implications of the war are manifested in diverse ways and
degrees in the contemporary Nigerian body politic. Biafra comprised
mainly the people of the Eastern part of Nigeria, who, led by Lt. Col.
Chukwuemeka Odumegwu Ojukwu, attempted to secede from the federation of Nigeria on account of several grievances prominent among which
was acute marginalization. According to Atofarati (2003),

> Under normal circumstances the amalgamation [of the three regions in Nigeria
> in 1966] ought to have brought the various peoples together and provided a firm
> basis for the arduous task of establishing closer cultural, social, religious and
> linguistic ties vital for true unity among the people. [Rather] There was
> division, hatred, unhealthy rivalry and pronounced disparity in development.

The apparent bitterness and discontent of the people of Biafra about
the way they were treated, and the total waste that the Nigeria–Biafra war
portended, come alive in the fiction on the war. Nigerian fiction on the
war, written mostly by scholars and intellectuals from Eastern Nigeria,
specifically the Igbo, who directly suffered and still bear the pains of the
war, reveals that the war was avoidable. The symbols within which the
stories are couched are profound. They indicate a close affinity between
the Nigerian civil war and madness. The symbols underscore the people's
recrimination of their Igbo leaders, on the one hand, who plunged into a
war for which they were ill-prepared and ill-equipped. On the other
hand, the symbols launch a reproach to and scorn of the then Federal
Government in Nigeria that in its irresponsibility and capriciousness
remained insensitive to the atmosphere of anarchy, manifest as severe
intertribal hatred, which engulfed the land and culminated in the Igbo-
led secessionist attempt. This study, in examining some of the war
stories published in *The Insider* edited by Chinua Achebe et al. (1971),

49

explores the symbolic inference of the situations that allude overtly or covertly to insanity. Insanity here, therefore, serves as the framework for the reader to apply in decoding the peculiar dynamics of the Nigeria–Biafra war. Other literary works on the Nigeria–Biafra war include Cyprian Ekwensi's 'Minus Everything' and *Survive the Peace*, Wole Soyinka's *The Man Died*, Chinua Achebe's short stories *Girls at War and Other Stories*, Ken Saro-Wiwa's *On a Darkling Plain: An Account of the Nigerian Civil War* and Peter Onwudinjo's *Women of Biafra*. The significance of *The Insider* lies in its pioneering status and role. The volume was the first published work of fiction on the Nigerian civil war and post-war periods. This paper sets out to unravel the symbols in the relevant stories as a way of, first, explaining the relationship between the civil war in Nigeria and madness, and second, evolving a vision for the future of Nigeria.

The version of Achebe's 'The Madman' (pp.1–8) in *The Insider* seems to be the original one, which he later modifies into a more extensive form in his collection of short stories, *Girls at War and Other Stories*. However, the thrust of the theme in both versions is the same. Achebe's succinct depiction of the madman in this story is noteworthy:

> He was drawn to markets and straight roads. Not any tiny neighbourhood market ... but a huge, engulfing bazaar beckoning people familiar and strange from far and near. And not any dusty, old footpath beginning in this village, and ending in that stream but broad, black, mysterious highways without beginning or end ... (p. 3)

The extract above defines the physical operating framework of the madman clearly portraying from the outset 'particular features that describe a person who is mad: drifting and aimless' (Uko 60). He holds conversations with himself, and the omniscient narrator reveals that the madman actually regards other people as insane. He has suffered diverse forms of what he considers to be mistreatment and humiliation, directly and indirectly, from his fellow Ogbu people, particularly from Okafo Nwibe. Nwibe led three other hefty men to whip the madman out of a stall at the Afọ market; he also beat up the madman to force him from the middle of the highway when a lorry was passing by; and he once sent his children to stone and taunt the madman, thereby causing him tremendous humiliation. The madman now finds an opportunity for revenge: he meets Nwibe bathing in the stream with his clothing on a boulder beside the stream. The madman takes them, ignores Nwibe's threats and runs away with them. Nwibe runs after him stark naked, shouting at him to return the clothing. While the madman runs, clothed in Nwibe's outfit, Nwibe is fully naked pursuing him. Nwibe is thus taken for the madman. They run into the crowded market on the big Eke market day, and Okafo Nwibe's nakedness and tenacious pursuit of the actual madman who is now clothed, as well as his continuous bumping against people inspire, various reactions as well as raising significant traditional issues:

Everyone looked at him first in surprise and then less surprise because strange sights are common in a great market. Some of them even laughed.
...

'That's a new one I'm sure. He hardly looks mad yet. Doesn't he have people ...?' (p. 5).

'People are so careless these days. Why can't they keep proper watch over their sick relation, especially on the day of the market?' (p. 6)

Further still, as people from Nwibe's Ogbu home see and recognize him, one throws down his long basket of yams, another abandons his calabash of palm-wine and they desperately chase him 'to stop him setting foot irrevocably within the occult territory of the powers of the market' (p. 6). Unfortunately, Nwibe is caught only after he has got to the heart of the market. His nakedness is covered with a wrapper donated by an Ogbu woman. His people, grief-stricken, lead him home. The popular and proficient native medicine-man declares Nwibe's insanity irreversible, and although it is eventually cured by another practitioner, therafter 'Nwibe became a quiet withdrawn man avoiding whenever he could the boisterous side of the life of his people' (p. 7). Two years later, the elders covertly deny his request to be considered for the ọzọ title, the highest title in the land. Nwibe becomes the metaphorical outsider, a recluse, stigmatized and merely tolerated and patronized.

Achebe in 'The Madman' skilfully configures a symbolic dimension into the whole corpus of discourse of madness. The symbolism can be decoded through the formula of the civil war in Nigeria. The actual madman represents Nigeria. The insanity manifests itself in the way Nigeria was embroiled, following the attainment of independence from Britain in 1960, in excessive corruption, nepotism, a thirst for power, authority and dominance that bordered on audacious fatality. These excesses degenerated into the coup and counter coup of 1966 that resulted in a pogrom of the Igbo in Northern Nigeria in 1966. Unfortunately, the Nigerian leadership of the time did not show appropriate concern about stemming the tide of violent tribal attitudes and callous avariciousness, and thus the socio-political equation of Nigerian history of that period became distorted. The events constitute a symbolic state of insanity that provoked the Igbo to such a degree that they sought to secede, declaring a sovereign nation of Biafra.

Evidently, the Igbo (Biafra) recognized their inadequacies and shortcomings in the war, like Nwibe who 'ran a hand swiftly over his face to clear his eyes of water' (p. 5), Biafra was poised to fight to attain its envisioned nationhood outside of Nigeria. In fact, Biafrans regarded the war as a struggle for survival and so they fought with the same fervour that Nwibe runs after the madman, with 'his chest ... on the point of exploding from the fire and torment within' (p. 5). The 'fire and torment within' serves as a catalyst to both Biafra and Nwibe in their pursuits. When eventually Nwibe is cured of his 'insanity', he becomes withdrawn and quiet, and the elders tactfully deny him the privilege of obtaining the ọzọ title; 'had they received him, perhaps he might have become at least partially restored' (p. 7), but in being denied this he remains marginalized. Also in a symbolic transmutation, although Nigeria declared at the end of the war that there were 'no victor and no vanquished' between Biafra and the national government, the Igbo are hardly fully accepted and integrated into the national fabric. However, as a strong-willed, tenacious and ambitious people, they become energized to work and succeed to over-come all encumbrances and be recognized in society, as evidenced in the significant roles and positions of the Igbo in the Nigerian socio-political, economic and religious schema. Here lies the uniqueness of the Igbo spirit.

In 'A Village in Agony' (pp. 9–20), Andre Aletta explores the pangs of war on Ameke in Eluama village. The story chronicles the acuteness and intensity of suffering among the people to a degree that threatens the people's mental balance. The undertones of insanity reverberate through the devastating consequences and conditions of the war: hungry children with large round eyes, *kwasiokor* [sic] children, air-raids causing enormous loss of lives and property, truncated education, the intimidation and brutality of civilians by soldiers and a general spirit of despondency. Such conditions turn men into beasts as Ofoegbu sings in *The Love of Money*:

I went to war with my brother and comrade-in-arms:
On our way he sold me to the enemy,
For the love of money. (p. 12)

The song is highly thought-provoking, validating Emenyonu's opinion that during the war, 'human reason had fled to brutish beasts. The world is peopled by unthinking human beings and thoughtful beasts with fore-sight.' (1973: 20). In reality, as observed by Brown (1968: 26), the Biafrans were exhausted by hunger and had few medical facilities. They lacked the clothing and individual equipment to combat the superior weapons of their opponent.

Chukwuma Azuonye's 'The Lost Path' (pp. 21–32) tells the story of fourteen-year-old Achike who was conscripted into a war six months before. Determined to return to his Okom home to reunite with his mother and brothers, he escapes from the camp and walks for a whole day, but loses his way. After the first six hours of relentless trekking, Achike encounters 'a maze of crisscrossing village paths ... now, he no longer knew his bearing. Still, he walked on ... [and] stopped there and decided to go no further' (p. 23). At this point, Achike definitely needs some assis-tance from a person familiar with the geography of the area. This being his tenth attempt to return home during the six months, Achike is afraid of being caught and forced again into fighting. He is also conscious that his imposing stature at his young age works against him: being so 'tall and big, he was an easy prey to the Military Police' (p. 24).

Fortunately for Achike, a man suddenly emerges from a nearby bush, but strangely, the man is talking to himself and laughing. The man is very dirty, with matted hair; his beard, specked with yellowing grey dust of hairs, is as dirty and unkempt as the hair on his head, and he gives out a pale yellow smell of castor-oil:

> Achike took him to be one of the *war casualties*; one of the village-folks whom *the war had turned beasts* – with no soap to wash, no clothes to wash; beasts crazy with hunger ... (25) (emphasis mine).

Achike's efforts to begin a conversation with the man so as to obtain information on the correct path to Okom are initially futile as the man does not talk to him. When eventually he begins to talk, his utterances are incoherent:

> Achike said, 'I want to ask you something ...'
> ...
> Then the man spoke: 'My name is Izreani nwa Dimoji. But why? Everybody has been asking me my name today.'
>
> 'I want you to show me the correct path to Umuna [that leads to Okom]', said Achike. 'I didn't ask you your name ... I have been walking since morning, but I cannot find the tarred road.'
>
> 'Your name? Are you asking me your own name! You must be crazy!'
> 'The road ... I said, the road ...'
> ...
> 'Ha! What strange beasts I meet today? Look! Are those ears of yours ornaments? Didn't you hear when I said it – that my name is Izreani nwa Dimoji?' ... (pp. 25–6).

Izreani's ranting and incongruous replies to Achike's questions bring to the foreground this underlying theme of madness in this story. He abuses Achike as stupid and hard-eared. From a distance, some people are watching and are amused at the unfolding encounter between Achike and the strange man. Achike becomes confused, feels foolish and embarrassed, and wonders what might be wrong. His consternation is reminiscent of Nwibe's in Achebe's 'The Madman'. Nwibe, stark naked, expects people to know that the properly clothed man he is vigorously pursuing is the madman, but people believe otherwise and act according to what they see.

In 'The Lost Path', it is ironic that the man regards Achike as mad: 'there are many mad people in this world' (p. 27); you must be a mad man!' (p. 25). It is also frustrating for Achike that the onlookers divulge no information to help him out of the hands of the man or to assist him proceed on his journey home. While Achike is convinced that Izreani is an eccentric, a half-wit, or an outright lunatic (p. 28), Izreani on his part, believes that Achike and the onlookers are mad, 'all floating about ..., swarming like maggots on nightsoil from dawn to dusk ... Is it just the war? Is everybody in this our land mad?' (p. 29). In spite of this, Izreani invites Achike to stay with him because 'you do not know what bad snake you're pursuing with a short knife' (p. 29). Achike ignores him, his wise counsel and prediction; and walks on, because 'home called and urged him on .... Time pressed. The threatening rain sapped all his hope, and he feared the prospects of getting benighted in the land of Izreani nwa Dimoji' (p. 30).

As Achike treks along, he feels Izreani's shadow following him and is reminded continually of his invitation to stay. He meets a Military Police Corporal and the Civil Defenders who inform him that Izreani is a madman. Achike continues 'through the oilbean-flanked corridor, through the thickening jungle' (p. 32) until 'the corridor suddenly terminated in the open market where women and children stood wailing and pleading amidst a large squad of soldiers and five lorries filled with able-bodied men of the village' (p. 32) who are being conscripted into the army. Achike is sure he is seen by the captors and is ultimately taken away as well. Achike's long and tiring trek, encounter with Izreani and ignorance of Izreani's lunacy and his eventual captivity denote diverse significations in the Nigeria–Biafran war paradigm. Emenyonu observes that though the lunatic is jeered by everyone around him and he becomes the laughing stock, ironically, it appears that in the Biafra–Nigeria conflict, the only philosophical and strategic heroes were the lunatics – they were the only people with vision and insight. They were the only people free in the true sense of freedom, yet they were the only people who commanded no respect and no attention (Emenyonu 1973: 19–20). This authenticates Izreani's proverbial prediction through the proverb of Achike's unfortunate recapture into the army.

Achike's escape from the soldiers' camp and tortuous journey through uncertain routes to get back to his mother and brothers are indicative of his search for freedom and identity. In symbolic terms, prior to the Nigerian civil war, the people of the Eastern region, in particular the Igbo, felt marginalized and relegated in the national polity. That the state of Biafra was declared was a manifestation of their lack of a sense of belonging on the one hand, and a climax of their feeling of dissatisfaction, on the other. Achike's unfortunate encounter with Izreani yields nothing positive, but rather, infuriates him, thereby symbolizing the unsuccessful attempts by the Igbo community to dialogue with the Federal Government of the time to reverse its policies on derivation of the national oil wealth and spread of development based on these resources. Achike's recapture into the war implies that he neither stays with Izreani nor attains freedom and reunion with his family. It signifies the fact that even though the war in Nigeria has been over since 1970, and a 'no-victor-no-vanquished' declaration was made to douse all nerves and tempers, Biafrans, the people from Eastern Nigeria, though still in Nigeria, neither fully belong nor are they independent and free to harness their resources for their own welfare.

Closely linked with the sense of disappointment and disillusionment in Aletta's 'The Lost Path' is Victor Nwankwo's 'The End of the Road' (pp. 33–50). This story is the closest to reality in its direct references to the authentic Nigeria-Biafra clash. It recounts the condition, welfare and psychology of the Biafran soldiers during the Nigerian civil war:

> There were about sixty boys altogether, all loaded with spades, picks, axes, tunnel diggers, mines, booby traps, and grenades. (p. 40)
>
> ...
>
> Troops comprised half-starved, rag-tag young men with sunken eyes and protruding ribs, armed with bolt-action rifles. ... There were altogether four hastily and poorly dug trenches, no support weapons and no morale. Nobody seemed to be in charge. I was immediately reminded of a bunch of newly hatched chicken abandoned by their mother. (p. 41)

Apparently, young boys were forced to serve in the Biafran army. They had no training or uniforms, and inadequate food and arms. Malnourished, poorly clothed and poorly armed, often abandoned by their senior Officers and Commanders, the soldiers become frustrated, disillusioned and desperate. The appalling conditions of the Biafrans were caused by two major factors: first the loss early in the war of their oil revenues (two-thirds of the total Nigerian production); hence they were denied the means to finance the war; second, Nigeria converted to a new currency during the course of the war. Biafra's ability to purchase arms was limited, thus it depended largely on what it could capture from both civilian and enemy camps, and what it could improvise (Atofarati, p. 18).

In the story, in spite of the soldiers' deplorable circumstances, as well as their inferiority in manpower and machinery, they walk continuously for sixteen hours to locate the squadron Headquarters in Ukworji. The troop is commanded by 'a tall, lean, hungry-looking individual with bushy face, bloodshot eyes, and bad tempered as a rattle-snake' (p. 43). At night, the soldiers, weary from hunger and the long trek, sleep in the bushes or at open market places. At dawn, they are awakened by kicks from the officer and Sergeant Major, and the trek continues. These acutely inhuman conditions force some soldiers, then called 'saboteurs', to defect and join the opposing group that has well-equipped and highly motivated soldiers. The phenomenon of the saboteur in the Biafran camp was a statement of protest and of a desire to live. In many cases, the protests were against the soldiers' poor conditions in the debilitating war; and the desire to live drove them to detect from the Biafran camp, that was characterized by excessive intimidation, starvation, lack of incentives, to the Nigerian camp. Defection and sabotage were a consequence of the overwhelming and excruciating odds against success, despite the soldiers' identification with the Biafran philosophy and cause.

In the story, the weary soldiers encounter a group of people, 'not soldiers. Not stragglers. Not even saboteurs – but people. Just people:

men, women and children, talking and laughing unarmed!' (p. 48). Two
words that surfaced from their banter were 'One Nigeria ...' (p. 49). 'One
Nigeria' was the slogan used during the tense period of chaos and anarchy
before and during the civil war, which in itself was an attempt by the
Nigerian government to quash secessionist ambitions led by the Igbo.
Nigeria sought to retain national unity. 'One Nigeria' implied the failure
of the Biafran secessionist effort, and the control by the Nigerian Federal
Government of all mineral resources from all parts of the country. In 'The
End of the Road', the reference to 'One Nigeria' means that the war has
been settled in favour of Nigeria. One man in the group of people encoun-
tering the soldiers informs them that the war is ended, that Biafra has surrendered. Lt. Onoh disbelieves the man and regards him as insane, but
when the truth becomes obvious to him,

> ... he turned abruptly and strolled off. ... A hundred yards off, he stopped. He
> unbuttoned his trousers, tucked his shirts in properly and buttoned up again.
> He adjusted the two stars on his shoulder. (p. 49)

Lt. Onoh carefully straightens himself up. His self-consciousness
indicates that the madness is over. He walks away, and with no formal
announcement on the end of the war, or the likely gains and prospects of
the veterans, Lt. Onoh has nothing to look forward to after having fought
against Nigeria, and lost. The sense of loss and hopelessness culminates
in total disenchantment as 'suddenly in a swift movement, the nozzle of
his rifle came against his head. A shot rang out. He slumped to the
ground, the rifle falling with him' (p. 49).

Essentially, Lt. Onoh's suicide contradicts his earlier indication that as
the war had ended, the madness that symbolized the war was also over.
Yet his suicide is in accordance with the anti-climactic end for Biafrans of
the war. He has reached the end of the road, he has been pushed to the
wall, he has not only been disarmed and disempowered by the Biafran
surrender to Nigeria, but he has actually been emasculated. He is like a
lone ranger in the forest, unrecognized, irrelevant and his efforts unap-
preciated. Lt. Onoh remembers the numerous lives lost in the war; he is
bitter at the waste of time and resources, and at the huge numbers of men
turned to beasts by extreme hunger and disease. It is important to note
here that despite French assistance to Biafra in 1968, the International
Committee of the Red Cross estimated that 14,000 people were dying each
day (Cervenka 1971: 54). In fact according to Atofarati (2003), estimates
on the total number of deaths from the war range from 500,000 to
2,000,000. There is no way of knowing with certainty the exact number of
the dead. The vast majority of fatalities, however, were starvation casualties among Biafran civilians (17).

It is significant that like Silas in Felix Okeke-Ezeigbo's story 'Caught in
the Web' (pp. 97–108), Lt. Onoh feels dejected and abandoned by Biafra,
which he has served all along with utmost dedication. He typifies many

Nigerians who were caught up in the tragedy of the civil war. Silas 'had never believed in heroism through death. Yet [he prayed] let whoever opted to die do so without dragging unwilling people into it' (p. 108). Silas represents those who were forcefully conscripted into the army. They were disgruntled because they were deprived of their freedom of choice.

In his analysis of Nigerian politics, Dudley (1973) explains the reality of conscription and says of the enlisting of young inexperienced boys into the Biafran army that 'most Biafrans considered their men as "fighters" instead of "soldiers" because they viewed warfare naively as inter-village free-for-alls' (p. 88). Lt Col. Ojukwu, the army commander who led the Biafran secessionist movement, promoted the idea that it would be civilians who would be called on to fight and win the war in Biafra:

> It has all along been my conviction that it is the civilians who will fight and win this war [for Biafra] and not soldiers. From all that has happened already, it would be foolish to expect the soldiers to satisfy the aspirations of this new [Biafran] republic (cited in Cervenka 1971: 131).

Ojukwu's calculated falsehood deludes the Biafran masses into a false feeling of hope, protection and victory in the futile war. In the context of the grief, gloom, trauma and agony of the war depicted in the stories in *The Insider*, it is a vision of optimism for the future of Nigeria for the book to end with Arthur Agwencha Nwankwo's 'To Lagos with Hope' (p. 109), it is an essential vision of hope for Nigeria. This story portrays post-war Nigeria: Emeka, who had fought on the secessionist side of the war, goes to Lagos; he has high expectations; he meets and intends to stay with his old friend, Danny, to find a job. It soon becomes clear to Emeka that 'Danny's façade of success was a sham' (p. 114). Danny lives with a distant brother-in-law and cannot provide Emeka with accommodation, but he does arrange for his friends, Tunde and Audu, to host Emeka. Emeka shares his war experiences with his new friends. He explains to them the psychology of the soldier in a war situation, but Tunde insists on partisan interpretations:

> **Emeka,** To a fighting soldier, the enemy is faceless. He is neither black nor white; tall nor short. ... The enemy is just the other party. I cannot tell you about the war without talking about the enemy ... even if we've turned out to be brothers. ... We were enemies while it lasted. We killed ourselves ...
>
> **Tunde,** Now hold it. Whom do you call the enemy? You mean, your countrymen are your enemies. ... Are we [from other ethnic groups] your enemies? (pp. 115–16).

Unfortunately, their friendship soon breaks down. Tunde and Emeka quarrel and fight, bringing back the bitterness that characterized the war, with Emeka representing Biafra, and Tunde, Nigeria. Audu (from the North) displays a higher sense of maturity than Tunde (from the West). This manifests itself through Audu's ability to tolerate, and Audu speaking about the notion of enemies during the war, says, 'but it's all over, we have to forgive and forget. ... This is no time to open old wounds ...' (p. 116). On the other hand, Tunde insists that the people from the East, the Igbo, the rebels, in fact, all Biafrans that sought to secede should be treated accordingly. He orders Emeka: 'Go to *your* Biafra. ... This is *our* Lagos' (p. 116), but Emeka argues that 'this is *one Nigeria* ... We should not start apportioning blames ... All Nigerians bear a responsibility in the war' (p. 116) (Emphases mine).

At the climax of their friction, Tunde makes good his threat of 'I'll show you this is our Lagos' (p. 117), by getting Emeka arrested by the police on undisclosed charges. Though illegal, the arrest costs Emeka all his money as the corrupt policemen collect Emeka's five shillings to free him, warning him against returning to Tunde's house. Emeka learns afterwards from Danny that the policemen were imposters. Now homeless and jobless in Lagos, and with Danny unable to help him, he is lucky to run into his old friend Alhadji in his Mercedes taxi who takes him in and then gives him twenty pounds and a job. It is Alhadji who rehabilitates him, thereby making an important statement about the disunity and animosity that exist among the major ethnic groups in Nigeria. It is clear from this story that the hope for Nigeria lies in: a sincere reconciliation among the ethnic groups; the ability to excise the madness that can emerge as a response to even a mention of the civil war in Nigeria; the readiness among Nigerians to protect and sustain Nigeria's sovereignty, and help Nigeria to succeed and have a credible place in the Committee of Nations in Africa and beyond.

'To Lagos with Hope' is emphatic about the need for a positive change of attitude among Nigerians as a means of averting the consequences of inflexibility such as the one that resulted in the civil war. As highlighted by Atofarati: 'the tragedy [of the war] was built on Ojukwu's inflexibility and the consequent inability to effect compromise on the political side. He fuelled the disaster with his ambition, desire and inability to control the situation in Biafra' (2003: 4). According to Emenyonu, the Nigeria–Biafra war was a camouflage designed by the oppressive leadership on both sides to shield from detection their excesses and crimes against the common man (1995: 452)

Technically, the kinetic imagery in this collection of stories derives from the portrayal of the road, crossroads, path and the long, winding and tortuous trek of the soldiers, escapees and veterans (in the post-war story). It translates symbolically into Nigeria's journey towards a true and authentic nationhood in spite of its diverse constituting ethnic groups and interests. The stories studied in this paper stress that as long as the Nigerian civil war remains a potent source of outrage, inter-ethnic hatred, discrimination, and intense nepotism, the bogey of insanity will remain among Nigerians, and the proper healing and development of the brutalized Nigerian mind and spirit, as well as the land, will continue to be an illusion.

WORKS CITED

Achebe, Chinua. *Girls at War and Other Stories.* New York: Bantam Doubleday, 1972.

Achebe, Chinua et al. *The Insider: Stories of War and Peace from Nigeria.* Enugu: Nwankwo-Ifejika & Co, Publisher Ltd., 1971.

Atofarati, Abubakar A. Home Page on 'The Nigerian Civil War, Causes, Strategies and Lessons Learnt. May 2003 <www.Ypforum.org/history_civilwar2>

Brown, Neville. 'The Nigerian Civil War.' *Military Review,* 48, October 1968.

Cervenka, Zdenek. *The Nigerian War, 1967–1970.* Frankfurt: Bernard and Graefe Verlag für Wehrwesen, 1971.

Dudley, Billy J. *Instability and Political Order: Politics and Crisis in Nigeria.* Ibadan: Ibadan University Press, 1073.

Ekwensi, Cyprian. 'Minus Everything.' In *Okike,* 1, 1971: 41–4.

—— *Survive the Peace.* London: Heinemann, 1976.

Emenyonu, Ernest N. 'Post-War Writing in Nigeria'. Studies in Black Literature. Vol. 4. Issue 1, 1973: 17–24.

—— 'Visions of the Nigerian Writer on the Nigerian Civil War.' In *The Writer as Historical Witness: Studies In Commonwealth Literature.* Ed. Edwin Thumboo and Thiru Kandiah. Singapore: UniPress, 1995: 445–59.

Onwudinjo, Peter. *Women of Biafra and Other Poems.* Port Harcourt, Nigeria: Double Diamond, 2000.

Saro-Wiwa, Ken. *On a Darkling Plain: An Account of the Nigerian Civil War.* Port Harcourt: Saros International Publishers, 1989.

Soyinka, Wole. *The Man Died: Prison Notes of Wole Soyinka.* Harmondsworth, Penguin, 1972.

Uko, Iniobong I. 'Artistic and Pedagogical Experimentations: Chinua Achebe's Short Stories and Novels.' *Emerging Perspectives on Chinua Achebe.* Vol. 2. Ed. Ernest N. Emenyonu and Iniobong I. Uko. Trenton, NJ: Africa World Press, 2004: 57–70.

Uwechue, Ralph. *Reflections on the Nigerian Civil War.* New York: Africana Publishing Corporation, 1971.

Becoming a Feminist Writer: Representations of the Subaltern in Buchi Emecheta's *Destination Biafra*

Oike Machiko

The Nigerian civil war (aka the Biafra War), which was fought between Biafra, located in southeastern Nigeria, and the rest of the nation from 1967 to 1970, has provided a fertile ground for African writers to dramatize the problem of the African nation-state. As expressed by Eldred Jones (1983), committed writers have taken it as their responsibility to confront 'this traumatic conflict', and consequently, have produced 'a whole corps of new novels' (p. viii). Central to the present discussion is that most of these 'new novels' have been written by men, and that studies of Biafra war literature have been male-focused. Craig McLuckie, for example, does not mention even a single woman writer in his (1990) book-length study except in two brief notes. Another book-length study by T. Akachi Ezeigbo is even more disappointing, since the critic is a well-known feminist, and still she provides only a diffuse survey on war literature without any clear feminist perspective. This critical neglect can be partly ascribed to the women writers themselves, for most of their texts are no more than autobiographical sketches.[1] The reason why few 'authentic' works about war are written by women is that instead of describing terrible battlefields or the dirty politics behind them, they tend to delineate the home front and familiar everyday life in a plain, down-to-earth style using their own experiences, as exemplified in *Never Again* by Flora Nwapa. Such works by women writers have not been paid serious critical attention except from feminist perspectives, and indeed, Chidi Amuta (1983) judges *Never Again* as a failure due to Nwapa's 'preoccupation with feminist propagandising' (p. 95).

In contrast to these marginalized, mostly autobiographical, texts on war by women writers, *Destination Biafra* (henceforth *Destination*) is perhaps the sole serious work of fiction composed by a well-known woman writer, Buchi Emecheta (1982). Its fictionality distinguishes the text from others, and is doubly focused by its meta-fictional characteristics. The novel follows the feminist quest of a heroine from the elite class. She evacuates to Biafra with refugees, and from that experience decides to write a novel, itself titled, *Destination Biafra*. The present paper intends to demonstrate how *Destination* dramatizes the problem of representing subaltern women. First, it aims to consider Emecheta's feminist positionality in writing *Destination* through examining its Foreword and Dedication. Second, it proceeds to a detailed analysis of *Destination* in order to position the heroine in her relations to, and differences from, the subaltern.

First of all, it is necessary to map the trajectory of the writing positions Emecheta has taken since her first work. Emecheta started her writing career with two semi-autobiographies *In the Ditch* and *Second Class Citizen*, in which she wrote in thin disguise of the economic hardships and mental agonies she experienced as a poor black immigrant mother with five growing children in the UK. After these semi-autobiographical experiments, she undertook genuine works of fiction, and represented the colonial history of Africa from a woman's perspective. Her fifth work, *The Joys of Motherhood* (1979), published during the UN Decade of Women, brought Emecheta international fame as a writer who spoke to the world for African women oppressed by what was called 'third-world tradition'. Then, after this masterpiece, Emecheta tackled the civil war in *Destination*. In short, in her early semi-autobiographies Emecheta expressed her *ressentiment* as an oppressed black woman, while she wrote *Destination* as an established writer who represented poor African women.

Emecheta's consciousness as a third-world woman writer who represents her less fortunate sisters is deliberately invoked in the author's Dedication and Foreword to *Destination*. In the Foreword, Emecheta privileges this novel and the second of her early two semi-autobiographies as stories that 'simply had to be written' (p. vii), and thus underlines her proxy status in *Destination*. What is important here is that one is self-representation by a poor black woman struggling against discrimination, while the other is a representation of subaltern women by an eminent feminist writer. Also, Emecheta apologetically confesses that unlike other writers, she was in Britain at the time of war; and that without first-hand experience of the war, she had to make up a story from what people told her later. Expressing her gratitude to people for providing her with material for the novel, she summarizes several anecdotes in the Foreword, and indeed, the readers are called to recognize the significance of the material she fictionalizes in the novel. Emecheta further admits that she could not integrate all the episodes people imparted to her into the novel. Most importantly, Emecheta dedicates the novel to the memories, not only of the war survivors, but also of the war victims. In this sense, Emecheta grounds the novel on the memories of the dead who cannot speak. Emecheta mentions the memory of her namesake niece first among her relatives innocently killed in the war, implying that she has survived in place of the girl. Then, after referring to the memory of her relatives, she continues to dedicate the novel to 'the memory of those Ibuza [Emecheta's home town] women and their children' (p. vi), and ends with prayers for the souls of the dead.

The Foreword and Dedication makes it clear that Emecheta takes responsibility for speaking for others, that is, the war survivors and victims who cannot speak for themselves. She gives a voice to the memories of these people in the form of a story. Of course the story an outsider represents over a distance in time and place, differs from the memories of those who experienced the events and thus Emecheta shares the burden of writers, especially third-world women writers, to represent the Other.

Having clarified the author's position, this paper will now analyse *Destination* in terms of this representation of the Other. The heroine, Debbie Ogedemgbe, is an elite woman, who in turn attempts to clarify her position in relation to subaltern women in writing about the war she has experienced with them. The novel is composed of two parts. The first part describes the dirty state politics leading to the war, which Debbie takes part in, first in the 'masculine' role of a soldier for Federal Nigeria, and then, in the 'feminine' role of a secret peacemaker dispatched to Biafra. The second part narrates the clandestine journey Debbie risks to Biafra disguised as a fugitive. Experiencing life and death with fellow refugee women, she learns their philosophy of survival, and decides on the last night of the war to help rebuild the nation as 'a woman of Africa' (p. 258) and to hand down the story of the war to subsequent generations. It is clear that the heroine depends on subaltern women for leading her through this feminist quest, and it remains disputable if the heroine finds her agency as an African woman without appropriating the subaltern. On her journey to her 'destination' she has to encounter subaltern women, who ask her, 'Where does the African woman you purport to represent stand, and where do we fall into?'[2] She, who has education and therefore voice, has *responsibility* to answer this question. The following discussion will trace the feminist odyssey of the heroine to her agency as an African woman and posit the problem of representing the subaltern.

The first half of *Destination* tells the inside story of the troubled independence which led to the war from the multiple perspectives of politicians, industrialists and military officers of Africa and Europe. The heroine, Debbie, is an Oxford-educated woman, and thus, as part of the elite is qualified to participate in this male-centered, post-independence power game, if only as a second-rate player. Her peripheral status in the men's circle is clarified, for example, when a group of high-status men of high positions talk about her at the wedding reception of Abosi, a fictional version of a future Biafran General. Here, one of his colleagues sarcastically remarks that she could be a parliamentarian when he watches her 'talk and behave like a European' (p. 44); then, an industrialist responds that she could be a secretary only; while her politician father jokes that she would rather be 'a lady Prime Minister' (p. 45). Her second-class status within the elite is emphasized by contrasting her close friend Abosi, an army officer in his stern army uniform, which he wears even as the bride-groom. Debbie attracts people in her gorgeous dress. Though not a full-fledged member of the elite, she is still very different from Emecheta's previous low-profile heroines.

To conquer the disadvantages of being a woman, Debbie sets about a feminist crusade, armed with her academic and family background, and enlists in the army.[3] She believes in gender equality, and hopes to exercise equal rights including the right to fight and kill. Thus she decides to 'help the Nigerian army – not as a cook or a nurse, but as a true officer!' (p. 45). Knowing that as a woman she is considered a second-rate player in nation-building, Debbie obeys the masculine rules of war and politics and embarks on being more manly than the men.[4] She shouts commands to the captured officers of Biafra 'at the top of her voice', in order to make her voice authoritative, revealing 'the sinews of her thin neck' (p. 79) in sharp lines. Confronted by a woman officer, the prisoners of war are almost amused, 'as if to say, "Whatever you do, however much you are armed and in command now, you are still a woman"' (p. 79). For this relegation to low status as a woman, she torments the haughty officers, and demonstrates her allegiance to male rules of war as a result of which, all the prisoners are tortured to death.

This tragic outcome alters Debbie's manner of participating in politics as an equal partner with men. When she realizes her imitation of men does not fulfill gender equality, but rather reinforces the status quo in the misdistribution of power, she decides to work for peace. In this role she takes on a secret mission given to her by the men to go to Biafra to dissuade the Biafran leader, Abosi, from secession. Interestingly, her feminist belief in her feminine role as a peacemaker is shared by the male chauvinist leaders. They agree with her involvement in war only if she is assigned a peripheral and feminized role, and so one of them warns her not to 'meddle in things bigger than you' (p. 129). He continues: 'don't forget, my dear, that you are a woman. That is why we are giving you this delicate mission' (p. 129). It should be noted that she is mobilized not only as a peace negotiator but also as a sexual ploy, for Abosi would have married Debbie, had it not been for her boyfriend. In the words of the male leaders, she should 'use [her] feminine charms to break that icy reserve of his [Abosi]' (p. 123). She knows her peripheral status, and chooses to use her sexuality as a strategy for the cause of peace, not only when she is ordered to do so by men, but also whenever she sees its effectiveness. For example, when she needs to elicit information from her boyfriend, a British officer, she dresses up the way he likes, in African traditional attire, and plays a gentle sweetheart on a romantic beach (pp. 111–14). Thus it is in these essentially feminized roles, the mother as peacemaker and the dangerous whore as sexual bait that she re-enters the war.

Nevertheless, in the battlefield she loses control over her sexualized body to the armed men, and is exploited by rape. On her way to Biafra on her mission she encounters a group of soldiers. The irony is that she works as an officer for the Federal Nigerian Army, while soldiers in the same uniform treat her only as war booty. The confrontation between Debbie and the soldiers is represented as that of a conflict between the sexes, irrespective of their political interests. Debbie declares to the soldiers that she is a Nigerian soldier in 'her harshest voice' (p. 130) dressed in 'her trousers . . . too baggy and her shirt's shoulders . . . too wide for her slim frame' (p. 131). The leader of the soldiers imitates her self-identification with laughter 'like the roaring of many fierce lions' (p. 131). Defeated, she is forced to throw down the gun, the symbol of her participation in the masculine cause of nation, and is raped. Hearing the men's derisive laughter, she realizes that whatever position she assumes, manly woman or feminine woman, in the male-dominated war, she is of very low status as a woman. Her belief in her participation in masculine politics is torn to pieces, just like her uniform, and she is reduced to being the naked body of a woman. After the rape, she is nursed at her friend's house by a seventeen-year-old servant, who mothers a child by an unidentified soldier. The servant feels superior to Debbie and satisfied to know that some women are 'worse off' (p. 158) than she. In spite of their class difference, both Debbie and the servant are despised as contaminated women, and in fact, Debbie is given a lower social position than the servant. Thus despite her intention to utilize her sexuality, men usurp it and fix her as their sexual object.

Deprived of her social identities and reduced to a sexualized body, Debbie resumes her journey to Biafra for a new position equal to, *and* different from, that of men. In her mother's words, Debbie, 'born a girl, wants to be a man, and wants the men to know she wants to be like them, and still retain her womanhood' (p. 161). The destination she is heading for is no longer the truly liberated nation the men allegedly seek (p. 60), but the Biafra of her 'dreams' (p. 160) where she can find her position. The transformation of her journey is symbolized in her discarding of her army uniform and putting on of *lappa*, common dress among African women, to disguise herself as a daughter visiting her mother in Biafra, travelling not in her private car with a driver, but in an old bus packed with Igbo refugees.

On this new journey, Debbie again confronts sexual assault,[5] but this time, instead of accepting the masculine power hierarchy, she subverts it.[6] One evening, Debbie and her fellow refugees encounter Nigerian troops, whose leader, Lawal, attempts to rape Debbie. While in the first rape case previously analysed, Debbie is treated as an anonymous woman; in this second rape, the rapist has known her personally and rapes her with clear recognition of her social position in order to divest her of her superiority and position her as a proper woman. Lawal claims to be an African nationalist. According to him, educated, and therefore Europeanized, African women like Debbie diverge from their original status in wanting to be like men and insult African men through their coquettish behaviour with European men. Through rape they should learn their appropriate position and obey African men. Lawal threatens her: 'I am going to show you that you are nothing but a woman, an ordinary woman' (p. 175).

However, the rape attempt fails, as Debbie is too dry to accept any man. This denial of pleasure in heterosexual intercourse empowers Debbie to subvert male-centred power relations. When Lawal gives up penetration with a curse, she slaps him, and to the 'dumbfounded' (p. 176) rapist, she restates her sexual status as defined by men in this power hierarchy: 'You thought you were going to use a white man's plaything, as you called me, only to realize that you held in your arms a woman who has slept with soldiers' (p. 176). Lawal has attempted to rape Debbie to teach a Europeanized feminist that she is just a woman inferior to men, and to elevate himself, an African man of an elite class, over Europeans. Now that Debbie proves to be a contaminated woman gang-raped by African soldiers, raping her would in turn mark him as being as vulgar as soldiers of the lowest rank. However, because he gives up his attempt at rape, he still boasts his moral superiority over Europeans, who have sex with any women, and says that his mother would die to know he had sex with such a dirty woman as Debbie. Debbie reformulates his words and points out his colonial mentality: 'would she [Lawal's mother] think better of me if I was raped by white soldiers?' (p. 177) and his chauvinistic ideas: 'Suppose you had been the first to touch me, what would some other person's mother think?' (p. 177). She further notices that in his attempt to reduce her to a mere woman he rather proves himself to be a mere man: 'You poor, poor men have so many problems to solve, problems you created for yourselves' (p. 177). Note that the male-centred power relationship is subverted here only through restating that relationship as when she asks him if she should stay in his tent till the next morning to save his face as 'a real man' (p. 177). Hence, she doesn't entertain any sense of triumph, but rather feels 'exhausted' and 'empty' (p. 176) as she positions herself as a 'filthy' woman, having disrupted and subverted male-centred discourse and continues her journey to her 'destination Biafra.'

Later that evening, Lawal and his troops murder all the men of the refugee group, and consequently when Debbie resumes her journey it is only with the women and children of the group. The novel is realistic in its presentation of her difficulties, coming from an elite background, in forming solidarity with her fellow travellers. Debbie's isolation from the other women is indicated by her inability to carry a baby strapped on her back. Debbie asks herself, 'What kind of African woman was she, indeed?' (p. 191). Also, one of the women, Uzoma, (of whom more will be said later) calls Debbie 'You over-educated people' (p. 192), and wonders 'why *you* choose to suffer with *us*' (p. 191 my emphases). Due to '[her] education, the imported division of class' Debbie cannot 'belong' and feels 'lonely, surrounded . . . by other women' (p. 211).

However there are some moments when Debbie and the women surmount their differences and form a community. One of these moments is
when a baby, born on the way and named Biafra, and whom Debbie has
carried on her back and one mother has breastfed after the death of his
birth mother, himself passes away. At the moment of his death, Debbie
sees the women watching her:

> There was no doubt that they felt as she did. On this issue *their common
> Africanness* came to the fore; a child was the child of the community rather
> than just of the biological parents. Their eyes met hers. What was there to say?
> The baby, *their* baby had died. (p. 212, my emphases).

Through witnessing the death of the baby they all have nursed, Debbie
and the women establish their shared African philosophy that the
community nurtures the children. Here Debbie finds herself located in
the community as a member with mutual responsibility and respect. This
community spirit encourages the women to overcome the tragedy and
live on for the bereaved children. For example, Uzoma reminds the
mourning women how their foremothers have nurtured the younger generation and sustained their community:[7] 'We have children to look after.
Just like our grandmothers. They looked after our parents who had us. . . .
Your children have to live. Get up, women' (pp. 213–14). Thus, the subaltern women teach their philosophy of survival to Debbie, accepting her
as one of their caring and cared members. They survive together for the
future of their community.

The novel presents this philosophy as passed from generation to generation among women, for Uzoma is associated with an anonymous wise
old woman of the group who early in the novel, has become their leader
due to her 'age and fearlessness' (p. 188). Before Uzoma advocates the philosophy cited above, she slaps and awakens the addressee crying in
misery just as the woman had done earlier. The old woman had soothed a
furious soldier talking to him as if she were his mother (p. 172), and
comforted a despairing woman talking to her as if it was her daughter
(p. 187). Although she passes away on the journey, the philosophy she
represents is bequeathed to her next generation. In this sense, the old
woman of the subaltern is able to speak.

The philosophy is shared not only among ordinary women, but also
among the older generation of women from the elite class. While in times
of peace Debbie's mother and her friends are bound to the traditional role
of a good wife, pretending to be 'so frail and dependent' (p. 157); in times
of war they exhibit the same philosophy of survival.[8] Take Debbie's
mother, for example, who nurses, comforts and encourages gang-raped
Debbie from despondency back to her usual determined self (p. 157).
Similarly, the wife of a politician abandons him in order to survive and
see the future prosperity of her children and grandchildren (p. 253).
Uzoma experiences the same transformation from dutiful wife to bold

survivor. With her husband around, she is dull and reserved; but with her husband gone, she exercises leadership and encourages other women (p. 213). Thus privileged women such as Debbie's mother and ordinary women like Uzoma echo each other, and the traditional philosophy women share across classes is emphasized. Is Debbie also able to ally herself with subaltern women and achieve sisterhood? Do we hear the voice of the subaltern, not the representation of them by Debbie?

To the disappointment of feminist readers, the novel does not end in celebrating sisterhood.[9] It is true that at the end of the novel Debbie is able to position herself as 'a woman of Africa' (p. 258) after learning from her experience with the women refugees. Yet there are questions about the ambiguous way in which the novel reaches its climax after the refuge scene. Whereas Emecheta, as indicated in the Foreword, depends on the war memories people have imparted to her to describe the atrocities which Debbie encounters with other women, the remaining part of the novel is a pure creation of the author's imagination. After Debbie parts from the women to serve the men's scheme again, the plot proceeds with few conversations and little description of the inner turmoil of the characters. The novel flatly reports that the Biafran leader dispatches Debbie abroad to give a detailed account of the holocaust to the international journalists, but does not delineate how Debbie actually makes her appeal. After reporting on the aftermath of the atrocities in this detached manner, the novel then abruptly presents a picture of Debbie declaring her new position as an African woman in post-war nation-building. At the end of the novel, Debbie witnesses Biafran leaders secretly fleeing the country led by British officers. To these men, Debbie proudly declares her new awareness of her responsibility, which resonates with Uzoma's philosophy. The description is unexpectedly realistic, as if Emecheta has nurtured the image of this last scene before she set about writing the rest of the novel. What matters is that this last scene and the scene of refuge are not fully incorporated into the novel, so this last declaration sounds sudden, incongruous and inorganic. In other words, the declaration made by Debbie, an educated woman, is grafted onto that made by Uzoma, a subaltern woman, only at an abstract level.[10] Their uncertain relationship is in clear contrast to the powerful tie between the old woman and Uzoma. What does this rupture mean?

A more detailed analysis of Debbie's decree in terms of class and representation should explain the rupture. In the final scene under discussion, her British boyfriend invites her to go to Britain with him and the defecting Biafran leaders. She declines the offer and clarifies her decision to live with her country-women as 'a woman of Africa' or 'a daughter of Nigeria' (p. 258) in contrast to the male leaders or 'black white' men who 'need to be decolonized' (p. 258). The British man warns her about her elite isolation that '[there's] no place for you here' (p. 258), to which she retorts that she plans to rear refugee boys and 'many other orphans' and to publish 'my manuscript' (p. 258). This declaration by Debbie about her post-war aims corresponds closely to Uzoma's words in that both of them intend to survive to raise the children and build their community. In addition to nurturing the future generation, Debbie takes on another responsibility as an educated African woman – to write a story of the war and pass on the memory of the people.

The novel has thrice referred to the responsibility of the elite for writing. The first reference occurs in the early days of Debbie's journey, though at this stage Debbie has not yet gained an awareness of her responsibility, and only wonders if the world has been informed of the predicament of common people (p. 195). She does not examine either her elite position or the role of the international community. However, in the second reference, as she suffers life and death with the women, she grows conscious of her responsibility as an educated woman to represent their experience at the risk of her own life. She hides her notes deep in her tattered dress, recording only key words of their experience in her personal code, because the story is too dangerous to write down in plain words. She tells herself, 'If she should be killed, the entire story of the women's experience of the war would be lost. . . . She must try to live, not just for the women but for the memories of boys [killed in the war]' (pp. 223–4). This sense of commitment, however, is lost when she talks about writing her would-be novel for the third time in the text. After she separates from the women, Debbie lodges at a residence of a family friend, and there she converses with the hostess about a story she is writing under the title of *Destination Biafra* (p. 246). Away from the site of experience, Debbie wields her authorial pen, reconstructs the memory of the women as a 'very interesting' (p. 246) story, and titles it as a coherent narrative. The story Debbie thus controls is different from the events the women experienced. The discrepancy is reflected in the two incompatible environments under which Debbie expresses her decision to write: one occurring while she flees for life with other women during an air raid, the other taking place at a safe residence of an affluent family friend. Debbie does not pay attention to this gap, and the readers are left with a question: 'Has the mission of Debbie as an elite woman desiring to represent subaltern women failed?'

The question is not easy to answer, for the story the readers have been reading is written no less by Debbie than by Emecheta. At one level of interpretation, *Destination* is not the self-representation by the subaltern but the story which Debbie, an elite woman, has composed from the memory of the subaltern. All the words including those of Uzoma and the old woman are arranged to be a coherent novel *post factum* away from the field.

At another level of interpretation, the novel shows the impossibility of representation. Few would dispute that the description of evacuation impresses readers with its realism and poignancy. The easy and relaxing atmosphere surrounding the writing desk of Debbie – and probably of Emecheta – is made the more incompatible with the anxiety and terror of the bush. The discrepancy threatens the novel and points to its forced coherence and false completeness. When memory of the Other is represented as a story, something is left unsaid. It is something which is unnamable, lurking at the border of intelligibility and representability, and threatening the story from within with its inherent absence. In the sense that the story exposes the limit of storytelling, *Destination,* as an already failed story, records the impossibility of representing the Other.

NOTES

1 For works by less known writers, see Acholonu (1985); Meniru (1987); Njoku (1985); Ofoegbu (1985); Onwubiko (1988); and Umelo (1978).

2 Nwagbara (2000: 147), Okereke (1994: 155–6) and Umeh (1978: 199) also note the journey motif in *Destination.*

3 For positive views of Debbie's enlistment as liberating women, see Frank (1987: 25), Nwagbara (2000: 144–6) and Okereke (1994: 150–2). For an analysis of women soldiers, see Kerber (1998).

4 For an analysis of the relationship between masculinity and militarism, see Reardon (1985). For an analysis of post-Cold War international politics in terms of gender, see Enloe (1993).

5 This paper owes a great deal to the insightful interpretation of another story of rape, 'Draupadi', by Spivak (1988).

6 Interpreting the second rape scene, Ojo-Ade (1988) argues that Debbie accepts the male-centred power relationship (p. 81), while Allan (1996) notes its subversion (pp. 216–17).

7 Bryce (1991) also focuses on the philosophy of survival in women's war literature as does Ezeigbo (1998) in analysing Nwapa's texts. However this philosophy could be appropriated by essentialists, as in the case of Odege (1999), who praises traditional motherhood and wifehood *uncontaminated* by the western feminism represented in Acholonu's war poetry. See also Wilentz (1992) and Trin (1989) who focus on women of the African diaspora and Asia, respectively, as storytellers and guardians of their community.

8 For a contrasting view of Emecheta's mother and her generation, see Fishburn (1995: 136).

9 Porter (1996) glorifies sisterhood without a critical class perspective (p. 323), while Nwachukwu-Agbada (1996) criticizes *Destination* for lacking class consciousness (p. 394).

10 Even Emecheta's critical admirers acknowledge flaws in her characterization of Debbie. See Allan (1996: 215–16), Frank (1987: 27), Nwachukwu-Agbada (1996: 392-4) and Porter (1996: 326). Needless to say, male critics give Emecheta's powers of characterization only superficial attention at best. See, for example, Chinweizu.

WORKS CITED

Acholonu, Catherine Obianuju. *Into the Heart of Biafra.* Owerri, Nigeria: Totan, 1985.

Allan, Tuzyline Jita. 'Trajectories of Rape in Buchi Emecheta's Novels'. In Umeh (ed.), 207–25.

Amuta, Chidi. 'The Nigerian Civil War and the Evolution of Nigerian Literature.' *Canadian Journal of African Studies* 17.1 (1983): 85–99.

Bryce, Jane. 'Conflict and Contradiction in Women's Writing on the Nigerian Civil War'. *African Languages and Cultures* 4.1 (1991): 29–42.

Emecheta, Buchi. *Destination Biafra*. Glasgow: Collins-Fontana, 1983 [1982].
——. *In the Ditch*. London: Barrie, 1972.
——. *The Joys of Motherhood*. London: Allison & Busby, 1979.
——. *Second-Class Citizen*. London: Allison & Busby, 1974.
Chinweizu. 'Time of Troubles'. Review of *Destination Biafra*, by Buchi Emecheta, *Times Literary Supplement* (London) 26 Feb. 1982: 228.
Enloe, Cynthia. *The Morning After: Sexual Politics at the End of the Cold War*. Berkeley, CA: University of California Press, 1993.
Ezeigbo, T. Akachi. *Fact and Fiction in the Literature of the Nigerian Civil War*. Lagos, Nigeria: Unity, 1991.
——. 'Vision and Revision: Flora Nwapa and the Fiction of War'. *Emerging Perspectives on Flora Nwapa: Critical and Theoretical Essays*. Ed. Marie Umeh. Trenton, NJ: Africa World, 1998: 477–95.
Fishburn, Katherine. *Reading Buchi Emecheta: Cross-Cultural Conversation*. Contributions to the Study of World Literature 61. Westport, CT: Greenwood, 1995.
Frank, Katherine. 'Women Without Men: The Feminist Novel in Africa.' *Women in African Literature Today* ALT 15 (1987): 14–34.
Jones, Eldred. Editorial. *Recent Trends in the Novel* ALT 13 (1983): vii–x.
Kerber, Linda. *No Constitutional Right to Be Ladies: Women and the Obligation of Citizenship*. New York: Hill, 1998.
McLuckie, Craig W. *Nigerian Civil War Literature: Seeking an 'Imagined Community'*. Studies in African Literature 3. Lewiston, NY: Edwin, 1990.
Meniru, Teresa E. *The Last Card*. Lagos, Nigeria: Macmillan Nigeria, 1987.
Njoku, Rose Adaure. *Withstand the Storm*. Onitsha, Nigeria: Africana-FEP, 1985.
Nwachukwu-Agbada, J. O. J. 'Buchi Emecheta: Politics, War and Feminism in *Destination Biafra*'. In Umeh (1996: 387–94).
Nwagbara, Augustine Uzoma. 'Women and the Dialectic of War: A Comparative Study of the Portrayal of Women in the Nigerian Civil War Fiction'. *Men, Women and Violence: A Collection of Papers from CODESRIA Gender Institute 1997*. Ed. Felicia Oyekanmi. Gender Institute Ser. Dakar, Senegal: CODESRIA, 2000: 125–52.
Nwapa, Flora. *Never Again*. 1975. Trenton, NJ: Africa World, 1992.
Ofoegbu, Leslie Jean. *Blow the Fire*. Enugu, Nigeria: Tana, 1985.
Odege, Ode S. 'Exile and the Female Imagination: The Nigerian Civil War, Western Ideology (Feminism), and the Poetry of Catherine Acholonu'. *Neohelicon* 26.1 (1999): 125–34.
Ojo-Ade, Femi. 'Women and the Nigerian Civil War: Buchi Emecheta and Flora Nwapa.' *Études Germano-Africaines* 6 (1988): 75–86.
Okereke, Grace Eche. 'The Nigerian Civil War and the Female Imagination in Buchi Emecheta's *Destination Biafra*'. *Feminism in African Literature: Essays on Criticism*. Ed. Helen Chukwuma. Enugu, Nigeria: New Generation, 1994: 144–58.
Onwubiko, Pauline. *Running for Cover*. Owerri, Nigeria: KayBeeCee, 1988.
Porter, Abioseh M. 'They Were There, Too: Women and the Civil War(s) in *Destination Biafra*'. In Umeh (1996: 313–32).
Reardon, Betty. *Sexism and the War System*. New York: Syracuse UP, 1985.
Spivak, Gayatri Chakravorty. Foreword. 'Draupadi', by Mahasweta Devi. Trans. Spivak. *In Other Worlds: Essays in Cultural Politics*. New York and London: Routledge, 1988. 179–87.
Trin T. Minh-ha. *Woman, Native, Other: Writing Postcoloniality and Feminism*. Bloomington, IN: Indiana University Press 1989.
Umeh, Marie, ed. *Emerging Perspectives on Buchi Emecheta*. Trenton, NJ: Africa World Press, 1996.
——.'The Poetics of Thwarted Sensitivity'. *Critical Theory and African Literature*. Ed. Ernest N. Emenyonu. Calabar Studies in African Literature 3. Ibadan, Nigeria: Heinemann Nigeria, 1987: 194–206.
Umelo, Rosina. *Felicia*. Pacesetters. London: Macmillan, 1978.
Wilentz, Gay. *Binding Cultures: Black Women Writers in Africa and Diaspora*. Blacks in the Diaspora. Bloomington, IN: Indiana University Press, 1992.

Politics & Human Rights in Non-Fiction Prison Literature

Sophie Obiajulu Ogwude

> When he is purged from the long deception and has begun to express new visions, the gates of the preventive detention fortresses open up and close on him. (Wole Soyinka, *Art, Dialogue and Outrage*, p.18)

> Democracy and justice can only be achieved when the various interest groups voice their positions and fight for them. (Ngugi wa Thiong'o, *Detained*, p. xv)

Social as well as political scientists have variously defined politics. If we call to mind Laswell's (1950) contention that politics is the struggle for power, acquisition of power, retention of power and the exercise of power, or even Easton's (1965) view that politics is the authoritative allocation of scarce resources, then it becomes easy to see why governance must be burdened with expectations, demands and counter/opposing demands. Our concern in this paper is to bring our erstwhile nascent and, now not so new, African democracies into perspective as we examine these against the backdrop of fundamental human rights. There is an obvious limitation to this objective since it would appear merely to be looking at one half of a problem, whose source is in the second, unmentioned half. In other words, for any discussion of politics and human rights in any African nation once under colonial rule to make sense, the nature of that colonial administration and its legacies must form an integral part of such a study.

The Universal Declaration of Human Rights (UDHR) dates back to 1948 following the Second World War and derives from the wider concept of natural rights, which every civilized society accepts as fundamental to each person as a human being. These rights are thus guaranteed by the Fundamental Laws of such countries through their constitutions. The substantive and basic rights include the right to life, liberty, health and expression. Others include freedom from torture, inhuman and degrading treatment as well as the right to a safe environment. Significantly, these procedural human rights include the basic principles of the legal system, which ensures the enforcement, and the protection of these substantive rights.

Prison literature from Africa generated by political prisoners and detainees constitutes a vast body of work. This fact alone is an eloquent testimony to the repressive state of governance in the continent. The earliest political prisoners were patriots who had found the overall governing principles of the colonial masters an unacceptable imposition. Resources, which had not been scarce, became so under the greedy governance of the local colonial administrations. Foreign nationals who hoped to make their fortunes in this new Eldorado were encouraged and their actions abetted in every conceivable way; the primary owners of the land were reduced to second-class citizens and made to work for the white masters, often for a pittance. Records abound of the plundering of the colonized nations and the despicable denegration of the colonized. The thefts of whole portions of the well-watered Shire Highlands in Nyasaland (present day Malawi), the occupation of the arable lands of Kenya, Central, East and Southern Africa, and the acquisition of the land rich in precious stones, along with numerous other indices of intolerable governance, fuelled resistance efforts, which were in turn met with murders and imprisonments. Direct literary products of preventive detention from this sub-region of Africa include among others: *Facing Mount Kenya* (Jomo Kenyatta, 1938), *Mau Mau Detainee* (J. M. Kariuki, 1963), *A Simple Lust* (Dennis Brutus, 1973), Strike *a Blow and Die: The Story of the Chilembwe Rising* (George Simeon Mwase, 1967; rpt. 1975) and *Sacred Hope* (Agostinho Neto, 1974) The West African climate was hostile to white settlers and thus the fight with the colonial regime in that sub-region was on a comparatively smaller scale. The most celebrated political prisoner of those times was Kwame Nkrumah and his autobiography *Ghana* (1957) was written from his cell at James Fort Prison.

An acute sense of right and wrong, justice and injustice and the attempts to fight against perceived wrongs are easily recognizable as the motivating factors behind the action of every political prisoner. The *Chambers Twentieth Century* dictionary reveals the current usage of the word 'hero' to refer to a person of 'distinguished bravery or any illustrious person'. Many political prisoners are heroes in the sense that they willingly take on the challenge of fighting for the good of others without regard either for personal gains or even of personal injury. In the face of right and wrong, people react differently. Some recognize evil for what it is, denounce it, resolve not to be a part of it in any way but lack the wherewithal to spear-head any form of organized resistance against it; for these people, the hope is that if everyone acts in fair conscience, evil will ultimately be defeated by good. Many belong in this group. Then there are the extremes, there are those who connive with the perpetrators of evil in the hope that immediate and future gains can accrue to them therefrom, and then we have the lion hearted; who see evil, and in the denotative heroic sense of 'extreme courage', use 'extreme or elaborate means to obtain the desired result', the desired result being always to reverse the wrong-doing and re-establish justice. To these groups we might add a third, comprising the separatists who are not concerned with the larger public interest and are largely insensitive to the demands of nation-building but are consumed with passion for the interests of the section of the society to which they belong.

The singular most devastating political principle of our time was the obnoxious apartheid policy in South Africa, which encouraged a huge corpus of protest literature. Many South African writers served prison sentences at one time or another, many were incarcerated more than once. According to Lewis Nkosi (1981), 'Dennis Brutus was the first South African poet to acquire a reputation abroad for his writing and for his opposition to South Africa's race laws' (p. 166). Dennis Brutus is of particular interest to the present study because in resolving to communicate effectively, he had decided (a) to strip his poetry of every form of superfluity that might impede understanding and (b) to aim to write for the 'ordinary person' (see Nwoga 1979: 48–9). Unfortunately, other writers from parts of Africa in which apartheid was absent were soon to be disillusioned as well. As Wole Soyinka notes, in experiencing the newly independent African nations' 'seductive experiment in authoritarianism' (1988, p. 16) and the ruthless suppression of any writer who dares to 'express a sensibility and an outlook apart from, and independent of, the mass direction', these writers came 'to the terrible understanding that it was not [their] South African comrade who was the object of compassion' (p. 16). This was over twenty years ago; at that time, for him at least, it was only a statement of fact. Now in retrospect, we can also credit this statement with a prophetic vision. Ironically, whereas the unwholesome political set-up in South Africa has been effectively dismantled since 1994, dictatorships still thrive in some 'independent' African states with life presidents often bereft of ideas and hopelessly impatient with alternative suggestions for government.

This wish to be able to reach the common man through creative works leads us into a discussion of the status of nonfiction in art. Non-fiction, alternatively called the 'new journalism', is now a favoured genre because it provides freedom from the limitations of fiction 'for there are limits to what a writer can create and to what he can meaningfully communicate through fiction', writes Ime Ikeddeh (1992: xii) in the *Foreword* to Ngugi's *Homecoming*. This paper proposes to examine Soyinka's *The Man Died* (1973) Ngugi's *Detained: A Writer's Prison Diary* (1978) and Ken Saro-Wiwa's *A Month and A Day* (1985) in the light of politics and human rights. Like the early protest writing from South Africa, these works are intended to communicate with ordinary people; the ultimate purpose being to correct and to urge better governance of the African nation states of Nigeria and Kenya. All three writers have employed different genres at various times. Soyinka and Ngugi are celebrated playwrights; Saro-Wiwa is probably best known and best remembered (by Nigerians at least) for his successful play *Basi and Company*, serialized on national television in the late 1980s. Soyinka and Saro-Wiwa are poets even if of varying seriousness and accomplishments. Saro-Wiwa's *Songs in a Time of War* (1985) is a collection of war poems written around the battlefront of the Nigerian civil war. Likewise, Soyinka's *Shuttle in the Crypt* (1972) contains poems written in prison detention to which he was consigned for his efforts to abort or avert the war itself. All three have written novels as well as non-fiction.

The question of language use is of primary importance to every committed writer since he or she aims first and foremost to achieve a wide and relevant readership. Ken Saro-Wiwa's experiments with language are too well known to justify repetition here. Nnolim (1992) has dealt with Saro-Wiwa's language and craft and Okere (2000) has done an equally interesting study of his poetry. In order to engage the ordinary Kenyan more effectively in his plays and other writings, Ngugi now writes in his native Gikuyu as well. Interestingly, his experiment with the Kamiriithu Cultural Group has an antecedent in Soyinka's Guerrilla Theatre of 1963, which was characteristically improvised to engage Nigerians in the political dialogue of the times. In all these efforts, the target audience determined the message and language.

Ime Ikiddeh (1972) delineates three distinguishing characteristics of non-fiction as containing explicit statements, informed and carried through by a passion and intellect which are only in circumscribed evidence in creative works, and finally, a clarity of commitment (p. xii). Taken all together, these factors help to ensure a better engagement with the populace for whom these writers have written. The narratives represent aspects of the writers' personal histories and so can be deemed to be autobiographical and to bear historical authenticity to the socio-political situation under which they have been written. The advantages of non-fiction are obvious, but there remains the difference between lived experience and recorded experience in that one is rooted in chaos and the other fashioned after a human dream – the dream of order. The order brought to bear on recorded experience renders it creative either in the also imaginative or fictional sense. Ime Ikiddeh has used 'creative' to denote fiction. Non-fiction is also imaginatively created art.

Human rights abuse came with colonial administration. It is non-existent in our indigenous judicial system, which recognizes that even a slave is the child of another person. The political and human rights history of Africa and particularly of the Eastern and Southern parts of the continent is too well-known and well-documented to justify its reproduction here. However, the point should be made that the early detainees on the continent (and specifically in Kenya) were not criminals and brigands but patriots whose primary objectives were 'to drive out the Europeans, seize the government, and give back to the Kenyan peasants their stolen lands and property' (*Homecoming*, p. 28). Many supported the initial efforts at decolonization long before it took the form of Mau Mau guerrilla warfare, and it was expected that the exemplary figure of the revolution, Jomo Kenyatta, would become the first African President of the country, as he did in 1963.

Six years before *Detained* appeared, an angry Ngugi had as it were set its course in his earlier work *Homecoming* (1972). Even the most perfunctory study of Ngugi reveals him as having a consistent vision and an unwavering commitment to decolonizing the African psyche both ideologically and economically. The two main forces in the socio-political life of Kenya (apparent in much of the rest of Africa also) are:

1. a foreign imperialistic bourgeoisie, in alliance with its local Kenyan representatives turning Kenyans citizens into slaves and
2. the historical struggles of people against economic, political and cultural slavery.

The disillusionment is based essentially on the fact that reforms, the equitable redistribution of national wealth and sound common sense principles of governance to bring these about, just never materialized. Instead, and contrary to the promises of election campaigns, efforts were being concentrated on maintaining the status quo in economic terms, as well as on continuing the imposition of colonial culture and foreign values. Ngugi has correctly argued that awareness and reorientation is important if a people are effectively to be urged to take their fates into their own hands:

> No country can consider itself politically independent for as long as its *economy and culture* are dominated by foreign interest. (*Det*: xv, my emphasis)

Ironically, this is a position that Kenyatta had himself once argued when he wrote in *Facing Mount Kenya* that:

> It is the culture, which he inherits that gives a man his human dignity as well as his material prosperity. It teaches him his mental and moral values and makes him feel it worthwhile to work and fight for liberty. (p. 317)

Indeed Amilcar Cabral's balanced view in this regard reproduced in Jeyifo's (1988) 'Introduction' to *Art, Dialogue and Outrage* is significant:

> A people who free themselves from foreign domination will not be free unless without underestimating the importance of positive contributions from the oppressors' culture and other cultures, they return to the upward paths of their own culture. The latter is nourished by the living reality of the environment and rejects harmful influences as much as any kind of subjection to foreign cultures. We see therefore that, if imperialist domination has the virtual need to practice cultural oppression, national liberation is necessarily an *act of culture*. (viii)

Cultural revival and promotion was the root cause of the stand-off between Ngugi and the Kenyan national government under Kenyatta. The defunct Kamiriithu youth centre, now re-organized and renamed the Kamiriithu Community Education and Cultural Centre, demanded activities satisfying to the yearnings of a people discontent with policies maintaining and furthering the status quo left behind by the British. The establishment of the centre in itself with its stated objectives *shows* that it was a project of empowerment. For example, in one year alone 55 ordinary peasants learnt to read and write! It had on overall 'ambitious programme' for changing the lives of the villages and the participants had the following guiding principles summarized as follows: that they were to achieve their set goals through 'a *Harambee* of sweat; that money was not the basis of development; that human hands and brains were the basis' (*Det*: 71). The offending play (to the Kenyan government) *Ngaahika Ndeenda* was written in Gikuyu, and on the content of this production, Ukpokodu suggests that it is the 'evolutionary history of oppression in Kenya from foreign masters to native masters: how the future of Kenyan children was already hopelessly mortgaged by living Kenyan exploiters' (quoted in Ukpokodu 1997: 56). Implicitly therefore, it reflected of the various social classes within the society as well as the inevitable class struggles which 'were the very essence of Kenyan history (*Det*: 72). The play was originally embarked upon for the purposes of entertainment and collective self-evaluation; as follow-up reading material for the new literates and finally, for the purpose of raising money for other projects. It accomplished these and much more. Two additional gains stand out; first, it gave the participants a sense of increased self-worth, and it also awakened latent talents, spelling hope where once there was none. It also helped to reaffirm the belief in Kenyan culture and added impetus to the peoples' struggles for the assertion of their culture and value. Ordinary peasants and workers at Kamiriithu by their activities and collective celebration of their culture revealed 'the putrescent impotence' of the alien culture (*Det*: 72). Unfortunately, the national government, like 'their colonial counterpart, ... had become mortally afraid of the slightest manifestations of [the] people's culture of patriotic heroism and outspoken indomitable courage' (*Det*: 71).

In retrospect, Ngugi had given the rationale for *Ngaahika Ndeenda* in his observation that 'it is when people are involved in the active work of destroying an inhibitive social structure and building a new one that they begin to see themselves' (*HC*: 11). Ngugi also asserts that, 'political freedom from foreign rule, essential as it is, is not *the* freedom. One freedom is essential. This is the freedom for man to develop into his full potential. He cannot do this as long as he is enslaved by certain shackles' (*HC*: 23), whether these are the chains of a colonial power, or worse still of an indigenous government. It is lamentable that a man brought to power through support 'from the peasant masses and urban workers because he was a symbol of their deepest aspirations' (*HC*: 29) could betray this common hope and trust and unleash the same punitive laws he had vowed to expunge from the Kenyan judicial system.

For the activities outlined above Ngugi was, on 31 December 1977 thrown into Kamiti Maximum Security Prison where he remained for the next twelve months. *Detained: A Writer's Prison Diary* is a product of that period of incarceration. Significantly, he has written about detention as he intimates in the Preface, not as a personal affair but 'as a social, political and historical phenomenon' (p. xi). That preventive detention 'is a direct heritage of the colonial era' as Rhoda Howard (1986: 9) has observed is not in question. Neither can there be any doubt that any government willing and able to resort to preventive detention as a weapon against patriots cannot be a government of the people for the people. It is reprobate and deserves to be treated as such.

Repressive African national governments abhor political awareness because enslaved nationals whose collective birthrights are plundered and concentrated in very few hands are safer and easier to contend with than a politically aware citizenry capable of demanding and expecting good governance. Ngugi summarizes this position in his observation that the intimidation, persecution and finally, the destruction of the theatre were all part of a calculated programme of 'rooting out critical elements and the suspension of the democratic process in politics, education and culture' (*Barrel of a Pen*: 47).

The point has already been made that the inherited laws of governance are responsible for the clash between indigenous progressive patriots and the conservative ruling powers in Africa today. Ngugi forcefully brings to the reader the 'sadistic brutality' of a colonial government symbolized by the rickshaw, the dog and the *syambok*. Seventy years of such a destructive alien presence is capable of fostering a draconian idle class unlikely to be receptive to class struggles, and the Kamiriithu theatre for which Ngugi was detained is in his own words 'crucial to Kenya's history of struggle' (*Det*: 73). Writing further, he remarks that writers in Africa and the third world 'are the modern Cassandras of the developing world, condemned to cry the truth against neo-colonialist and imperialist cultures and then be ready to pay for it with incarceration, exile, and even death' (*Letters from Prison, Det*: 191). All the three writers in the present study have selflessly embraced the role of acting as the bearers of the collective burden of their peoples.

In addition to forcibly excluding its victims from the people's struggles, preventive detention is often regarded as a sure means of breaking a non-conforming person's spirit and will power. Significantly, prison experiences in Kenya and Nigeria are similar and Ngugi sums this up effectively when he writes:

> A narration of prison life is, in fact, nothing more than an account of oppressive measures in varying degrees of intensity and one's individual or collective responses to them. ... physical beating with the possibility of final elimination;

strait-jacketing to ensure total bodily immobility; sleeping on cold or wet cement floors without a mat or blanket so the body can more easily contract disease; denial of news or books to weaken the intellect; bestial food or a starvation diet to weaken the body; segregation or solitary confinement to weaken the heart; such and more are the sadistic ways of prisons and detention camps. (*Det*: 100-1)

Undeniably then, preventive detention violates every single substantive basic human right: the right to life, liberty, health and expression, freedom from torture, inhuman and degrading treatment and even the right to a safe environment. Justice delivery and prison administration have a big impact on human rights protection and are indicators of the level of civilization and respect for human rights manifest in every society.

Soyinka wrote *The Man Died* in response to his preventive detention for his role in working to avert the Nigerian civil war. The period of the Nigerian civil war is yet our darkest in history and even 30 years on, the socio-political super structure still resonates with some of the ugliest vibrations of the war. The moderate historians and politicians have had their say but it is essentially true that this war was between two ethnic factions: the Hausa/Fulani and the Igbo/Ibo (*TMD*: xv). Although Soyinka is Yoruba, he was involved because, as a patriot, he deemed himself first and foremost a Nigerian. He was nabbed and detained by state agents who were determined to go through with the war and were desirous of blocking any avenues that could make withdrawal from the stand-off possible.

The first Republic following Nigeria's independence in 1960 ended in a fiasco barely six years after. The military came, eliminated sections of itself, midwifed the civil war and for more than 30 years lived to enjoy the fruits of the wreckages of the war and the wealth of a hapless nation. In direct contrast to the Kenyan situation, the devastation meted out to Nigeria was not so much from the British legacy of governance as the military, accused with justification of humiliating the nation by 'a treason promoted, sustained and accentuated by forces that lacked purpose or ideology beyond self-perpetuation through organized terror ....' (*TMD*: 20).

The Nigerian civil war soon proved to be more economic than political and there were two main beneficiaries namely, a 'profit-motivated mafia' and 'an arrogant, raping, murdering, terrorizing soldiery' (*TMD*: 150). Together they formed 'an unbreakable alliance of mutual, lucrative guilt and with a successful philosophy of genocide' (*Ibid*: 177). While in prison Soyinka saw first-hand the princely treatment given to Ambrose Okpe and Gani Biban, soldiers of the 3rd Battalion for their cold-blooded murder of the Igbo photographer Emmanuel Ogbona in Ibadan. The intention is clearly that unlawful detention would first serve temporarily or even permanently to silence the 'offender', since while in seclusion and under the government's malevolent eyes he could be effectively restrained from further generating provocative or undesirable material. However, in the unshaken belief that 'the man dies in all who keep silent in the face of tyranny' (*TMD*: 13), Soyinka 'wrote and smuggled out a letter setting out the latest proof of the genocidal policies of the government from detention' and for this reason, 'they sought to compound their treason by a murderous conspiracy' (*TMD*: 29). Without justice there can neither be true peace nor meaningful development in any nation.

'Justice is the first condition of humanity', states Soyinka (*TMD*: 95) and preventive detention is conceived and executed through injustice. It should be abrogated and expunged from our books of jurisprudence for this reason alone, but especially because in addition the poor infrastructure for the administration of criminal justice, and the absence of adequate legal aid to litigants result in undue protraction of trials as well as over-population in the prisons. A government that deliberately misgoverns, denies empowerment through education and that consciously plunders the nation through unpatriotic financial dealings and engagements, perpetually enslaves the citizenry and ultimately emasculates its people. The two African nations under focus in this essay are culpable. To a very great extent, they are responsible for the nonchalant attitude of the masses towards injustice. Directly, they encourage official cover-ups through bribes as well as by a careful cultivation of the cult of sycophancy. The apathy is such that there are no demands for medical personnel to be brought to book and held responsible for the unethical discharge of their medical duties in the prisons or any where else for that matter. In these texts, the deplorable conditions of our prisons assail the reader. In *The Man Died,* a woman is delivered of her baby completely unaided by any qualified attendant or personnel, a man dies of medical inattention and callous indifference on the part of state agents, exposure to sun is rationed and meals are barely fit for scavengers.

Disease is used as a weapon 'to extort information or confession' and 'a means of vindictive humiliation, or of breaking a person's will' (*Det*: 104). Martin Shikuku's pathetic case etches an indelible mark in the mind. Another inmate in Kamiti prison suffered for seven years from swollen veins. He was uncured. Yet another bled from advanced piles and lived in agony for years and he, too, left the prison untreated and uncured. Significantly, we also find an obvious parallel in the Nigerian government's deliberate refusal to inoculate Soyinka against the much dreaded cerebral-spinal meningitis in the hope of its becoming 'one more "natural" possibility of the ultimate solution' (*TMD*: 190).

Oil was discovered in Nigeria about the same time that the military made its debut in the Nigerian political scene; from that time on unfortunately, proceeds from the sale of this commodity have not been used judiciously for the common good and welfare of the nation as a whole. Infrastructure

put in place from its gains has not been commensurate or equitably distributed. The gap between the rich and the poor has widened; other cash
crops like groundnut, cocoa and cotton have been neglected by our rulers
who have one and all become so rich that even their children and other
hangers-on have turned millionaires. To our chagrin we learnt that some
of these more equal Nigerian animals fly frequently to more exotic West
African countries just for lunch! Significantly, these sickening displays of
wealth were happening at a time when many working families could
barely earn enough to ensure one meal a day. Even as I write this,
intensive negotiations are taking place to retrieve the billions stashed
away in Swiss and other European banks by members of one family alone
– the late Nigerian Head of State, General Sani Abacha. He may have
beaten Mobutu Sese Seko in this game of greed and avarice. Shortly before
his death, Abacha was in a murder dance with the Nigeria Labour
Congress over the minimum wage. His predecessor's Structural Adjust-
ment Programme (SAP) and its consequences were furiously gnawing at
the hearts and homes of most Nigerians including those employed by the
government. Yet Abacha could not find it in his heart to increase the
minimum wage without first laying off workers.

Ogoni land houses a recognizable percentage of the Nigerian oilfields.
However, the Ogoni have not even found the derivative formula of allocation of adequate help. Their men cannot farm viably because of the devastating effects of oil prospecting; even the little food stuff produced in
these areas cannot easily be taken to markets as there are no access roads.
Their young people are not included in the running of society and it is
difficult for them to find work. At the time of writing, the Cable Network
News (CNN) carried the Breaking News that some youths in one such oil-
producing area in Nigeria had taken hostage some employees of
Texaco/Chevron. What the news failed to add was that these youths acted
in desperation; they asked for jobs and not for a ransom; they want to be
self-reliant and they know that the natural resources from their home-
lands can adequately ensure that. This was Ken Saro-Wiwa's fight – to
bring to the fore the plight of the Ogoni and win for them well-deserved
rights.

A major index of human rights abuse is the degree to which writers are
censored. Inevitably, censorship is followed either by the detention or
imprisonment of particular writers, and all restrictions of this type constitute a despicable infringement of the victims' human rights. 'The fact is
that detention without trial is not only a primitive act of physical and
mental torture of a few patriotic individuals', writes Ngugi, 'but it is also a
calculated act of psychological terror against the struggling millions'
since it 'means the physical removal of patriots from the people's
organized struggles' (*Det*: 13–14). The history of Ken Saro-Wiwa corrobo-
rates this contention; his fight for the rights of the Ogoni people was
found irksome by our 'indigenous colonizers' (*AMD*: 7) and fear of his

success maddened the government run by a 'minority, but one with a reckless concentration of power' (*AMD*: xvii). His eventual execution coming as it did at the peak of these struggles only helps to reaffirm the truth in Bernard Shaw's dictum that 'assassination is the extreme form of censorship' (1921 rpt 1971: 708). It is in the same vein that fearing Ngugi's unconventional Kamiriithu theatre as a tool that could possibly stir up class struggles, which would ultimately pave the way for equitable resource control and a power-sharing formula, he too was clandestinely thrown into preventive detention for months without trial and in a farcical display of warped logic, refused re-entry into the university system where he had been a professor before his abduction. Soyinka describes 'the crippling mind-scattering impotence that came from such encounters [with abusive state agents], the knowledge that one individual, all in his own right, without the need to justify his action to you or the society of which you are both a part, *that such a power exists to stultify your private life by circumscribing your movements and jeopardizing your livelihood* (*TMD*: 28, my emphasis).

Ken Saro-Wiwa's *A Month and a Day* documents such harrowing experiences. When the Nigerian civil war and the genocidal activities that took place within it are considered against the backdrop of Kosovo and ethnic cleansing allegations, it becomes difficult to understand why some, and not others have to face the International Court at the Hague. Consider the state of the prisons in which political prisoners have been held in Nigeria and Kenya against the ones housing even the most vile of criminals elsewhere, and disturbing insights into human rights questions emerge. Today there is concern for the prison conditions of those accused of grievous crimes against humanity. Specifically, international human rights bodies continually visit Guantanamo bay in Cuba to monitor whether prisoners suspected of being members of Al Quaeda and the Taliban are held there live in acceptable conditions. This point brings to mind Soyinka's (1988) essay 'Religion and Human Rights' in which he asks:

> What is the unique perspective of any race or nation on the reality of human pain and suffering ... is pain experienced in cultural terms? ... Perhaps we should translate into every spoken language in the world, emphasizing their sheer ordinariness, the words of the much abused *Merchant of Venice*. 'Hath not a Jew eyes? Hath not a Jew hands, organs, dimension, senses, affections, passions? If you prick us, do we not bleed? If you poison us, do we not die?' (p. 84)

I have since been persuaded to consider whether or not there is a social context to human rights issues. For instance, does any one race or ethnic group feel pain more than another? Why is it that some people are more able to empathise with human rights violation victims than others? How does the political set-up on the ground affect the fight for the preservation of basic human rights? It could be argued that unjust governments thrive only because the citizenry refuse their responsibility of at least speaking out against it. In defining a nation as 'a unit of humanity bond together by a common ideology' (*TMD*: 183), Soyinka does not imply a people of the same political persuasions but rather a people having certain basic universal principles, which are accepted and respected equally by all. We have seen that, outraged by the events of the mid-1960s in Nigeria, he worked to end both 'the secession of Biafra, and the genocide-consolidated dictatorship of the Army, which made both secession and war inevitable' (*TMD*: 18). Unfortunately, for every Soyinka, we had ten or more 'power prostitutes', parading as intellectuals but who were in reality 'young opportunistic bourgeois, who lack any sort of conviction or commitment' (*TMD*: 35–6). For his part, Ngugi carried his professorial gown to town, to work with ordinary Kenyan citizens to raise their awareness and empowerment, thus, exposing the sham of the Kenyan post-colonial, or more appropriately, neo-colonial administration. For this crime as we have seen, preventive detention was clamped on him and while in prison under deplorable conditions, 'petty-bourgeois intellectuals ... who hide ethnic chauvinism and their mortal terror of progressive class politics behind masks of abstract super-nationalism, and bury their own inaction behind mugs of beer and empty intellectualism' (*Det*: xxi) vilify him, especially through the state-sponsored media.

Sadly, our people are more adept at copying evil than good; more criminally ingenious at improving power-backed atrocities than in improving governance. What is particularly unnerving is the fact that these kinds of African governments have intensified the obnoxious policies meted out on the African peoples by their erstwhile colonizers, thus perpetrating the master/servant relationship of the past, only this time it is the case of 'indigenous' colonizers turned predators within a single nation state. The list of African leaders absurd in their fastidious and brutal policies against their own is long. In Malawi we had Kamuzu Banda. We have seen Jomo Kenyatta and Arap Moi in Kenya. We cannot forget Idi Amin of Uganda or Mobutu Sese Seko of Congo in this generation. General Ibrahim Babangida's (our local Maradona) military administration in Nigeria is alleged to have committed the most heinous act of inhumanity against a citizen. Dele Giwa a high-ranking journalist was killed in the sanctuary of his home with a letter bomb. Babangida was soon to be followed by General Sani Abacha, the deaf and dumb *Ogidinga* who made history at death; Nigerians took to rejoicing openly in the streets and bars as news of his death was confirmed. During his time in power, people got murdered in all sorts of places: while asleep in their bedrooms, in crowded streets and undoubtedly, in the quiet of prison cells and, moreover, government functionaries were often implicated in these murders.

Professor Tam David-West (1992: A7) has argued, among other things, that 'justice elevates a nation or an institution. Injustice like a wasting cancer slowly but persistently destroys the fabric of society and leads on to eventual demise' (p. 58). Justice is the hallmark of any great nation and until justice is elevated to a prime position in our political sphere, meaningful growth and development will forever elude us. Pain is not an emotion circumscribed by cultural or ethnic boundaries and the nation of which Soyinka speaks would be a community of human beings able and willing to recognize this as a fact. 'Injustice stalks the land like a tiger on the prowl', writes Saro-Wiwa. 'To be at the mercy of buffoons is the ultimate insult. To find the instruments of state power reducing you to dust is the injury' (p. 18). Two years after the publication of these words in *A Month and a Day*, he was executed in defiance of world opinion. Saro-Wiwa's execution brings to mind the Russian Bolshevik's definition of power in the notorious question 'who-whom?' In other words, this simply means: who will get whom? One cannot simply conclude in this case, as in many others before it, that the state got the artist, since the song like all art lives on even after the singer/artist is long gone.

Soyinka has remarked that the Nigerian writer has from the outset remained 'articulately watchful' and that all things considered, the African writer should against all odds have 'the courage to determine what alone can be salvaged from the recurrent cycle of human stupidity' witnessed in our nation states (*Art, Dialogue and Outrage* 1967; rpt 1988, 19–20). Helping to mould a nation's consciousness appropriately and with the overall and paramount interest of the nation at heart is to my mind, not only noble but also unquestionably patriotic.

The socially productive function of works such as these is illuminating. Not only are the reasons for the writers' preventive detention intimated, but we are also told how they were imprisoned, and why they felt compelled to write in prison. Like all political prisoners, they wrote in defiance of oppressive regimes. Writing helped to keep demons of the mind at bay. And they knew that they had to keep their minds and hearts together and protected from the brutality of near demonic states. They wrote, 'partly to wrench some ease for [their] own mind[s]. And partly that some world sometime may know' and they wrote to assert their 'will to remain human and free despite the official government programme of animal degradation of political prisoners' (*Det*: 6). They wrote because they refused to 'submit willingly' to the 'daily humiliation of fear' (*TMD*: 15).

If some African writers are accused of a lack of vital relevance between their literary concerns and the overwhelming reality of most of our modern nation states, neither Soyinka nor Ngugi nor even Ken Saro-Wiwa can justifiably be accused in this manner. These writers have exposed and decried human rights abuses in their respective nations and thus they must be seen as performing the critical function needed to bring forth responsible governance. Every political detainee is at heart a patriot and herein lies the irony of preventive detention; those who in all earnest should be put in prison for unpatriotic acts run the government and 'own' the state machinery to put the patriot behind bars. In discussing the state national prisons and police blocks, these writers are eloquent in their agony over the history of our nations. Through indictments and positing alternative and contrary viewpoints to that of the state government they offer the way forward to an emancipated and empowered polity. In short, three major strands of pre-occupation are manifested in each of the three works examined in this study, namely:

(a) Political and social statements about things as they are
(b) Actual lived experiences in prison
(c) Hopes / images for a better future.

Unquestionably therefore, these writers have combined to speak as the voice of vision for our time. They have spoken in short of the need for re-instating human dignity, the need for an answerable political leadership and the need for a socially responsible citizenry.

They have done this in different ways. Whereas Saro-Wiwa's style is for the most part ordinary and conversational, Ngugi's is pungent, strident and more overtly recalcitrant, for example in his opinion that true Christianity is antithetical and opposed to national patriotism. In contrast, Soyinka tempers vehemence with moderation in such a manner as to respect, for example, his reader's right to be a Christian.

Black humour and satire run through Ngugi's rendering of aspects of both the colonial administration and their excesses in Kenya, and Kenyans encounter with the post-1963 nationalist governments. Pain assails the reader in a long tortuous and unabated manner except in one humorous instance:

> There is a warder who hardly ever talks. But when we start reading news of exploits of the Red Brigades in Italy, his mouth suddenly opens. He can talk endlessly about them with only one constant refrain. 'And they are not touching the poor,' he would say, laughing until tears flow down his cheeks. Then he would describe graphically, in minute detail, how they shot this or that rich Italian person, as if he had been present when the deed was done. 'And to know that they are not touching the poor,' he would repeat. About Kenya or Africa, however, he is absolutely mum. No words. No opinions. (*Det*: 141)

Even here indictment against inhibiting government is not far removed.

Such pain is mitigated with humour in *The Man Died* and relieves its intensity without diminishing or undermining its import. Once, the writer shocks his reader with the announcement: 'I made a strange discovery this morning. I'm pregnant' (*TMD*: 215). This is not a witty rendering of malnutrition manifesting as kwashiorkor. Five weeks of one of his numerous periods of hunger strike had resulted in such weight loss as to require an unconscious extension of his abdomen in order for him to be able to hold up his trousers. Soyinka's running battles with state agents before he submits himself to them, his near dare-devil tactics to obtain a pen from a prison doctor and more paper than he officially signs for from state agents, pale before his account of the buffoon called the governor of the Kiri-kiri prison. 'I nearly swore that he was a Biafran agent secretly employed to entertain the detainees', he writes (*TMD*: 100). So cinematographic is the description of this encounter that at the end the reader is quite unable to restrain himself or herself. However, the whole sickening picture remains: the stench, the inhumanity, the impotence of the agent of a bestial administration, the defiant will of a people with their backs to the wall who knew there was nothing else to lose – all these and more remain vivid in the background of this comic display.

The three writers studied here have questioned the unacceptable culture of fear enforced through the abuse and misuse of power. Dictatorial African governments work hard to instill the fear to fight injustice and the fear to promote authentic indigenous African culture, which they find recriminatory. The writers have been outraged by indices of injustice in the socio-political situation of their times and in writing their feelings and experiences, they enjoin us to become engaged in the dialogue necessary to move us forward.

WORKS CITED

Brutus, Dennis. *A Simple Lust*. London: Heinemann, 1973.

David-West, Tam 'Of Justice and Peace', *The Guardian on Sunday*, 10 May 1992.

Easton, David. *Framework for Political Analysis*. Englewood Cliffs NJ: Prentice-Hall 1965.

Howard, Rhoda *Human Rights in Commonwealth Africa*. Totowa, NJ: Rowman and Littlefield, 1986.

Ikiddeh, Ime. *Foreword*, in Ngugi wa Thiong'o, *Homecoming*. London: Heinemann, 1972.

Jeyifo, B. 'Introduction'. In *Art, Dialogue and Outrage: Essays on Literature and Culture*. Ibadan: New Horn Press, 1988.

Kariuki, J.M. *Mau Mau Detainee*. Oxford: Oxford University Press, 1963.

Kenyatta, Jomo. *Facing Mount Kenya*. London: Secker and Warburg, 1938.

Laswell, Harold and Caplan A. *Power and Society*. New Haven, CT: Yale University Press, 1950.

Laswell, Harold. *Politics: Who Gets What, When and How?* Cleveland: World Publishing, 1950.

Mwase, G. Simeon. *Strike a Blow and Die. The Story of the Chilemlowe Rising*. London: Heinemann.

Neto, Agostinho. *Sacred Hope*. Dar es Salaam: Tanzania Publishing House, 1974.

Ngugi wa Thiong'o. *Barrel of a Pen*. Trenton, NJ: Africa World Press, 1983.

—— *Homecoming*. London: Heinemann, 1972. Rpt. 1982. (All references are to the 1982 ed. and are cited as *HC*.)

—— *Detained: A Writer's Prison Diary*. London: Heinemann, 1981. (All references in the text are to this edition and are cited as *Det*.)

Nkosi, Lewis. *Task and Masks: Themes and Styles of African Literature*. London: Longman, 1981.

Nkrumah, Kwame. *Ghana. The Autobiography of Kwame Nkrumah*. London: Panaf Books, 1957.

Nnolim, Charles. *Approaches to the African Novel: Essays in Analysis*. London: Saros International Publishers, 1992. pp. 158–72.

Nwoga, D. I. 'Modern African Poetry: The Domestication of a Tradition'. In *African Literature*

Today. ALT vol. 10, 1979: pp. 32–56.

Okere, Augustine. 'Ken Saro-Wiwa's Art in *Songs in a Time of War'. The Literary Griot*, 12 (1), Spring 2000: pp. 6–36.

Saro-Wiwa, Ken. *A Month and a Day: A Detention Diary.* Ibadan: Spectrum Books Ltd. 1985. (All references in the text are to this edition and are cited as *AMD.*)

—— *Songs in a Time of War.* London, Lagos and Port-Harcourt: Saros International Publishers, 1985.

Shaw, Bernard. 'The Rejected Statement' – Part 1. *Collected Plays.* London: Bodley Head, 1921 (1971) pp. 697–726.

Soyinka, Wole. *Art, Dialogue and Outrage: Essays on Literature and Culture.* Ibadan: New Horn Press, 1988.

—— *The Man Died: Prison Notes.* Ibadan: Spectrum Books Ltd, 1972. (All references are to this edition and are cited as *TMD.*)

—— 'Religion and Human Rights'. *Index on Censorship*, 17 (5) 1988.

—— *A Shuttle in the Crypt.* London: Rex Collings, 1972 (rpt New York: Hill and Wang, 1977).

Ukpokodu, I Peter. 'Theatre as Socio-Political Power in Africa: Some Contemporary Experiments'. *The Theatre Annual* xlv, 1992: 39–64.

—— 'Performing Artists and the Question of Human Rights in Africa: Ngugi wa Thiong'o and Wole Soyinka', *The Literary Griot*, 9 (1&2) 1997: 49–74.

Problems of Representing the Zimbabwean War of Liberation in Mutasa's *The Contact*, Samupindi's *Pawns* & Vera's *The Stone Virgins*

Maurice Taonezvi Vambe

In his foreword to *The Struggle for Zimbabwe* (1985), the then prime minister of Zimbabwe, Robert G. Mugabe commends the authors, David Martin and Phyllis Johnson, for writing a history textbook 'through ZANU's History' (Mugabe, 1981: v) but goes on to argue that the main limitation of the book is that it is written by 'onlookers', who according to him 'have the limitation that they are not the actors themselves' (p. vi). Here, Mugabe implies that those who did not wield the gun and were not necessarily linked to ZANU history cannot write a credible and an 'authentic' history of the liberation struggle. Dumiso Dabengwa (1995), writing from the ZAPU side contests the above view and suggests that the definitive history of the war cannot be written without taking into account the ZIPRA war narrative. Dabengwa however, reinforces Mugabe's view that the war can only truthfully be narrated by the 'actors', when he, Dabengwa calls for a new breed of 'historian, political scientist, economist [and] sociologist' (p. 24) to give Zimbabwe a truthful account of the contradictions of the war of liberation fought between 1972 and 1979. Neither Mugabe nor Dabengwa looks to Zimbabwean fiction for potentially truthful narrative accounts of the war. Rhodesian Front Files, ZANLA or ZIPRA war records as part of conventional history have laid exclusive claim to true representation of the past, or to narrating the 'real' history of the war, suggesting that within the discipline of History, there is a general consensus that social sciences such as History, Sociology and Political Administration can represent the past more accurately than any other formal narrative. In this 'social science paradigm',

> The implicit connection between African literature and social science episte-
> mology is so powerful that any suggestion that artistic production in Africa
> might actually work against the claims of society, history or culture is easily
> dismissed as a resort to formalism or the doctrines of art for art's sake (Gikandi,
> 2000: 1)

The notion of literature that *works for society by working against it* or contradicting 'claims of society, history and culture' is new to a Zimbabwean context. The mistaken assumption in conventional history on the war in Zimbabwe is that narrative in history is naturally invested with the capacity to give form to human experiences, endowing 'stories and events with coherence and meaning they do not possess as mere sequences (Wilson-Tagoe 2003: 151). This process of elevating the discipline of History attempts to subordinate other formal narratives such as fiction and relegate them to the *second order of truth bearing*, and yet historical narratives are also social constructs that order and rearrange human experience, and hence, influence the meaning and interpretation of historical processes in the way they narrate events. Approaches to literary narrative that have emerged from Zimbabwe have complicated these assumptions of History until they are no longer the only source of 'real' history. Zimbabwean literature has the ability to generate meanings which change with time but nonetheless, have equal claim to producing credible narratives of historical memories of the war whose claims are not beyond contest, but narrative true to life, and make up significant aspects of different people's lived experiences. While Zimbabwean literature can produce a 'history in its own right' (Wilson-Tagoe 2003: 158) the problem arises also, when critics begin to claim that fiction has a single mode of narrating historical memories of war. That literature has its own protocols of representing reality through images should not be taken to mean that it is totally an invented social construct without any relation to social existence. The materiality of metaphor/metonymy in fiction carries with it different, and sometimes conflicting temporalities of time, a fact that suggests that different ways of narrating the war can emerge from a body of texts originating in the same country. In other words, however seemingly 'full' or 'complete' a literary text appears to be, it is always based on a selection of material that excludes other 'histories' or memories of war. The 'real' is drawn into the text and *becomes* the text in a paradoxical way since 'real life can never be truthfully represented as having the kind of formal coherency, met with in the conventional, well-made or fabulistic story' (White 1987: ix–x).

The problem of representing the war of liberation in Zimbabwean literature is felt most acutely in critical essays that emphasize 'events', 'battles' and actual 'contacts' in the war at the expense of exploring the process of narrating the war as an ideological arena (O'Flaherty, 1997: 1–6). Other critical accounts of the Zimbabwean war have emphasized the violent nature of the war of liberation, despite the fact that not all violence originates from war (Dandy 2000: 91–100). It seems to me that Garikai Mutasa's (1985) *The Contact*, Charles Samupindi's *Pawns*, (1992) and Yvonne Vera's *The Stone Virgins* (2002) offer among them, and within each individual text, various versions of the war, and competing modes of representing the history of the liberation struggle. To investigate how each of these texts constructs its narratives of war and history and compares to other Zimbabwean literary texts, brings out the multiplicity of the war narratives within them and this denies those literary narratives interpretive closure.

Unlike the oral songs on war that circulated freely among the masses during the struggle, something that encouraged instant self-criticism among the cadres, *The Contact* is a product of intellectual reflection, an artifact written after the war. That creative distance from the actual physical war affects Garikai Mutasa's way of representing the war but does not make his novel less credible as an account of war. *The Contact* tells the story of seven ZANLA guerrillas who have come to liberate the town of Shiku in the district of Shabani, 'unofficially *Zvishavane*' (p. 10). The story of the war is narrated from the third person singular, a perspective that allows the omniscient narrator to supply the reader with detailed information about the potentially conflicting war narratives in the novel. *The Contact* highlights the physical and military prowess of the Zanla guerrillas and the author, Garikai Mutasa does not hesitate to award all the major military victories to the armed guerrillas. The guerrilla war machinery is portrayed as so efficient that it successfully undermines the military mighty of the Rhodesian Front (RF). In the novel, guerrillas suffer no casualties from the heavily armed RF, they can disarm Corporal Nhamoinesu's group and hold them hostage (p. 50). Comrade Hondoinopisa brings down a RF vampire and a chopper (p. 72), overrides the mercenary Colonel Gaskell and humiliates Turnbull, the RF commander, in his house in front of his daughters (p. 59). This highly picturesque depiction of the war was also confirmed by surviving guerrillas who used it to boost morale of other guerrillas at the front, as well as to persuade the masses that the guerrilla movement was the winning side. And yet, today with new accounts of the suffering of the guerrillas that are emerging in post-independence Zimbabwe (Kanengoni 1997) it is difficult to accept this glorious portrayal of the guerrilla without effecting significant modifications. Even a moderate nationalist who experienced the excruciating pain and suffering associated with the struggle is bound to question that depiction. Anyone familiar with the perilous war situation in Zimbabwe between 1972 and 1979 knows only too well that the RF army was well-armed and that in many cases it successfully overran guerrilla positions. In portraying the guerrillas as always winning the battles, Mutasa, is motivated by the desire to portray Africans as heroes emerging out of a historical process in which they are conceived as not only as having the upper hand, but as standing on higher moral ground. This highly romanticized literary version of the war, also typical of Edmund Chipamaunga's *A Fighter for Freedom* (1985), has been described by Chiwome (2001) as 'triumphalist literature' because it mimes the official mythology of the Zanla version of the war that valorized individual leaders as heroes. In this triumphalist 'official' version of the war, fiction is asked to serve the purposes of conventional historians since the presumption is that 'fictional narratives ... grow in respectability the nearer they approximate historical narrative' (Chennells 2001: 2). This assumption threatens to prevent fiction from exercising its right to doubt, or to generate its own *probable* war narratives that challenge the 'facts' proffered as evidence of war narratives in conventional history.

When *The Contact* was published in 1985, it was part of a larger discourse of African cultural nationalism that sought to reverse racist myths which portrayed Africans as 'comic buffoons, [who] cannot act effectively without whites directing them' (Chennells 1995: 119). What is absent in Mutasa's account of the war are the irreconcilable ideological conflicts that often threatened to derail the armed struggle between the nationalist leaders and the guerrillas, between the guerrillas themselves and among the masses. As a result, the unrealistic levels of literary invention of the war narrative in *The Contact* are bound, ironically, neither to satisfy some nationalists nor their critics. The accusation levelled at Martin and Johnson's *The Struggle for Zimbabwe* (1981), that in its narration of the official version of the war the book, 'obliterated ... popular memory ... [and propagated] an official mythology of war, with heavy emphasis on its abstract and 'glorious aspects' (Barnes 1999: 118) also applies to *The Contact's* account of the war. In Mutasa's desire to weave an 'authentic history' (p. 38) of the war, he has elided the problem of the uneven levels of consciousness among the guerrillas and their leaders. The net result of the propagation of ZANU-PF's official version of the war is that as fiction *The Contact* has rendered visible the ideology of the ruling class and this has resulted in the suppression of other alternative versions of the war memories. For instance, while those who wielded the guns have been apotheosized, the masses who provided vital information to the guerrillas, who supplied material in the form of food and provided moral support are depicted as unreliable, passive, stupid, a gravid and unthinking mass of anonymous faces waiting to 'endorse' (p. 37) the guerrillas' messages of politicization. The ordinary women are dismissed as 'suckers to the manhood of Zimbabwe' (p. 52) thus revealing the misogynistic tendency that is being promoted in the novel against growing evidence that the war could not have been successfully executed without the involvement of women as both guerrillas and *chimbwidos* or couriers (Nhongo-Simbanegavi, 2000). The climax of the novel's official narrative version of the war is the elevation of the leadership to individual heroism when Gadzirai, the leader of the seven guerrillas in Shiku, has after the war in 1980, no moral scruples in working for 'large multinational firms in Harare ... [while] the wife is teaching at Mount Pleasant High.' (p. 125). What the officially sanctioned narrative of war in *The Contact* has achieved has been the creation of a new middle class that displaces the former whites. The organic and stable official narrative of war is, in the novel, finally validated by 'nature' that is depicted as being restored to its tranquil self:

> Life pregnant with life. Butterflies and beetles crawling in the earth. The revolt became a co-ordinated order with the green sprouting of life and foliage. Beautiful flowers from trees and shrubs, miniatures from the carnage. The lords

and gods of the earth were on seasonal strike, creating and recreating what the gods of the heavens had destroyed. They filled the earth with life in a vengeance of the rain. Rebellion. Revolt. The storm had destroyed only to strengthen its adversary; the earth. The earth; now flowing and glowing with animals, insects and blossoms. (p. 67)

This beautifully evocative passage from *The Contact* balances 'rebellion' and 'revolt' with the restoration of the 'natural' order in which the leaders, the ordinary guerrillas and the masses occupy a hierarchical 'metaphysical' position in the order of things. This schizophrenic imagination that informs *The Contact* reflects the novel's capacity for resistance to as well as ideological containment of potentially radical war narratives. The order and conformity that the passage evokes as the legitimate denouement of the war is predicated on the suppression of individual as well as some collective memories of the masses that fall outside the novel's official narrative. For example, the peasant Old Fukidza continues to farm the same old tired plot of land, and Comrade Hondoinopisa, now unemployed, living a life of a vagabond has gone back to a life of stealing (p. 125). The anti-climactic final statement of the novel that 'not everyone was lucky' (p. 125) neutralizes the hegemonic official narrative of triumphant nationalism while at the same time condones the historical betrayal of the majority of Zimbabweans in 1980.

Pawns, a novel by Charles Samupindi published twelve years after independence complicates the simplistic picture of war depicted in *The Contact*. *Pawns* refuses to play second fiddle to accounts of war contained in conventional historical records, which, in David Moore's words would have made the war of liberation 'a singular and celebratory narrative buttressing ZANU-PF'S claims to power' (Moore 1995, 6). *Pawns'* literary strategy is to create space for the different voices competing to give meaning to the war of liberation. The novel is about Daniel, alias Fangs' spiritual/physical/mental journey to manhood until he joins the liberation forces on the side of Zanla. Fangs' experiences in the war are less glorified and are far from the Hollywood version presented in *The Contact*. Awaiting training and deployment at Seguranza, a guerrilla camp in Mozambique, Fangs and his comrades face hunger and disease, and he witnesses the death of Peter, his friend. During the long months of waiting for training to become a freedom fighter, there are also 'defections, naturally – some heading for home. A home that could not be reached. Some are captured by Frelimo and handed back for the dreaded ritual' (p. 69) that involves brutal physical beating. This frustration is compounded by the fact that after training, while at the war front, guerrillas are exposed to deadly napalm from RF raids. The medics, Comrade Mabhunu, Comrade Toitora and Pasi die in the human carnage (p. 134), all suggesting the guerrillas' humanity and their vulnerability to enemy fire power. Vulnerable, in the thick of the battle, Fangs desires immortality because of his love for Angela, one of the *chimbwidos*: 'for the first time in their encounter, Angela tries to see the commander, (Fangs) as a man and not as a combatant' (p. 132). Further, the narrator comments that 'a combatant is a human being before he is a combatant. The human in him will continue to surface ... (p. 139). The humane dimension shown by Fangs' love for Angela contrasts sharply with Mutasa's guerrillas who act like automatons in an uncontrollable war machine. Even as Samupindi's guerrillas are humane, ironically, they too are violent to the masses 'from which, for the most part, they also come – and for whom the war is purportedly waged (Moore 1995: 376). In *Pawns* this violence against the masses is evidenced by comrade Logistics who murders the old peasant, Mhangira, even when the guerrilla had no tangible evidence that the old man was a traitor. Samupindi's refusal to accord every act of his guerrilla-creations the status of heroic deeds in an 'unsullied' war narrative is part of his desire to debunk official nationalist myths that portrayed the guerrillas' relationship with the masses as always positive, while depicting the Rhodesian forces as always the cruel characters. In this endeavour to demystify the portrayal of the war, Samupindi 's efforts are complemented by Alexander Kanengoni's short story, 'The Man from Chibwe' (1993) that depicts a ZANLA guerilla who is saved from death by a Rhodesian security man, whom the guerrilla was later to meet in post-independence Zimbabwe as a pauper. In other words, the conscious way in which Samupindi narrates the war, exploding some of the ZANLA war myths is the writer's way of smiting the official populist ideology which continually sustains its legitimacy by peddling the myths of the invincibility of the guerrillas. In *Pawns*, Samupindi rejects the notion that military factors alone could have guaranteed freedom for the guerrillas. As Ngwabi Bhebhe and Terence Ranger (1995: p. 3) note, 'the guerrillas always had a keen appreciation of the supreme importance of the social, ideological and political "fronts"' of the war.

Part of the ideological knowledge that the guerrillas acquired during the struggle had to do with contradictions deep-seated within the ZANLA movement. In *Pawns*, the old guard of the ZANLA movement is represented by Robert Mugabe, whose 'blue tennis shoes were no more than fibres tied round his feet' (p. 52). Mugabe is constructed as a sober leader and as one who employs 'precise syntax' (p. 61). In the official war narrative that *Pawns* presents, Mugabe is portrayed as a social democrat who does not believe in talking behind his fellow guerrillas' backs; he does not hide from his comrades what he believes, which is that the other political parties such as Joshua Nkomo's ZAPU, Ndabaningi Sithole's *Zanu Chimwenje* and Bishop Muzorewa's African National Congress (ANC) are historical sell outs:

> Comrades, as you are all aware, Muzorewa, Nkomo and Sithole initiated the dialogue which precipitated the 1975 détente. But ZANU has learned from the past that dialogue is futile and will not give us back our land ... Only an armed struggle, only the barrel of the gun, will get us our land back. (p. 73)

In this, Robert Mugabe's ZANU version of the war given voice to in *Pawns*, some of the official myths are rearranged and reconstituted as ideological absolutes at a potentially harmful level. The thematic refrain 'in the end, the hand of ZANU shall rule!' (p. 23) builds into a mythic potency and reinforces the legitimacy of the party in the eyes of its followers. On the one hand, ZAPU which has contributed significantly to the war effort against colonialism particularly in Matebeleland is shown as being in the penumbra of nationalist politics. ZAPU is bedeviled by internal strife, and disorganization. On the other hand, the destructive politics of attrition pursued by Bishop Abel Muzorewa's army, Dzakutsaku or Pfumo Revanhu have not been adequately explored.

If the interpretation of *Pawns*' meaning potential is limited to the official Zanu version of the war, it would be easy to conclude that the novel is imaginatively committed to a one-party state and as such constructs a war narrative that operates as a theoretical justification or ZANU-PF under Robert Mugabe to rule Zimbabwe *ad infinitum*. In this way, Samupindi's authorial and aesthetic perceptions of the war would have to be considered as merging into an anti-pluralistic tendency typical of official thinking in post-independence Zimbabwe. The reality of the complexity of *Pawns*' multiple modes of narrating the war is that the novel has deliberately highlighted this official ZANU-PF account of the war, upstaging that version so as to introduce the alternative narrative voice of the Vashandi. Though Angus Shaw (1993: 11) believes that *Pawns* is imaginatively conceived from the 'ZANLA side' the presence of the Vashandi guerrillas – a group of young, educated cadres committed to dismantling privilege within the struggle – complicates the nationalist narrative of war favoured by the old guard of ZANU who claim to speak in a unitary voice. The Vashandi are an idealistic group that wants to abolish potential privileges in post-independence Zimbabwe. Joseph, one of the converts to the Vashandi cause believes that theirs is a 'guerrilla warfare within guerrilla warfare' (p. 100). The Vashandi set their goals as the rejuvination of the war, particularly between 1975 and 1976 when the old guard of nationalists are jailed and the war efforts are almost stalled. The young cadres also seek to fight the tribalism believed to have been perpetuated by the old guard, and that had resulted in the death of Herbert Chitepo, the ZANLA Chief strategist in 1975. As the omniscient narrator notes, the new Vashandi:

> Recruits appreciated the need for effective execution of the war, but felt there had to be clear political direction. [Besides] the language of the trainers, strange to most, was Korekore liberally smattered with Mozambican words and phrases. This leant a further dimension to the conflict. If you did not speak it, you were outside, you did not belong, you did not come from Mount Darwin. (p. 85)

The Vashandi guerrillas within ZANU seemed way ahead of the old nationalists politically, in so far as the Vashandi combined the idea of the 'war of manoeuvre' aimed at taking control of the state machinery, with the 'war of position' (Gramsci 1973: 238) that sought to effect social transformation of the relations between guerrillas and among the masses during the struggle itself. In *Pawns*, the question of ideological self-criticism was central to the Vashandi because the old guard believed that 'as for ideology, this can be decided after independence'(p. 102). In another context of struggle similar to that of Zimbabwe's, Amilcar Cabral (1966: 2) bemoaned what he calls the 'ideological deficiency ... within the national liberation movements', that in *Pawns* the Vashandi saw as the greatest weakness of the struggle. Although Fangs is not a convert to the Vashandi cause, Fangs can see sense in their ideological programme: 'it is difficult not to acknowledge that they have a good case' (p. 76). Fangs is being ironic when he tells Joseph that he, Fangs cannot 'countenance dissidence' (p. 20) because, by giving voice to the Vashandi narrative, *Pawns*, Samupindi has been accepting the idea that 'a people's war'(p. 72) ought to acknowledge contradictions within it and that war can only meaningfully be narrated, written from and given multiple meanings to, from a multiplicity of ideological positions. Stanley Nyamfukudza commenting on *Pawns* supports the above observation when he argues that

> the war of liberation can never be one person's story: the scenario was much too complex for that, the sides and realities too various, so that every authentic version that is added is another nuance in the maturity of the flavour of the wine'. (1993: 11)

Unfortunately, for the old guard nationalists, the Vashandi could only be dealt with by a ruthless suppression of their war narrative, and the person to execute them was ironically General Josiah Magama Tongogara, the guerrilla who has entered into African song, dance, drama and folklore as the hero of the struggle for liberation in Zimbabwe (p. 102).

Historically, the Vashandi movement was violently dismantled during the liberation struggle, losing key members such as Nhari and Badza (p. 70). According to David Moore, that process of 'silencing' the Vashandi signalled that the old guard of ZANU began to 'create its monopoly on violence from the conception of the guerrilla war and to take the possibility that ...' the various groups contending for the leadership of the movement [would] be resolved by a tension ridden combination of coercion and consent' (Moore 1995: 376). But in *Pawns*, Samupindi refuses to depict the suppression of the Vashandi as the successful containment of alternative war narratives by the new nationalist government. After independence the governing elite's national romance of an authentic history is further undercut by the presence of Fangs' poverty. Fangs has emerged battered from the war, and scrounges for morsels of food in the street-bins of Harare. He fights with ferocious lean-dogs of the city which accuse him of foraging in their territory. Fangs' ex-comrade-in-arms Kufa receives cruel treatment from the father-priest whose expensive car reduces Kufa to a smudge of blood – a formless, broken lifeless body before him. The priest deals kicks out at Kufa's dead body and springs to a ferral frenzy as he inspects the extent of the damage to his car. After the war it is not only Fangs who is harshly rejected and remains unaccommodated by the country whose liberation he fought for. His mother is ruthlessly harassed and fined for selling vegetables by the roadside, and along with the less advantaged women and prostitutes described in the novel, Fangs' mother is crushed by the country's skewed and cruel laws that protect the few and victimize the majority. The simmering discontent of the majority of Africans who feel betrayed by their leadership metaphorically transforms itself into urban guerrilla warfare in Marechera's *Black Sunlight* (1985) and perhaps more mimetically, the historically documented war carried out by 'ZAPU dissidents' that rocked Matebeleland between 1981 and 1986. The story of an 'illicit version of the war' (Vera 2002: 73) told from the perspective of ZIPRA women is one that *The Stone Virgins* pursues.

The Stone Virgins, a novel by Yvonne Vera, further complicates the picture of a Zimbabwean war narrative by refusing to depict it as a distinctly male affair, and a largely ZANLA history that *Pawns* paints. In *The Stone Virgins*, the author narrates from the point of view of ZIPRA female guerrillas, the liberation war (1972–9) and the civil war fought in Matebeleland from 1981–6, between the new black government forces and the so-called 'Zapu dissidents'. The novel itself is about Thenjiwe and Nonceba, two sisters who become victims of the post-independence disturbances in Matebeleland. *The Stone Virgins* also gives voice to the 'dissident' war narrative as narrated by Sibaso, one of the 'dissidents' who after witnessing the betrayal of independence goals, returns into the hills of Gulati as a sign of defiance to the rule of Robert Mugabe, the new prime minister of Zimbabwe.

Conventional ZIPRA history begins with the formation of ZAPU in 1961, progressing linearly into how that party was built into a huge guerrilla war machine, until the party began to train soldiers for a conventional war in 1978 (Dabengwa 1995: 24–35. This picture of 'official' ZIPRA history is confirmed by Brickhill (pp. 48–72), whose account of the ZIPRA war narrative dutifully follows ZANLA accounts in the ways it underplays the role of black women in that war. In contrast, *The Stone Virgins*, 'remembers' these two wars differently (p. 82). In the novel, Vera suggests that the roots of ZAPU lay as far back as the '1950s' in which African woman struggled to maintain some sort of cultural space in the face of threat from colonialism. The author registers the changing perceptions of women, how they became part of a new urban popular culture defined by 'bottles of shield deodorant and Tomesai Shampoo. And Ponds' (p. 23). In their struggles to domesticate the city and adapt to the new city culture, Vera's women of the 1950s display contradictory perceptions. They feel entrapped by the new culture of the 'ambi generation' and yet when the

1970s come, the women redefine that space, occupying it as guerrillas, to the perplexity of colonialism and the African patriarchs. Vera's women of the '1950s' reject the notion that African women were simply underdogs during colonialism. They were, ironically, vectors in promoting some aspects of colonial culture, even as the same women fought the colonial system (p. 49), and challenged African male stereotypes that viewed the women as passive onlookers on the creation of history.

In *The Stone Virgins*, Vera deliberately searches for female heroines 'because the country needs heroes, and flags, and festivities' (p. 4). That the author finds the heroines among black township women of Thanda-bantu validates the roles of women as significant during the struggle. This point that has also been emphasized by Tsitsi Dangarembga in *Nervous Conditions* (1995), and in Irene Mahamba's *Women in Struggle* (1985) is all the more significant because it has been consistently downplayed in other literary works such as *The Contact* and *Pawns*. In *The Stone Virgins*, Vera subverts both 'official' ZAPU and ZANLA war accounts, and the novel suggests a reversal of roles between African women and men. In her novel it is the historical urgency of the African women, their 'memories of anger and pain' and their desire for total freedom that are emphasized. The ways in which the war narratives, memories and contribution of Vera's female characters are portrayed in the novel becoming *the* text that interrogates the 'official' Zapu war narrative reveals the latter as relent-lessly fragmented (p. 82), fragile and one-sided. Recounting the war narrative from the position of ZAPU woman constitutes an act of sub-version of ZAPU official mythological version of the war. This revisionist sensibility in *The Stone Virgins* is effected so that it would take on board what the narrator describes as other 'illicit versions of the war' (p. 53). These illicit versions of the war are the novel's inchoate but *probable* nar-ratives that deny the novel interpretive closure. In the words of the narrator 'to acknowledge that there are other narrative versions of the war is itself an act of refusing to bury the memory [of] the bones [of Nehanda] rising' (p. 59). This statement connects *The Stone Virgins* to Chenjerai Hove's *Bones* (1988) in which Nehanda prophesies that even when the colonialists kill her, her 'bones' shall rise in the name of African women and men to avenge her death.

And yet, Vera's womanist war narrative is not without its own 'undis-turbed histories' (p. 50) and 'burnt portions of ... memory' (p. 71) of pain and anger. When the civil war breaks out in 1981 and curfew is imposed in Bulawayo (p. 59), black women suffer from the new government's desire to extend its hegemony to the people of Kezi. After the civilian population of Kezi refuse to submit and confess where the 'dissidents' are, 'soldiers shoot them, without preamble – they walked in and raised AK rifles: every shot was fatal' (p. 121). And in the process, Kezi is reduced to 'a naked cemetery' (p. 143). In this account of how the new government trans-gressed, violated and killed its own people, with women suffering the most, the triumphalism and celebrations that mark the new leader's rule in the new nation is radically subverted and ridiculed. In fact, in *The Stone Virgins* Vera refuses to describe the war of 1981–6 as a civil war, or 'dissident' menace, because to have done so would have confirmed the official account of the disturbances in Matebeleland as a product of ZAPU 'malcontents' who, as the government-controlled media suggested only deserved to be treated like beasts (*The Herald*, 28 June 1984). Vera also refuses to explain why that war took place, because that would lock her novel within the 'social science paradigm' which emphasizes causation, continuity and closure in the explanation of social reality. Through this conscious way of withdrawing knowledge the novel denies conventional historians the opportunity to confirm their conclusions and prejudices that it was simply the new government's brutality that was to blame for that war. Vera is not concerned with apportioning blame, rather with the desire to open channels for fruitful dialogue. Refusal to dwell on the 'historical causes' means that Vera runs the risk of dehistoricizing the war of 1981–6 because she relies extensively on creative invention. This technique of withholding information on the causes of the disturbances portrays the new government as extremely xenophobic and tribalist, which again might not convey all the complexity of that war, but significantly allows Vera to concentrate on describing the intense brutality meted out to the people of Matebeleland by the ZANU government: the murder of Thenjiwe, and the rape and mutilation of Nonceba by Sibaso, the new 'bandit' that has emerged out of the conflagration of the early eighties.

The triumphalist ZANU war narrative, and post-war stability is put to further severe test when Robert Mugabe sends the fifth brigade to quell the Matebeleland disturbances. Vera captures this tragic moment in the new nation's history through the desecration of the cultural life of Thandabantu by the soldiers of the new government. In the novel the violation of Thandabantu is in fact the violation of Matebeleland, the attempt at 'burying of memory' (p. 59) of the war narrative of ZIPRA women. For Vera the new leaders turn out to be rogues or a 'gang of bandits' because they use coercion to define the cultural life of the new nation. That the new prime minister sustains his legitimacy in Matebeleland not through people consenting to his rule but through force underlines the fact that although the nation is a source of new identities, the same nation paradoxically represses the memories of the people of Matebeleland that it defines as dissident, and cannot therefore exist alongside. The banality of the leader's power is revealed by the soldiers who carry out systematic torture to 'intimidate, to kill, to extract confessions, to resurrect the dead' (p. 124). Two soldiers chillingly force a wife to axe her husband to save her two sons from death (p. 80). The brutal torture to death of Mahlathini (p. 123) is described in ways that suggest that it is the new government that is illegitimate and consequently is made up of a group of bandits.

Although Ranger (2002: 209) argues that Vera has severely restrained her pen because, according to him, what happened in Matebeleland was even more grotesque than fiction could imaginatively handle, Vera's accounts of the fifth brigade's brutality in Matebeleland tends to subserve the conclusions of conventional history (Alexander and others, 2000). What Vera is doing in recreating the war narrative of Matebeleland in terms that confirm the conclusions in conventional history is to suggest that the war was a planned, atrocious but purposeful (p. 124) ethnic cleansing of the people of Matebeleland led by a predominantly Shona government. This mode of depicting the conflict challenges the ZANU government's claims that it was dealing with bandits and not dissidents; the lack of coherent political motivation, attributed to bandits it was used to justify dealing with them in an inhumane way. Such a negative portrayal of the new government in negative terms enables Vera in *The Stone Virgins* to create and validate a new official 'Ndebele' historiography that is predicated on what the author perceives as violence instigated by Shona against the Ndebele. In this way, Vera participates in the reinvention of tribalism and unfortunately, at this point in the narrative, the author's mode of revising the official war narrative does not to step outside of stereotyping the new government as callous, through and through. That this new 'Ndebele historiographical war narrative' also fails to resist the lure of objectifying other narratives, typical of the dominant ZANU's war narrative, is clear in *The Stone Virgins'* fascination with carefully selected episodes depicting the new government's heavy hand towards the Ndebeles and their suffering as the victimized minority people. What the novel elides in this counter-narrative is that some Shona people also suffered in the Matebeleland disturbances, and that the picture painted of total neglect and of lack of development in Matebeleland is far from the truth on the ground.

The process of destabilizing ZANU political hegemony also involves subverting what Vera perceives as errant Shona cultural nationalism. For Sibaso in *The Stone Virgins*, the Matebeleland debacle is a result of a hegemonic but delinquent Shona cultural nationalism that has been allowed to suppress other cultural memories. It is for this reason that Sibaso rejects *Feso*, a Shona novel that has been used by nationalists to contest colonial hegemony (p. 109). What Sibaso, and by extension Vera, rejects in *Feso* is, first, Solomon Mutswairo's claim that Zimbabwe historically belongs to the Shona people, and secondly, *Feso's* projection of the First and Second *Chimurengas* as distinctly Shona discourses of cultural nationalism. The mere existence of *The Stone Virgins*, its giving of voice to the 'dissident' narrative is the process by which the author transfers spiritual anchorage of the new nation to Bulawayo. The new nation that is to be installed at Lobengula's kraal (p. 165) needs to restore the past, and the cultural symbols that will give this new nation form are depicted as coming from Matebeleland.

The paradox that Vera in *The Stone Virgins* has to come to terms with is that her novel cannot destabilize Shona/ZANU's triumphant narrative of war and peace, via a recreation of a 'stable' Ndebele account of the war. It is to Vera's credit that she registers an acute awareness of the fragility of the 'Ndebele' war narrative from Matebeleland which she has constructed in the novel through her descriptions of Mahlathini's death at the hands of the army. Vera does not write *The Stone Virgins* as if she was present during the political disturbances that rocked Matebeleland between 1981 and 1986. For example, there are different accounts – potentially conflicting as well – of what actually happened to the people of Kezi during those fateful days:

> some of the men who are missing in the village *are said* to have certainly died there, the others, *it is said*, walked all the way from Kezi to Bulawayo ... having managed to escape, carrying with them the memory of a burning body and an impeccable flame ... *Others insist* that nobody fled to Bulawayo ....(123–4) (my emphasis)

On the actual killing of Mahlathini Vera does not write as if she was present but uses reported speech: 'those who witnessed the goings-on at Thandabantu on this night said Mahlathini howled like a helpless animal' (p. 123). Vera deploys the genre of reportage because of its ability to unravel potential discrepancies between fact outside the text and 'reality' imaginatively constructed in the novel. Reportage also introduces the multiplicity of narrative voices, all vying to capture the problematics of re-presenting a civil war narrative that can never be complete when uttered from one side or position. The frailty of memory is a permanent feature of the oral mode within which reportage speech is inscribed. Within the instability of the oral narrative suggested by the reported speech in the novel, the desire to represent ZANU/Shona 'violence' on Ndebele as absolute and natural is contestable and, ironically necessitates a preliminary critique of *The Stone Virgins*' own mode of representing the war narratives it has constructed.

As a counter-history of the official war narrative of what actually happened in Matebeleland, Yvonne Vera's *The Stone Virgins* can be said to be keenly aware that individual oral testimonies from 'dissidents' like Sibaso contain potential distortions because these stories have been edited, and facts reordered during the process of narration in order to produce preferred interpretive meanings from the actual events of the war. It is for this reason that the novel refuses to endorse Sibaso's claims as a helpless victim of what is in Matebeleland perceived as the brutality of the new leaders. The 'dissident' war narrative is thus denied the privilege or monopoly of absolute 'truth'. Though a product of a brutal history the novel rightfully insists that there is no justification for Sibaso to murder the innocent Thenjiwe (p. 73) as he does, or to rape and mutilate Nonceba (p. 62). The inconsistency of Sibaso's war narrative, and its inherent instability as a credible source of the meaning of 'history' is metaphorically hinted at when he, Sibaso, looks at himself in the mirror. What he sees is not a neat, uncontestable identity of the self but 'an apparition' (p. 71) and as Sibaso says, 'the mirror looked cracked. I could see my own broken face behind it' (p. 76). By linking Sibaso to a 'post-war spider, a hungry spider' [that] is fragile like 'the membrane around dreams' (p. 76), Yvonne Vera is commenting on the predatory nature of men and women. Associating Sibaso's war narrative with a 'cracked' mirror, 'broken face and 'fragile' dreams is Vera's way of casting doubt on the authenticity of that narrative. For Vera, writing or interpreting the war is highly problematic because of the affiliation of the process of narration to specific ideologies that threaten to impose stability and closure to the narrative, whereas in real life, 'history has [no] ceiling' (p. 74). *The Stone Virgins* concludes by narrating a different kind of war; one of healing and 'delivery' between Cephas Dube and Nonceba. In this new war of healing the two are supportive of each other; they both avoid defining each other. Even in this new war, *The Stone Virgins* insists on the open-endedness of historical processes as well as acts of representing the multiplicity of human identities that emerge from war narratives in Zimbabwe.

In conclusion, there are ideological and imaginative problems in representing the Zimbabwean war of liberation in *The Contact*, *Pawns* and *The Stone Virgins*. First, this problem emerges from conventional history that has tended to lay exclusive claim in terms of representing what it terms the 'truthful' war narrative in Zimbabwe. The mistaken assumption that war narratives are mere sequences elides the fact that narrative in conventional history orders and rearranges events and social reality so as to meet the preferred conclusions of those who construct them. Zimbabwean fiction complicates the mistaken assumptions of conventional history because fiction has the capacity to produce credible, truthful, believable and meaningful war accounts and represent these war narratives using images, metaphors and metonyms. Within Zimbabwean literature an *ideological war is waged* in the multiple ways in which various authors create a body of literature representing the war narratives in ways that confirm, and interrogate, each other.

The Contact constructs a war narrative that portrays the leaders of the nationalist struggle as the main heroes of the struggle. The masses who worked assiduously to make independence realizable have their roles underplayed. The unsophisticated picture of ZANLA armed guerrillas always winning the battles they engaged in against the powerful Rhodesian army that the reader saw in *The Contact* has been more subtly portrayed in *Pawns* where Samupindi depicts guerrillas as vulnerable to enemy fire power. In *Pawns*, the official ZANLA war narrative is presented as a mythology that is meant to justify the continued rule of ZANU-PF under Robert Mugabe *ad infinitum*. The novel undermines this official account of the war by introducing the Vashandi war narrative, showing that within the ZANLA nationalist movement there were ideological struggles between the old guard and the young educated cadres of the movement.

The triumphalist official narrative of war and peace in post-independence Zimbabwe is further undercut in *Pawns* by the fact that Fangs emerges out of the war battered and foraging for leftover food in Harare's bins. Independence is not economically meaningful to him and to his mother, who with other women is persecuted by the new nation's laws that victimize the majority and protect the few powerful people in positions of leadership. *The Stone Virgins* by Yvonne Vera adds further layers of complexity to both the assumptions of conventional history and to the modes of representing war narratives in *The Contact* and *Pawns*. In *The Stone Virgins*, the war is narrated from the viewpoint of ZIPRA women, and Vera participates actively through *The Stone Virgins* to create a 'Ndebele' war narrative of post-independence Zimbabwe. The war narrative complements and undermines efforts by conventional historians from Matebeleland by erecting a new 'official' Ndebele mythology of the Matebeleland disturbances. Fortunately, in *The Stone Virgins* Vera is aware that even this version that puts all the blame of the disturbances on the new government cannot be sustained. Individual stories by 'dissidents' such as Sibaso cannot be accepted at face value. They have inherent internal instabilities that arise from the fact that they too, are ordered, rearranged and narrated in ways that make them *become* texts that are influenced by social ideologies meant to satisfy certain aims that might or might not coincide with the goals of Zimbabwean nationhood. *Pawns* and to a large extent, *The Stone Virgins* prefer literary open-endedness as an ideological and artistic technique that denies interpretive closure to the reading of war narratives of Zimbabwe.

WORKS CITED

Primary Texts

Mutasa, Garikai. *The Contact*. Gweru: Mambo Press, 1985
Samupindi, Charles. *Pawns*. Harare: Baobab Press, 1992
Vera, Yvonne. *The Stone Virgins*. Harare: Weaver Press, 2002

Secondary Texts

Alexander, J. (*et al.*) *Violence & Memory: One Hundred Years in the 'Dark Forests'of Matebeleland*. Oxford: James Currey, 2000
Barnes, T. *'We Women Worked so Hard: Gender, Urbanization and Social Reproduction in Colonial Harare, Zimbabwe, 1930–1956*. Oxford: James Currey; Portsmouth, NH: Heinemann, 1999.
Bhebe, N. and Ranger, T. (eds), *Soldiers in Zimbabwe's Liberation War*. Harare: University of Zimbabwe Press, London: James Currey, 1995.
—— *Society in Zimbabwe's Liberation War*. Harare: University of Zimbabwe Press; London: James Currey, 1995.

Brickhill, J. 'Daring to Storm the Heavens: The Military Strategy of ZAPU 1976 to 1979'. In Bhebe, N. and Ranger, T. (eds) *Soldiers in Zimbabwe's Liberation War*, Harere: University of Zimbabwe Press; London: James Currey, 1995: 48–72.

Cabral, A. 'The Weapon of Theory'. Address delivered to the First Conference of the Peoples of Asia, Africa and Latin America. Havana, January, 1966.

Chennells, A. J. 'Introduction to the Essays on Zimbabwean Literature'. Unpublished paper from a conference on 'Scanning our Future, Reading our Past.' A Centennial Celebration of Zimbabwean Literature. Harare: University of Zimbabwe Press, 10–12 January, 2001.

—— 'Rhodesian Discourse, Rhodesian Novels and the Zimbabwe Liberation War'. In Bhebe, N. and Ranger, T. (eds) *Society in Zimbabwe's Liberation War*, Harare: University of Zimbabwe Press; London: James Currey, 1995: 102–29.

Chipamaunga, E. *A Fighter For Freedom*. Gweru: Mambo Press, 1985.

Chiwome, E. 'Modern Shona Literature as a Site of Struggle, 1956–2000'. Unpublished paper presented at the conference on 'Scanning our Future, Reading our Past': A Centennial Celebration of Zimbabwean Literature.' Harare: University of Zimbabwe Press, 10–12, January, 2001.

Dabengwa, D. 'ZIPRA in the Zimbabwe War of National Liberation'. In Bhebe, N. and Ranger, T. *Soldiers in Zimbabwe's Liberation Struggle*, Harare: University of Zimbabwe Press; London: James Currey, 1995, 1: 24–35.

Dandy, J. 'The Representation of Violence, the Individual History and the Land in Chinodya's *Harvest of Thorns* and Nyamfukudza's *The Non-Believer's Journey*'. In Jones, E. D. and Jones, M. (eds), *South & Southern African Literature* ALT 23. Oxford: James Currey, 2002, pp. 91–100.

Dangarembga, T. *Nervous Conditions*. Harare: Zimbabwe Publishing House, 1989.

Gikandi, S. 'African Literature and the Social Science Paradigm'. Michigan: University of Michigan, Seminar paper, 2000, 1–20.

Gramsci, A. *Selections from Prison Notebooks*. New York: International Publishers, 1971.

Herald, 'Dissidents Worse than Beasts' 28 June, 1984: 4.

Hove, C. *Bones*. Harare: Baobab Books, 1988.

Kanengoni, E. 'The Man from Chibwe' in *Effortless Tears*. Harare; Baobab Books, 1993.

—— *Echoing Silence*. Harare: Baobab Books, 1997.

Marechera, D. *Black Sunlight*. London: Heinemann, 1980.

Martin D. and Johnson P. *The Struggle for Zimbabwe*. New York and London: Monthly Review Press, 1981.

Mahamba, I. *Women In Struggle*. Harare: Zimfep, 1985.

Moore, D. 'The Zimbabwe People's Army: Strategic Innovation or More of the Same?' In Bhebe, N. and Ranger, T. (eds) *Soldiers in Zimbabwe's Liberation War*. Harare: University of Zimbabwe Press; London: James Currey, 1995 Vol. 1, 73–86.

—— 'Democracy, Violence, and Identity in the Zimbabwean War of National Liberation: Reflections from the Realm of Dissent', *Canadian Journal of African Studies*, 29 (3), December 1995: 375–402.

Nyamfukudza, S. *The Sunday Gazette Magazine*. Harare, 28 November 1993,

O'Flaherty, P. 'War Literature in Rhodesia/Zimbabwe as a Metaphor for the African Postcolonial Experience: The Case of *The Non-Believer's Journey* by Stanely Nyamfukudza and *Karima* by T. O. McLoughlin', *Mots Pluriels*, 1 (4), 1997, 1–6.

Ranger, T. O. 'History Has its Ceiling: The Pressures of the Past in *The Stone Virgins*'. In Muponde, R. and Taruninga, M. (eds) *Sign and Taboo: Perspectives on the Poetic Fiction of Yvonne Vera*. Harare: Weaver Press, Oxford: James Currey, 2002, 203–16.

Nhongo-Simbanegavi, J. *For Better or Worse?: Women and ZANLA in Zimbabwe's Liberation Struggle*. Harare: Weaver Press, 2000.

Shaw, A. 'Review of *Pawns*'. In *The Sunday Gazette Magazine*. Harare, 28 November 1993, p. 11.

White, H. *The Content of Form: Narrative Discourse and Historical Representation*. London and Baltimore. John Hopkins University Press, 1987, pp. ix–x.

Wilson-Tagoe, N. 'History, Gender and the Problem of Representation in the Novels of Yvonne Vera', in Muponde, R. and Taruvinga, M. (eds), *Sign and Taboo: Perspectives on the Poetic Fiction of Yvonne Vera*. Harare: Weaver Press, Oxford: James Currey, 2002, 155–78.

The Need to Go Further?
Dedication & Distance in the War Narratives of Alexandra Fuller & Alexander Kanengoni

Zoe Norridge

In 2004 Alexandra Fuller dedicated her second novel, *Scribbling the Cat* to Alexander Kanengoni. This was an intriguing gesture on many levels. Firstly, Fuller had never met Kanengoni but explains that he became the metaphorical 'godfather' to her novel after she came across his novel *Echoing Silences* in Johannesburg airport, shortly after it was published in 1997. Secondly, although both novels focus on the Zimbabwean liberation struggle, Fuller's is an autobiographical account of her travels with a white former Rhodesian soldier whilst Kanengoni's is a fictional exploration of the experiences of a black guerrilla soldier.

Such public declarations of cross-racial identification are relatively unusual in the context of post-independence Zimbabwean war literature, which remains scarred by legacies of racial division. This said, of course there has been much cross-pollination between writers from a wide range of backgrounds in Zimbabwe (as elsewhere), facilitated by forward thinking dynamic editors such as the courageous Irene Staunton. There have also been fictional explorations of cross-racial identification and indeed both Fuller and Kanengoni published short stories on this theme in a recent volume of new writing from Zimbabwe entitled *Writing Still* (Staunton 2003). But even with these precedents, Fuller's decision to dedicate her second novel to Kanengoni forms both a provocative political statement and an attempt to open up new dialogues. This article looks at both the motivations for Fuller's identification and its implications for her identity as an 'African writer'.

Alexandra Fuller's parents moved to Rhodesia in 1965, a year after Ian Smith's Unilateral Declaration of Independence. However, after the death of their second child, Adrian, in 1968 the family returned to England, where Fuller was born in 1969. Leaving the grey and miserable poverty of farming in Cheshire behind, the Fullers then moved back to Rhodesia in 1972. Fuller's first novel, *Don't Let's Go to the Dogs Tonight* (2002) tells the story of her childhood growing up on various farms in Rhodesia and later in Malawi and Zambia (2002). Although her parents still run a fish farm in

Zambia, Fuller has now married an American and lives in Wyoming with her three children.

A generation older than Fuller, Alexander Kanengoni was born in Chivu in central Zimbabwe in 1951. He worked for a few years as a teacher but left to join the liberation struggle in 1974. Following independence in 1980, he returned to education and read English literature at the University of Zimbabwe. After university he worked for the Education and Culture Ministry where he managed education programmes for ex-combatants and refugees. Then from 1988 to 2002 he worked at the Zimbabwe Broadcasting Corporation as Head of Research Services. In 2002, as part of the controversial 'fast-track redistribution' of property programme, Kanengoni was allocated some land and became a farmer (Primorac 2005, Kanengoni 1997).

In her *Scribbling the Cat* dedication to Kanengoni, Fuller describes him as an African writer 'who stared war in the face and chose not to look the other way'. This fairly aptly sums up Kanengoni's literary career which has been a continual engagement with the ambiguities and horrors of war. He has published three novels (*Vicious Circle*, 1983; *When the Rainbird Cries*, 1988; *Echoing Silences*, 1997) and a collection of short stories (*Effortless Tears*, 1993).

Kanengoni's most recent novel, *Echoing Silences*, tells the story of a war veteran, Munashe, trying to reconcile himself with his traumatic experiences during the war. His memories of his actions as a guerrilla soldier haunt him, destroying his mental health with flashbacks and hallucinations. Immediately after being decommissioned, he had intended to travel to Mozambique, where he trained and fought, in an attempt to make peace with the past. However, he is found by his family and detained in Zimbabwe by domestic obligations. When his mental health continues to deteriorate, his young wife organizes a traditional healing ceremony, at the end of which Munashe dies.

Fuller's *Scribbling the Cat* on the other hand is an autobiographical story of her travels with 'K', a former Rhodesian Light Infantry soldier, who she met whilst staying at her parents' Zambian farm. Fuller and K undertake the voyage through Zimbabwe to Mozambique that Munashe never manages to make. As they travel together K explains his occasional flashbacks and tells Fuller about his war experiences. They also meet several of his former colleagues who tell their own tales. At the end of the novel Fuller is left both with a sense of her own complicity in the Rhodesian regime and the realization that however many questions you ask, the past remains incomprehensible.

After the opening dedication to Kanengoni, Fuller frames her novel with quotations from his *Echoing Silences*. The first quotation is particularly provocative given the nature of her narrative. It describes Munashe as a young soldier, discovering the history of his people for the first time:

So when he finally heard the section commander talking about civilisations that existed in the country before the coming of the white man, he was shocked to discover the history of his people did not start with the coming of the whites. The section commander began with Munhumutapa and the Rozvi empires during the Great Zimbabwe civilization and continued on to the coming of the white man and the first chimurengas, and on through the various forms of colonial government up to Ian Smith's UDI, when the last bridge between blacks and whites was burned down and the only way left to communicate was through violence: the war, the second chimurengas. (Kanengoni, 1997: 15 quoted in Fuller, 2005: 1)

Here we see race, history and war as inherently bound up together from the outset. Kanengoni clearly highlights the role of education in the war, the revalorising of black identity through the retelling of stories of the past. We also see that racial separation has a key role to play in these histories, particularly after UDI when 'the last bridge between blacks and whites was burned down and the only way left to communicate was through violence'. Fuller chooses to highlight the highly racialized barriers to communication between the different sides of the Zimbabwean liberation war by quoting from a text by a black Zimbabwean freedom fighter at the beginning of her novel about white Rhodesian soldiers. In doing this she may have several objectives.

This choice of quote may signal Fuller's desire to use contemporary writing as the means to re-open communication, reconciling the past through the sharing of stories in a non-aggressive context. The quotation may also carry with it a more personal agenda for Fuller's identity as a narrator. Both of Fuller's novels are strewn with examples of white racism, which forms part of her project of 'honesty' – describing things as she finds them. However, by dedicating her novel to Kanengoni and opening her narrative with such a provocative quote, Fuller seems to suggest that she herself has a more considered perspective on events. As such this quotation could serve as a counter to the racist opinions we will hear later in the novel by showing Fuller's own mixed allegiances from the start. It also seems to place Fuller firmly within the realm of the omni-scient narrator who can see reality 'for what it is' – from a multitude of perspectives. Perhaps finally it also situates Fuller's narrative on a meta-textual level. As such, the Kanengoni quotation both points towards the literary production of history in the Zimbabwean context, and flags up the selective, constructed nature of any process of writing.

Another level at which Fuller identifies with Kanengoni in order to enrich her own text can be seen in the narrative similarities between the two novels. As I mentioned earlier, both protagonists, Munashe and K, express a desire to return to Mozambique as a journey to the source of their troubles. Here travelling across space is allied with travelling through time and facilitates the expression of memory in a manner that is familiar for the reader of Zimbabwean literature (see for example Vera, 1994). These journeys through time and space are not always voluntary.

Both men recall being sent into conflict zones by their superiors during the war and subsequently fleeing from these sites in fear of their lives. Similarly, K and Munashe's memories of the past sometimes return to them involuntarily and leave them powerless in their wake. K talks about his 'spooks' and Munashe explains 'ghosts follow me wherever I go. I don't want to think about the war. I want to forget it, but I can't' (Kanengoni 1997: 60).

K and Munashe's traumatic memories of the war become focused around one central incident – an act of violence against a civilian woman that they cannot leave behind. Munashe is pursued by recollections of having been forced to beat a 'sell out' woman and her baby to death. Although this is one memory amongst many, it is the one that plagues him the most because it seems to be such a one-sided act of aggression:

> His life became a sequence of nightmares: horrible confused disjointed memories of the war. At first the memories were general, haphazard, random, but eventually they focussed on the woman with the baby crying on her back as he battered her with a hoe with a broken handle. She became his daytime nightmare. (Kanengoni 1997: 38)

As Munashe's dreams begin to tip over from sleep into daytime nightmares, so Kanengoni's text becomes fragmented, flitting between the past and the present, sometimes even narrating diverse episodes quasi-simultaneously, as if superimposing the past onto the present. Fuller achieves a similar juxtaposition of time periods by continually moving between K's memories of the past and her location in the present. As K tells her about his violent war experiences she constantly returns to the physicality of their current reality, grounding his memories somatically with phenomenological detail that anchors the characters between two worlds.

The central traumatic incident that K's horrific war memories circle is his torture of a civilian woman for intelligence about guerrilla soldiers' whereabouts. K 'shoves' hot sadza into the woman's vagina until she talks. She died two weeks later from her injuries and K was subsequently accused of manslaughter but acquitted without a trial following psychological reports. The key difference between this story and Munashe's is that K, in a position of authority, voluntarily wounds the woman, whereas Munashe is following orders he is powerless to resist, conscious of the inhumanity of his actions at the time. Although we are told about the psychological pressures upon K, the urgency of gaining information and his subsequent and perpetual remorse, we remain horrified by his deliberate actions. He tells Fuller the story as a form of talking therapy and she teases it out of him because she feels this core traumatic incident from the past must be the key to understanding the man she sees before her in the present (2005: 148).

By this point in the narrative we are well into the second part of Fuller's novel and she has already established her relationship with Kanengoni through her initial dedication, framing quotations, and multiple narrative similarities. When K has finished recounting his horrific actions of the past she chooses to make a further identification, this time with K himself, which in turn sheds light on her deliberate references to Kanengoni and reveals more about Fuller's identity as a writer.

Following K's narration of his story Fuller writes:

> And I thought, I *own* this now. This is *my* war too. I had been a small, smug white girl shouting, 'We are all Rhodesians and we'll fight through *thickanthin*'. I was every bit that woman's murderer. [...] I said, 'I had no idea...' But I did. I knew, without really being told out loud, what happened in the war and I knew it was as brutal and indefensible as what I had just heard from K. I just hadn't wanted to know. (2005: 152)

This quote raises fascinating questions about guilt, responsibility and ways of knowing. By declaring herself responsible, by suggesting she herself is 'every bit that woman's murderer', Fuller opens up the issue of civilian complicity in the Zimbabwean liberation struggle. Fuller revisits her childhood self, a 'small, smug white girl' shouting Rhodesian propaganda in order to expose what she perceives to be the reality of white life in Rhodesia in the 1970s.

In an e-mail to me in March 2006 Fuller explained that after *Don't Let's Go to the Dogs Tonight* was published many 'whites' felt very 'betrayed by that book'. She wrote:

> I had taken the lid off the lie that there had been a degree of sanity in the white community, or the lie that there had been liberal white families living in Rhodesia who did not support the Smith regime. Let's be clear about this: if you did not support the racist regime in Rhodesia and you were white you were kicked out of the country. So if you were living there during that time you were implicitly or explicitly racist and you know exactly how brutally racist and brainwashed the whites were. (Fuller e-mail, April 2006)

By declaring her own childhood racism and support of the Smith regime, Fuller now asserts her adult responsibility for atrocities committed in 1970s Zimbabwe 'in her name'. This declaration of complicity is an interesting political statement.

Mark Sanders, in the introduction to his carefully argued examination of intellectual complicity in apartheid South Africa, explores how the assertion of complicity is an important part of the reconciliation process. Sanders suggests that even the opponents to apartheid were implicated by its thinking and practices and had to 'shape their responsibility accordingly' (2002: 1). Sanders quotes from the first volume of the Truth Commission's report which suggests that one of the shortcomings of drawing attention to the extreme crimes of the apartheid era is that this obscures the potential of the 'little perpetrator' in each of us (2002: 3). He also argues that instead of the Truth Commission urging South Africans to wash their hands of personal responsibility, it actually encourages them to actively affirm 'complicity, or potential complicity, in the 'outrageous deeds' of others. Once cultivated, this sense of responsibility would, in the best of possible worlds, make one act to stop or prevent those deeds' (2002: 3–4).

Alexandra Fuller juxtaposes the outrageous crime with the small crime, a woman's murder with the flag waving racism of a young child. And she seems to suggest that one is the logical progression from the other. By declaring her complicity is she moving towards a form of reconciliation with or atonement for the past? On first reading, Fuller's declaration of guilt might seen to be disingenuous and potentially self-indulgent. But in the light of Sanders' comments about how the assertion of complicity can be read as a step towards reconciliation, this passage takes on a redemptive aspect. As Fuller herself points out, she has come to the difficult realization that she owes her life to the brutal actions of soldiers like K. This contagion of responsibility is also reflected in Kanengoni's writing where to be alive whilst others die becomes a recurrent motif of guilt: 'He was afraid that all the people he had known and even loved in the war were falling one after the other by the wayside whilst strangely he carried on, as if his survival was nurtured by their spilt blood' (1997: 69). In both Kanengoni and Fuller's texts the survivors of this war have traces of blood on their hands.

However, when we look to the wider context, and in particular at Fuller's audience and writing style, the situation is further complicated. Alf Ross, amongst others, has pointed out that guilt only exists within a normative system where contra-attitudes are greeted with negative responses such as disapproval, criticism, dissociation or anger (1975: 6–7). Fuller's profession of guilt for acts carried out 'in her name' whilst she was a child does not sit easily with the judicial view of childhood as a period of non-responsibility. For her assertion to function as a reconciliatory gesture it may require that her audience share both her distaste for the Smith regime and a sense of colonial guilt that is passed from generation to generation. As such she seems to be writing for informed readers who empathize with Kanengoni's perspective and distance themselves from the overtly racist opinions expressed by some of the unrepentant former soldiers she meets. Whether this is representative of her actual audience is another question entirely.

Fuller is aware of the ideological pitfalls she negotiates and falls into and writes self-reflexively about this process. Her sense of personal power and sensitivity to the dominant discourses of privilege is underlined by her repeated references to her easy lifestyle in the US. She comments on the complacency of her new home, referring to the 'innocent, deluded self-congratulation that goes with living in such a fat, sweet country' (2005: 73). However, at the same time she distances herself from this experience as someone who doesn't belong to such an unquestioningly luxurious life. This process of distancing is achieved through self-conscious statements about the inappropriateness of her actions in the face of the poverty and suffering she sees on the road. One particularly striking example is seen in the passage describing her drive through Zimbabwe where she reflects: 'under these circumstances, air-conditioning (like exorcism of war memories and the act of writing about it) was an unpardonable self-indulgence' (2005: 144). There seems to be a clever discontinuity in Fuller's comparison here, as air-conditioning and the exorcism of war memories are clearly not comparable forms of 'self-indulgence'. Surprising comparisons add a note of flippancy and humour throughout Fuller's writing but is this really what she is trying to achieve here? I wonder whether instead she is inviting the reader to disagree with her – to indulge and forgive her. The reader might be expected to agree that air-conditioning is a luxury, but disagree with the suggestion that war memories are too. Does this pattern of half agreement and indulgent dis-agreement set up a dangerous precedent for Fuller's later emotionally charged assertions of guilt? Does the dutiful reader of *Scribbling* come to that passage where Fuller declares herself as 'every bit that woman's murderer' and agree with her that war is 'brutal and indefensible' but disagree that Fuller is responsible? Perhaps there is something in the qualifying 'every bit' that invites us to believe that this is not what Fuller actually means, but is instead a heat of the moment gesture. If her childhood self can be held to be complicit it is surely for being a 'little bit' rather than totally responsible.

It also appears plausible that Fuller's declaration of complicity forms part of her assertion of involvement in Zimbabwe's past and therefore a reaffirmation of her identity as an African writer. As such, Fuller seems to assert her 'authenticity' in the present by laying claim to events in the past. She writes 'I *own* this now. This is *my* war too' (2005: 152). Could this be not so much a declaration of responsibility but a declaration of identity? As many theorists have pointed out, identification involves 'the detour through the other that defines the self' (Fuss 1995: 9). Does it then follow that Fuller's 'identification' with both K and Kanengoni can ulti-mately be read as an assertion of identity? In an e-mail to me she explains:

> I got fed up of being told I couldn't be an 'authentic' African voice because I am white – what a load of rubbish. Authenticity is not to do with skin color, it's to do with honesty. My world had been politically incorrect and ugly in a lot of ways, but if I write about it honestly, then it's a real contribution to the narrative of our history and it affirms Kanengoni's work. Do you see? I mean, if I write honestly about the white side of the war, it affirms the honesty of his work which was about the black side of the war, it's as if we've written mirror images of the same story and together the works make the story more concrete and complete. (Fuller e-mail, April 2006)

Then with a characteristically complex gesture, after her statements about honesty and authenticity, Fuller also points out that 'there isn't one truth at all'. The idea that Fuller's and Kanengoni's work forms mirror images of the same story raises issues on two accounts. Firstly, those fighting to maintain the Rhodesian white elite and those fighting for majority rule in Zimbabwe had very different histories and motivations for their struggle. Even if both sides of the war were brutalized by their experiences and ordinary people did become victims of circumstance, perhaps it would be wise to remember this essential difference. Indeed Fuller does herself frequently talk about being on the 'wrong side' of the war. Secondly, there are fundamental differences in terms of time period and narratorial perspective between the two works. Kanengoni's third person narrator gives us direct insight into Munashe's experiences during and following the war. And in *Echoing Silences* there is an immediacy and an urgency of personal struggle that comes from a wound still fresh. *Scribbling the Cat* on the other hand is a first person account of a woman bearing witness to a soldier's testimonies, to events that took place whilst she was elsewhere. This has some ground in common with the testimonial observations of the women in Munashe's life, but Fuller's ongoing witness role means that we can never receive unmediated insights into K's thoughts in the same way that Kanengoni's delves into Munashe's mind.

Kanengoni's dense elliptical writing leaves the reader with many uncertainties and unanswered questions. By contrast Fuller, with her customary bluntness, admitted in *Scribbling the Cat* that she hoped to write K into coherence through their travels and conversations together. She also hoped that in this process she would find out more about herself: 'And then I would know what I was doing here and how I had arrived here and I'd know more about who *I* was' (2005: 148). But as her quarrel with K and her disillusionment with herself at the end of the novel show, any coherent identity remains ultimately beyond her reach. Instead, her conversations result in what Kanengoni terms an 'erosion of certainty' (1997: 59). As we see in both Fuller's and Kanengoni's novels and short stories, dialogue reveals a sense of instability. It is perhaps this instability and 'erosion of certainty' that ultimately form the most fertile footing from which to re-examine the reader's own sense of changing identity and responsibility.

Fuller ends *Scribbling the Cat* with a chapter entitled 'The Journey is Now'. Reflecting on Rhodesian/Zimbabwean war wounds she comments: 'Those of us who grow in war know no boundaries [...] we are without skins, without membranes, without the usual containments of civilisation' (2005: 250). This is a wonderfully seductive piece of universalism that plays into ideas of shared identity created through suffering. But ultimately of course, despite Fuller's dedication to Kanengoni, there remains a wide distance between the two writers. A distance that is born of difference in personal and collective histories, artistic perspective and even current geographical location.

Fuller's dedication to Kanengoni is a gesture that opens up the potential for dialogue. But this dedication has yet to become a conversation. Finally, and perhaps most poignantly in a world characterized by such radical inequalities between Europe, the US and Africa, Fuller and

Kanengoni are divided by economics. Kanengoni's novel is out of print and available only second hand. Fuller's on the other hand has been through several reprints and is heavily marketed and promoted both in the UK and the US. Although Fuller is actively promoting African writers through her own novels and her interviews, if the texts she cites are under funded and unavailable then perhaps there is a need to go further. The increasing unavailability of African literary masterpieces is also a disservice to Fuller herself. *Scribbling the Cat* can only be read in its full complexity alongside other Zimbabwean accounts of the liberation struggle. If the only literary representations widely promoted in the West are by white former Rhodesians then something is fundamentally askance in the international representation of Africa. Conversely, there is a need for academia to be more embracing of these texts that clearly form opinions in the West, alongside more exclusive 'intellectual' literature, if we are ever to be able to examine how literature interacts with the realities of Africa in the world today.

NOTE

I would like to thank Alexandra Fuller for her lively responses to my questions, Irene Staunton for endeavouring to put me in touch with Alexander Kanengoni and Ayako Aihara for patiently commenting on the ideas in this article over many months.

WORKS CITED

Fuller, Alexandra. *Don't Let's Go to the Dogs Tonight*. London: Picador, 2002.
____ *Scribbling the Cat*. London: Picador, 2005 (US edition 2004).
Fuss, Diana. *Identification Papers*. London: Routledge, 1995.
Kanengoni, Alexander. *Echoing Silences*. Harare: Baobab Books, 1997.
____ *Effortless Tears*. Harare: Baobab Books, 1993.
____ *Vicious Circle*. London: Macmillan Pacesetters, 1983.
____ *When the Rainbird Cries*. Harare, Longman Zimbabwe, 1988.
Primorac, Ranka. 'Kanengoni, Alexander'. In *The Literary Encyclopedia* (online database). Published 19 January 2005: http://www.litencyc.com/php/speople.php? rec=true& UID=5878
Ross, Alf. *On Guilt, Responsibility and Punishment*. London: Stevens & Sons Limited, 1975.
Sanders, Mark. *Complicities: the intellectual and apartheid*. Durham and London: Duke University Press, 2002.
Staunton, Irene. *Writing Still: New Stories from Zimbabwe*. Harare: Weaver Press, 2003.
Vera, Yvonne. *Without a Name*. Harare: Baobab Books, 1994.

| History, Memoir & a Soldier's Conscience |
| Philip Efiong's |
| *Nigeria & Biafra: My Story* |

Isidore Diala

The postmodern interrogation of the very ontology of history continues to extend the frontiers of fiction. With the accessibility of history predicated on memory and its representation on textuality, history invariably tends to replicate the processes of fiction, given that memory is selective and that the textualized event is narrated. Noting this interface between fiction and history, the South African novelist and scholar, Andre Brink (1998), remarks that the (auto)biography like history is seen to be based on what is consensually approved as real but contends that

> Even when a story tacitly narrates an event 'based on reality' it is infused with, and transformed by, the notoriously unreliable complex of private motivations, hidden agendas, prejudices, suspicions, biographical quirks, chips on the shoulder, and conditions that constitute the idiosyncratic, individual mind. (p.39)

Yet if the (auto)biography is marked by a colourful reinvention of the past, official historiography, created to perpetuate the status quo, demonstrably derives its hegemonic power by professionally simultaneously 'mythologizing' history while reinforcing the myth of history as a disinterested and objective record of events. Thus the memoir, an individual's record of their perception of momentous public events, subjective, biased, represents an invaluable interrogation of and complement to official chronicles, even while remaining a *literary* event.[1]

Arguing that in the memoir it is the communal narrative rather than the private that is pivotal, McLuckie (1997) cites Holman and Harman to remark that a primary distinction between a memoir, a form of autobiographical writing, and autobiography proper is that the former engages personalities and actions other than those of the writer while the latter focuses on the inner and private lives of its subjects. Acknowledging the inherent subjectivity of the memoir, McLuckie nonetheless ranks it above the work of the historical ideologue and considers it a necessary intervention to regulate and challenge the authorized version of history:

> Heralding event, community, and character over date and campaign, the memoirist comes across more forcefully than the historian because minutiae and anecdote are a metalanguage. (p. 34)

He cites Roy Pascal to reinforce this view:

> ... yet a peculiar truth arises from restriction and bias. Without aiming at a self-portrait the memoirist gives an account of both circumstances and himself, thus enriching as well as distorting the historical situation. ... partisanship, bias, may be not only an attractive feature of memoirs but also a greater help than too strenuous straining after objectivity since the truth of what is written may be better assessed if the predilections and prejudices of the author are patent. (qtd in McLuckie 1997: 33)

Reminiscences are of course compelling to the extent that the events they recall are momentous or at least significant or that the personality of the memoirist itself elicits interest; when a major personality reminisces on an important public event in which s/he was a significant participant, the memoir generates a two-fold interest. Remarking on the intrinsic propensity for wars and other epochal events to give rise to considerable self-narratives, Remi Oriaku (1997) cites Thomas-Cooley to note that the fifteen years of the American Civil War, between 1850 and 1865, and the immediate events preceding it, generated more autobiographical writings than the previous two hundred years of American literary history. Noting the faithfulness of the Nigerian civil war to this pattern, Oriaku is fascinated that the vanquished in that war, the Biafrans, rather than the victorious Nigerian side, atypically, have generated most of the narratives on the war. Of Oriaku's explanations for this unusual trend (the defeated rather than the victorious telling the story of the war) his speculation on an apparent compulsion among Biafrans to disavow responsibility for failures, and the continuing fractious nature of Nigerian politics in the post-civil war era are very probably the most convincing (p. 61). (Moreover, the victor hardly needs to *account* for his actions; his memoir when he finds this necessary is invariably implicated in colourful self-lionization). The obverse of the passionate repudiation of responsibility for the failure of Biafra, in itself a subtle reaffirmation of belief in the Biafran cause, is the compulsion for self-exoneration for the conflict in the first instance: this guilt consciousness – an understandable human response to loss, a tribute to the victor inspired by the deep human craving for survival and rehabilitation – has indeed been the more productive inspiration of significant memoirs on the war, it would seem, from the Eastern minorities following the example of the Chief Secretary to the Biafran Government, Ntieyong U. Akpan's (1971) *The Struggle for Secession, 1966–1970: A Personal Account of the Nigerian Civil War.* Philip Efiong's recent memoir, *Nigeria and Biafra: My Story* (2004), is in this regard a focal text.

A biographical note at the end of the book (no doubt necessitated by the author's concentration on the events immediately leading to the civil war and the civil war itself rather than attempting his full autobiography) indicates that Philip Efiong enlisted into the army, the West African Frontier Force, as a private in 1945. A Lieutenant Colonel in the Nigerian

Army when the first coup d'etat led by Major Chukwuma Nzeogwu took place on 15 January 1966, Efiong served first as Principal Staff Officer in Major General J.T.U. Aguiyi-Ironsi's regime, then as Acting Chief of Staff Supreme Headquarters before his appointment at Kaduna as Deputy Brigade Commander under Lieutenant Colonel Wellington Bassey. Obliged to return to the East after the countercoup in May 1966, Efiong was in Enugu, the capital of the Eastern Region, when war broke out in 1967. As a Biafran officer, he served as Chief of Logistics, then Chief of Staff, Commandant of the Militia, and Chief of General Staff. He was in other words in the Biafran hierarchy second only to General Odumegwu Ojukwu, the leader of Biafra; and just before the end of the War, when Ojukwu left Biafra, Efiong was fleetingly the leader of the Biafran nation, and voluntarily led the delegation that officially surrendered to the federal side. One, presumably, can hardly serve a cause more devotedly! Absolutely contrasted with the recent resurgence of Biafran nationalism as embodied in the organization, Movement for the Actualization of the Sovereign State of Biafra (MASSOB), *Nigeria and Biafra: My Story* is not a token from a Biafran veteran in the heroic war adventure model aimed at rekindling pro-Biafran sentiments. Its appraisal of Biafra is indeed sombre; its propagandistic value is absolutely pro-Nigeria.

If Efiong designates his memoir 'story', he is rigorously intent on its being perceived as 'history'. In his 'acknowledgments' he thanks his former military colleagues 'for their encouragement and interest in this historical work' and for seeing

> in the publication of this book an opportunity to take a detached look at our history as a nation and apply the lessons we learn thereof for the benefit and better understanding of the past by ourselves and posterity. (x)

His aim in the work is to 'raise a number of interesting issues of historical importance and relevance' (p. 3) and by remaining faithful to 'what actually happened' to 'disentangle some of the complex and controversial issues' pertaining to the crises: 'My commitment therefore is to TRUTH, which I think will best serve our national cause and interest' (p. 3). He recurrently contests earlier accounts of the events he narrates and much later in the work (when asked to draw up a self-incriminating document on his activities in Biafra) abjures lying even at the peril of persecution or death. Efiong is mindful of the extensive corpus of writing on the civil war and perceptive in his delineation of the motivation behind the writings:

> This story has been told and retold in a number of shapes and forms and for varying motives. Some have written to prove their innocence and helplessness in the roles they had played even if in the event they wielded considerable influence and power on issues of the time. Some have written to show how they won or lost the War, some have written to make quick money because they had a good story to tell, while some have written to justify the principles and cause in which they believed and for which some others lost their lives. (p. 1)

Aware that his memoir could be read from one or a combination of these perspectives, he identifies his aim as a rebirth of sensibilities and hopes that his

> narrative should be seen as the pinprick of an injection needle. A fleeting pain (in our conscience rather than our flesh) which, one hopes, will bring in its wake a lasting relief and even initiate a cure for our socio-political and other attendant problems. (p. 1)

The soldier's access to truth no doubt is a frontal attack on facts and a dispassionate reflection on them. Yet as the memoir was written more than three decades after the events, facts are invariably refracted through memory, and interpretations are notoriously implicated in imagination. The soldierly vocation, especially in times of war, is notoriously associated with diverse forms of intoxication. And one can speculate that impressions formed in a state of distraction even when miraculously remembered perfectly will still be undependable. When Efiong writes, 'It is difficult, writing from memory, to be very accurate about dates and events', he clearly indicates an awareness of the limitations of human memory even in ideal situations.

Moreover, *Nigeria and Biafra: My Story* is not always entirely Efiong's story. When, for example, he offers the biographical sketches of the leaders of the 15 January coup d'etat, beginning from their childhood and early school career, he is certainly digesting his reading or drawing on popular accounts. Likewise when Efiong narrates in some detail the killing of Major General Aguiyi-Ironsi, including in the account a crucial dialogue between Major Danjuma and Lieutenant Colonel Gowon (reported through Danjuma's memory) and a revision of Lindsay Barett's account of Lieutenant Colonel Hilary Njoku's escape (based as Efiong says on 'My own information on this escape bravado' (p. 128), he leans on accounts he can only hope are dependable; indeed Efiong attempts to validate the account of Njoku's escape by noting that he later saw the scars left from the bullet wound inflicted on Njoku on the occasion. Effiong's promise of truth cannot be absolutely predicated on irrefragable eye-witness accounts; it is also fulfilled partly through the mediation of accounts whose credibility the memoirist can only hope for. The memoir as a type of the autobiography does not employ the omniscient narrator in its *conventional* form in fiction but the need is ever present, even urgent, highlighting the limits of personal experience and the yearning to make a coherent and harmonious narrative of life's apparently episodic experiences. This is a vital function of fiction and a deep motivation of the memoirist. The necessity to explore sources of information, the speculations on human motivations, the projections of anxieties and apprehensions inwardly known to be the writer's onto others, the virtual desperation to *understand*: these are consistent with a deep craving to transform the confusion of history into some meaningful and comprehensible pattern.

Efiong's involvement in Biafra is of course the primary occasion for *Nigeria and Biafra: My Story* and the Nigerian patriotism that is the motivation of this account is consistently foregrounded; he is deeply anxious that his roles in the crises which inspired the book be put in proper perspective:

> It is my hope that this book will help the people of this country and, in particular, my people of the former South-Eastern State, to understand the dynamics that helped shape my role in the Nigerian crises of 1966–70. (148–9)

Born in Aba in the Igbo part of the country, Efiong, an Ibibio, grew up and lived in Ikot Ekpene though he actually hailed from Ibiono in Itu, all in the former Eastern Region. Locating the 15 January coup at the heart of the causes of the civil war, Efiong's delineation of the ethnic character of the revolution and the emergent first Nigerian military regime is rather intriguing. He initially thinks (much like the Nigerian populace that celebrated the coup and regarded the coup leaders as true patriots and heroes) that ethnicity was not central in its motivation, only to characterize it later as essentially Igbo. Efiong acknowledges that Ironsi had been marked out for elimination by the coup leaders and is insistent that their unwarranted underrating of Ironsi was a major reason why the coup came to grief. He highlights Ironsi's painstaking efforts, on his assumption of the role of Head of the Federal Military Government and Supreme Commander of the Armed Forces, to assuage the anguish of the North which had borne the greater brunt of the failed coup. If Ironsi's policies were misunderstood and generally interpreted as revealing his weakness, Efiong has no doubts of Ironsi's 'sincerity and honest intentions' and discerns in his appointments 'an unimpeachable expression of faith in the unity of the country and his personal belief in North/South harmonic coexistence'. Efiong's examples are telling:

> The rapid promotion of Northern officers, including the appointment of Lieutenant Colonel Yakubu Gowon as chief of Staff, Army, was seen by the South as a policy of appeasement of the North and the betrayal of Ironsi's guilt-complex. Ironsi, however, did everything to reassure and promote confidence in himself and his Administration by those very acts. For instance, one of his secretaries was Ahmadu Hamza, a close relation of Sir Ahmadu Bello. His personal orderly and bodyguard was a Northerner, and one of his Aides-de-Camp was a young Northern officer. Anyone who is familiar with such offices will know that such appointments are always based on the absolute confidence reposed by the senior officer in the person so appointed. (p. 62)

Efiong never associates the Ironsi regime with nepotism with regard to the Igbo people. It was indeed at Efiong's own suggestion that the East was added to Ironsi's planned national tour. However, by designating the July 1966 coup that ousted Ironsi the 'reprisal coup', Efiong implicates Ironsi in the first coup which Ironsi himself played a central role to foil and in which he had escaped death; moreover, by characterizing Ironsi's regime as 'Igbo regime' (as when Efiong talks about his 'circumstantial involve-ment in the Ironsi and, by extension, Igbo regime' (p. 146)), Efiong delivers a very clear verdict – though he hardly makes any effort to sub-stantiate it in his memoir. But perhaps his presentation of his relationship with Ironsi is even more puzzling.

Deeply impressed by his portrait of Ironsi as objective if not essentially positive, Efiong is insistent that his judgement is dispassionate:

> I have no reason to love Ironsi as a military man. He was, after all, the one who deliberately denied me the rare opportunity to further my progress in the Army and, perhaps in my life, when he cancelled my university course tenable at Manchester University in Britain in 1965. If I had gone on that course, which he cancelled as soon as he became General Officer Commanding (GOC) the Nigerian Army (under the pretext that I could not be spared to attend the course), I would not have been involved in the crisis and its outcome. Not with-standing that, I cannot be prejudiced in my assessment of his political relevance and public stance during his tenure as Head of State. (p. 63)

Quite apart from Efiong's regret for and recantation of the roles he played in the crisis leading to the war and in the war itself, and his expressed preference to pursue personal goals and advancement while the country drifted, the above passage mysteriously dwells only on Ironsi's ostensible reason for cancelling Efiong's university course without indicating the real ones. Efiong recalls that when he and Major Kur Mohammed were on courses in the United Kingdom and Ironsi was Military Attaché at the Nigerian High Commission, Ironsi visited Major Kur Mohammed regularly and never visited Efiong even once though Mohammed and Efiong both lived in the same town in Surrey. However, Efiong confesses later that but for the three weeks in which he acted as Chief of Staff, SHQ in Brigadier Ogundipe's absence, 'I never really worked closely with the late Major Ironsi and consequently we knew very little of each other' (p. 90).

On Ironsi's assumption of office as Head of State, Efiong was appointed the Principal Staff Officer at the Supreme Head Quarters of Ironsi's State House. In this position Efiong's initiatives, resourcefulness, ascetic cor-rective posture and managerial skills were amply highlighted. And he seemed to have enjoyed Ironsi's confidence:

> I personally handled, actually on the Supreme Commander's instruction, delicate issues affecting corporate establishments like the Ministry of Works and the Lagos Development Board (LEDB). I was hardly involved in political affairs, except when I got involved in matters affecting state security. (pp. 59–60)

Ironsi's later appointment of Efiong as Deputy Brigade Commander at Kaduna (with a view to taking over command from the incumbent Com-mander, Lieutenant Colonel Bassey), as Efiong acknowledges was in recognition of his abilities:

> ... there was a lot of talk about Lieutenant Colonel Bassey's weakness in dealing with the Governor (Lieutenant Colonel Hassan Katsina). He was

alleged to be 'kow-towing' and deferring far too much to the Governor who was a junior officer to him. For the sake of good discipline it was thought that I would be less politically inclined and more military in my dealings with the Governor. (p. 91)

However, Efiong has his reservations about the position and appraises it as 'sweet nothing' (p. 91). Similarly, on the frustration of his efforts to contact Colonel Gowon who emerged as Head of State after the counter coup, Efiong's renunciation of his appointments under Ironsi is complete:

My 'crime' ... appeared to be more or less founded on fear and suspicion because of my recent post under Ironsi ... I was not an Ironsi man as such, and saw my service under him as a normal call to military duty – a thankless one for that matter. (p. 144)

Much later though in Efiong's narrative of a plot led by a man from Akwa Ibom to eliminate him, Efiong makes an acknowledgement that after all confers his appointment in Ironsi's regime with a measure of value:

This particular Akwa Ibom friend at Surulere, an ex-service man whom I loved and trusted, made his living from a job which I personally got for him when I was principal Staff Officer at Ironsi's SHQ. He benefited from that job until his death in the 1980s. (p. 148)

Efiong is anxious to account for his efforts to draw Ironsi's attention to rumours of an imminent counter coup, remarking that he was only performing his duty; he is in other words eager to disavow any implication in the alleged effort to entrench Igbo hegemony. His sympathy for the North is strong just as his condemnation of the massacre of mainly Igbos in the North is complete, though he suggests that the Igbos may well have provoked it in part. With the sincerest of intentions he sought to meet Gowon to find a resolution to the crises about to engulf the nation but was given a cold shoulder. He had to obey the order for army officers to return to their regions of origin. Efiong had already written to Ojukwu the Governor of the Eastern Region, dissuading him from secession and on getting to Enugu reiterated the point at his meeting with Ojukwu. He could hardly hope therefore to be taken into confidence any longer by Ojukwu in his plans for the war. As Efiong himself notes the creation of Rivers and South East States from the Eastern Region was a political masterstroke meant to isolate the minorities from the Igbo. Efiong was therefore not obliged to fight for Biafra which he hardly believed in. But frustrated in his bid to meet Gowon, barely managing to escape with his life in Kaduna, hunted in Lagos (with someone who bore some resemblance to him murdered in mysterious circumstances probably in a case of mistaken identity), Efiong was naturally apprehensive about the reception he would get on the federal side. His very return to the East was an act of anguished resignation:

It was then clear to me that my position in Lagos was no longer tenable. Gowon had said we should go back to our regions of origin and for me that meant the

East. I could not make any contacts with my former colleagues in the Army without being treated with suspicion and being exposed to the risk of being killed. Everyday I stayed in Lagos from 1 to 12 August 1966 was both hectic and a bonus. I had to keep on the move, constantly changing my abode for safety and anonymity. (p. 148)

On the destruction of his house at Ikot Ikpene by federal troops during the civil war, his anguish (arising only partly from a deep sense of hurt) derived mainly from his recognition that for him defection from Biafra was hardly a viable option:

I gathered that my house at No. 55 Umuahia Road at Ikot Ekpene was deliber- ately destroyed by federal troops and my properties jointly looted by soldiers and civilians alike. I should also add that my brother's soap factory standing at No. 61 Umuahia Road, which was the first and only industrial factory in the whole of Ikot Ikpene at that time, was also deliberately destroyed. It was indeed a field day for all and sundry and culminated in a mock funeral service for me. My father, an old man of at least 72 years, was forced to witness the destruction of the house after he had been manhandled, tried and publicly humiliated and mocked at ...The name Efiong was anathematised and anybody who bore it ran the risk of being lynched and or killed ... Nothing could better dramatise the depth of hatred for a man whose only crime was to try and call a halt to further bloodshed by his comrades-in-arms than the happenings at Ikot Ikpene. It is difficult to believe that in the midst of this, I should have defected to the Nigerian side, be given a red carpet treatment and hailed as a hero as some people later suggested I should have done. (p. 230)

It would seem that by the alleged roles of Efiong in the Ironsi regime, he had hurt the North mortally and estranged himself forever. Efiong's feet were virtually led to Biafra. *Nigeria and Biafra: My Story* is a true Nigerian patriot's painstaking account of the circumstances that compelled him to serve Biafra:

What I do know is that I believed neither in secession nor in an armed conflict in resolving the Nigerian crisis. *That I fought in the War on the side of Biafra had nothing to do with my belief.* As the patient reader goes through this book, he or she will discover why I had to be and fight where I was, and how I came to occupy the unique position I found myself in the conflict. (p. 330, my emphasis)

Nigeria and Biafra: My Story recurrently reads like a peace offering by a terribly misunderstood man.

If Efiong is passionate in delineating the circumstances that led him to the Biafran side, he nonetheless served Biafra devotedly. However, right from the onset of the hostilities he was deeply apprehensive of the state of Biafran preparedness for the war and remained obsessed first by the prospects and later by the spectacle of human waste and suffering. Typically, unappreciative of the total self-giving embodied by the poet Christopher Okigbo, characteristic of the high-minded enthusiasm with which Biafrans rallied round to defend their young republic without due process and barely armed only to fall victims to a determined enemy, Obasanjo, the General Officer Commanding the 3 Marine Commando

Division of the federal forces, in his arrogantly entitled memoir on the war, *My Command* (1980), dismisses it as 'unnecessary bravado' (p. 18). The moving spectacle on the other hand inspired in Efiong a deep sense of duty. By his involvement with the Biafran Militia, whose purpose and significance he articulates with clarity, Efiong assumed responsibility for those young men:

> I felt that if these enthusiastic young civilians must go into battle, then it was our [trained soldiers] responsibility to see that at least they received rudimentary military training to ensure that they were mentally and physically equipped to defend themselves. As it turned out in due course, the balance between immediate and total collapse of Biafra with unpredictable consequences and operational staying power was to be supplied by the 'rank and file of the Militia'. (p. 192)

He was part of a diplomatic mission to seek peace, and established refugee camps for dislocated Biafran populace from the Eastern minorities; he sternly indicts the General Officer Commanding the Biafran Army, Major General Alexander Madiebo, for the uncompassionate documentation in his memoir of the destruction of the houses of Annags alleged to be saboteurs and indicates how that kind of attitude estranged many Eastern minority communities from the Biafran cause. For Efiong, Ojukwu's will to prolong the war could only indicate vaulting ambition and the deepest insensitivity to the suffering of the people whom he led. His portrait of Ojukwu is as the antagonist of the struggle that he led and is therefore one of outright condemnation. The problem is that it seems occasionally a little inconsistent and rather uncompassionate.

Efiong depicts Ojukwu as Iago's 'bookish theorist':

> Ojukwu, as an historian, no doubt had read military history at Oxford University and happened to have fallen in love with the Chinese method of assaulting the enemy position in waves of human hordes. So, his idea of a skirmish was unleashing waves after waves of screaming civilians armed with 'pick-helves' and cutlasses against armed Nigerian soldiers. He felt that nothing unnerved a trained and well-armed soldier more than such a horde of screaming civilians. The soldier, he was convinced, would just turn and fly away from the screaming hordes. Having formulated this strategy, there was of course no need for logistical consideration. (p. 170)

It is doubtful that Ojukwu confided this 'formulation' in any person other than his Chief of General Staff, Major General Philip Efiong. But the paragraph immediately following this in Efiong's memoir comments further on Ojukwu's preparation for the war and records that 'clandestine recruiting became intensive in the Igbo speaking areas of the East' (p. 170). Efiong's intention is certainly to indict Ojukwu further for his distrust and wilful exclusion of non-Igbo Biafrans from his plans. However, he also reveals that Ojukwu apparently was not only preparing screaming human hordes for the war. At the Nsukka sector where Efiong felt the 'formulation' was put into practice, he significantly becomes rather unsure if Ojukwu had traced his inspiration for the 'formulation' to

the Chinese, prompting the self-interrogation at the end of his rehash of
the strategy: 'No doubt he [Ojukwu] was quoting, perhaps, from his
Chinese experience?' (p. 191). 'Quoting' certainly implies a text, oral or
written, which Efiong was privy to but only remembered imperfectly on
this occasion, unlike previously. Several replicated passages in *Nigeria
and Biafra: My Story* make the memoir rather reminiscent of an oral epic
tale narrated over a period of at least several days in which focal episodes
recur. As the passages are consistent, they mutually revalidate each other
but the slight hesitation in the second 'Chinese formulation' passage is
telling. Memory – its fluctuations, adventures, repressions, inventions –
is of course a major component in every memoir; and its imperfections
often regulate the quality of our grasp of the past.

Efiong represents Ojukwu as a military dictator who would not
delegate power. If Ojukwu required the people's mandate to declare
Biafra as a sovereign state and several times more to continue the war
effort, Efiong contends that the leader deliberately misrepresented and
distorted the facts so as to deceive the public and elicit the response he
sought. Efiong seems a little unsure of how to appraise Ojukwu's wartime accolades on (deserving) soldiers; he complains that the awards
bestowed on him were 'completely unnecessary' and 'had nothing more
than nuisance value' (p. 334) only to complain also that Ojukwu privileged 'bravado' and 'flamboyance' (p. 336) in selecting officers to be
decorated for bravery. Efiong hardly fell into such a category yet he was
decorated several times; moreover, why would it matter to Efiong who
got awards that had only nuisance value? Efiong reflects at length on the
factors that led to Biafran defeat, highlighting the impact of the new
twelve-state structure which separated the Eastern minorities from the
core Igbo East Central State, Obafemi Awolowo's legitimation of starvation as a weapon of war and the devaluation of the Nigerian currency
which was still legal tender in Biafra, the position of Britain, the dire
lack of arms and ammunition, and so on. However, he presents Ojukwu's
insensitivity and personal ambition as the crucial reason for the prolon-
gation of the war:

> the Biafra soldier fought an impossible war under conditions that were totally
> inhuman and uncalled [sic]. It was the result of one man turning what was the
> people's will to fight a war of survival into a desperate and reckless attempt to
> achieve a personal ambition – even if it meant destroying the very people he
> purportedly was fighting to preserve. (p. 237)

At the early Biafran misfortune at Nsukka, Efiong rose beyond a fleeting
inclination for macabre humour to offer characteristic professional
counsel:

> I could have said to him [Ojukwu] with a glint of triumph in my eyes, 'I told you
> so,' but that I did not do. He was not in the mood to appreciate such a costly, if
> salient joke. So, instead, I told him to take heart. He said he had no officers and
> no armament and was thinking seriously of surrendering. I said he was not in a

position to surrender, as that could prove too reckless and costly to lives. The timing was wrong. (187)

Understandably, Efiong's preferred moment of negotiation was one of military credibility. As the war wore on, Ojukwu's stature apparently became more threatening and one could feel his looming image imprisoning Efiong in a view the latter hardly shared even at the peace talks in Ethiopia:

> Ojukwu was able to monitor the proceedings at Addis Ababa and issue directives to the mission leader. It was really difficult to use one's initiative even in such a situation where discretion could have been used to supplement valour. (p. 241)

Even while he was in a private discussion with the Emperor Haile Selassie, Efiong evokes for the reader Ojukwu's presence, threatening and implacable.

Yet Efiong acknowledges the veneration in which Biafra held him: 'My own position in Biafra was highly respected and I had no problem coping with ethnic proclivities' (p. 227). On the few occasions he chose to assert his authority, Efiong's opinion was not contested: despite Ojukwu's initial attempt to intervene, Efiong's expulsion of Victor Banjo and Alale, at the time Ojukwu's close friends, from meddling with the Militia stood; he successfully intervened when refugees from the Eastern minorities were reported being molested and even killed as they tried to cross into Aba. His recollection of the episode highlights its sensitivity:

> I put the blame for the killings squarely on the shoulders of the leaders of Aba community ... It was an unpleasant task to perform, but it was remarkably well received and thereafter the molestation of people from these areas stopped. (p. 226)

A mere note from Efiong added Madiebo to the delegation that left with Ojukwu for Ivory Coast at the close of the war. One wonders if perhaps self-effacement or acts of self-defence kept Efiong from influencing the course of the war more decisively. However, he recognized and appreciated the opportune moment when it came. For federal Nigeria, Ojukwu, not Efiong, was the ultimate culprit yet Efiong was second only to Ojukwu and his heroic rejection of flight was in defiance of at least the possibility of persecution (which he endured heroically when Obasanjo incarcerated him for 77 days for granting an interview on Biafra to *Drum Magazine*).

Madiebo (1980) in his earlier memoir on the war, *The Nigerian Revolution and the Biafran War*, clearly implies that Efiong's final role of surrendering to the federal forces was prearranged:

> General Efiong was left behind to play the last honourable, but sad and difficult task of undertaker for Biafra, which we had all fought very hard, but without success, to create and preserve as the last sanctuary for the then oppressed peoples of Eastern Nigeria. (p. 373)

Efiong refutes this completely and claims the initiative as his: 'I should like to make it quite clear that the decision to surrender and end the War was not a plan I made with Ojukwu before he fled "Biafra"' (p. 30). He emerged as a clear hero of the War by his courage in assuming responsibility for stopping the phenomenal human misery and suffering in consonance with convictions of the Biafran leadership and people:

> Far from throwing 'Biafra' at the mercy of the Federal Military Government as some commentators (such as Frederick Forsythe in his book *Emeka* (p. 166)) have written on my surrender moves, the truth is that I stuck my neck out to salvage what was left of 'Biafra' and thus fostered the survival and unity of the Nigerian nation. I had at least two other options open to me. I could have left the country like others did, compelled by the realities of the situation; I could have taken over control of the Biafran Organization of Freedom Fighters (BOFF) (of which I know the Federal Military Government was greatly apprehensive), taken to the bush and prolonged the conflict and the sufferings indefinitely. Instead, I opted for peace in order to stop the inhuman sufferings of our people. I was fully aware that this option could also spell my doom as a person. I freely exercised my option to end the War with the full backing and support of 'Biafran' leaders. (pp. 2–3)

Efiong conceives of the tidal forces of historical movements as initiated and controlled only partly by human agency and in part by inscrutable metaphysical forces. Meditating on Governor Hassan Katsina's involvement in the massacre of Easterners in Northern Nigeria, Efiong does not absolve him of responsibility but notes nonetheless, 'one would have to concede the fact that what was happening was in consonance with the North/East power tussle and Governor Hassan Katsina was playing a fateful role from which he had very little choice' (p. 116). Again appraising Danjuma's role in the counter coup and the assassination of Ironsi, Efiong concludes on the attempt of Danjuma's biographer to exonerate him: 'Indeed, Danjuma needed no surrogate apologist to wash him clean. He simply had no choice in the matter, considering the part he played' (p.135). Similarly, there is a paring down of human responsibility in Gowon's connivance in the assassination of Ironsi and his host, the Military Govenor of the Western Region, Lieutenant Colonel Francis Fajuyi; Gowon may well have betrayed Ironsi who appointed him Chief of Staff, Army, over officers senior to him but then Gowon 'too had no choice but to bow to the grinding wheel of fate as far as Ironsi and Fajuyi were concerned' (p. 136). Ojukwu is appraised as a tragic character trapped in a matrix of circumstances that he could hardly control:

> Ojukwu himself had an inflexible commitment to destiny and a particular course of action, which was aided and abetted by tragic circumstances at the turn of events ... Ojukwu was not a fatalist but had a strong belief in destiny as far as safeguarding the lives and property of Easterners in general was concerned. (p. 173)

This may well be consistent with Efiong's insight about an innate endemic Nigerian mentality not easily amenable to modification. He warns in the preface about the threat to national unity which this mentality poses, noting that in spite of apparent political changes 'we have not changed from being Nigerians' (p. 2). In the final chapter, 'Reflections', he writes at greater length about this freak, *the Nigerian*:

> I see the Nigerian as a materialist with yearnings for spiritual upliftment; a capitalist with socialist pretensions and a democrat with dictatorial traits of insufferable guile and intolerance. He is a welfarist with traits of sadomasochistic junketing who has raised philandering to an art form; he is a guru who dines with the devil; he is an intellectual with fear of flying beyond the horizon of mediocre intellectual aspirations; he is proud but has a sickening awareness of his inadequacies. In short he is a very normal person and he has a personality all his own, which makes him stand out anywhere in the world as a Nigerian, regardless of his ethnic background and even his clothing. (p. 338)

For Efiong the individuals that embody the creative force that can enhance the growth of the nation are significant exceptions to this rule.

Phrases such as 'profile of tragedy,' (p. 123), 'tragic dilemma' (p. 124), 'unrealistic tragedy' (p. 179), 'irony of fate' (p. 343) recur in Efiong's memoir. He begins *Nigeria and Biafra: My Story* with a virtual supernatural narrative foretelling the imminent crises about to engulf the country and an otherworldly figure promising him protection as he was a good man:

> He looked at my palms and started telling me about the crisis the country was going to go through and the enormous bloodshed that was going to follow. Of course, I was very sceptical and told him he was probably seeing the bloodshed in the West. Operation 'wet-ie' was already on I pointed out to him. He shook his head and went on to say he had seen me in the midst of the crisis that was more like a war rather than the political killings I was talking about. (p. 5)

The prologue virtually recreates the atmosphere of a Greek tragedy of preordained events in which humans, hardly sovereign, had limited roles to play. Efiong characterized himself as 'a victim of circumstance' who had 'borne to a very great extent the brunt of being made unjustly the scapegoat of the Nigerian Civil War' (p. 341). Intrigued, that despite his sincerest of intentions to forestall the civil war and then to lead Biafra back to a united Nigerian nation he remained undeservedly the symbolic victim of that war, did Efiong perhaps seek an explanation in the concept of fate? By turning the major *protagonists* on the political *arena* of the country between 1966 and 1970 into *characters* in a tragic drama, Efiong offers a plausible *interpretation* of that history; but this of course fundamentally involves a process of *fictionalization*. The human lesson of history derives from our assumption of responsibilities for our actions.

That the moment of initial encounter between the victor and the vanquished in a conflict should be perceived differently is perhaps to be expected, and this accentuates the role of projections in turning perceptions of people into *character creation*. Obasanjo's self-conception and his perception of defeated Biafran soldiers contrast very sharply with

Efiong's impression of the self and of Obasanjo at the end of the war. Obasanjo's self-image is as the magnanimous conqueror reassuring the defeated and *therefore* routed, embattled, lachrymose Biafran suppliants of their personal safety:

> Fear and near-panic could be clearly read on the faces of the civilians standing by. I went unhesitatingly upstairs where all the officers whose colleagues we had been in the Nigerian army stood gazing at me uncomfortably with fear and surprise ... To break the ice, I put out my hand to Efiong and we shook hands warmly... By now everybody in the room had relaxed as a result of my unexpectedly warm and cordial approach. I had addressed all the officers in there by their first names or their nicknames and shook hands with each of them very warmly. (*My Command*, pp.124–5)

On the other hand, Efiong's perception of the victorious General Officer Commanding 3 Marine Commando Division of the federal forces inscribes him as the archetypal conqueror: 'Obasanjo's problem *as I saw it at the time* was that he was too anxious to impress us with his power and authority' (p. 297, my emphasis). Efiong's refutation of Obasanjo's imputation of tearful impotence to him is one of the rare moments of explicit self-adulation in *Nigeria and Biafra: My Story*:

> In Obasanjo's *My Command*, the impressions he has given that I grovelled before him saying, almost fearfully, 'We are a defeated people, what do you want us to do' (p. 126), was nothing more than ego-boosting and patronising attitude which had nothing to do with my personal courage at the time. That, certainly, was not my style. At least, I expected him to do me the honour and justice of admitting that at no time throughout our meeting at Amichi, Owerri and Lagos, did I display anything but exemplary calmness and courage in a situation that could crush most people. (p. 297)

Obasanjo's consternation at the firmness – he would prefer obstinacy – of the Biafran delegation in Lagos in their insistence that the surrender document be properly worded arose from the conflict in his *expectations* from the vanquished and the reality: he seemed baffled that even in physical defeat, the Biafran spirit remained exultant. Efiong's journey to Radio Biafra at Obodo-Ukwu to make the capitulation broadcast had already set this in full relief. The passage is probably the most moving in the whole memoir and inscribes Efiong as the People's General, the self-sacrificial saviour; it equally makes an impassioned statement on the resilience and triumph of the human spirit:

> Our route was through Orlu to Obodo-Ukwu village where the broadcast was to be made. Our soldiers were crest-fallen and tired. They were bewildered and uncertain. They were going, they knew not where. They had one consolation. Their Chief of General Staff was still around. As our convoy moved along, many others with their vehicles tagged along, many were anxious to know what I was going to say. The fleeing refugees were a study in human tragedy. No one can fully describe the spectacle we saw. The people were ragged, footsore and haggard form [sic] hunger and starvation. Some women were with babies and some of these were hanging on and sucking the dry breasts of their mothers. It was a scene of pathetic suffering and agonising endurance. I was deeply

perturbed and considerations of my own safety, in the wake of advancing federal troops, did not even occur to me in the presence of such human suffering and tragedy. To me, every single one of these people was a hero. They were the real heroes of the War. (pp. 293–4)

Efiong's stature is foregrounded by a self-effacing technique of subsumed analogy. If the indictment on Ojukwu for his gross insensitivity and abdication in the above passage is only oblique, the allusion in the broadcast to 'those elements of the old government regime who have made negotiations and reconciliation impossible have voluntarily removed themselves from our midst' (pp. 294–5) – is certainly precise. Ojukwu is depicted as the villain of the war story, Efiong the true hero.

The earliest commentators on *Nigeria and Biafra: My Story* have variously drawn attention to the dependability of the work as evidence of the sterling leadership qualities of the author. In his foreword to the text, General Ibrahim Babaginda, former military ruler of Nigeria, appraises the book as a 'significant historical work' and discerns in it 'an enormous amount of hitherto unpublished facts and factual details in meticulous sequence, with analytical fervour not affected by the simplicity of his delivery' (p. xiii). The historian, Toyin Falola, in his introduction to the book identifies a complex interplay between the objective and the subjective, the realm of verifiable facts and that of an imaginative striving to grasp the substance of the historical experience through analysis:

> Where he describes what he saw and heard, there is very little to disagree with each. Where he offers interpretations of what he observed or experienced, some may disagree. The potential disagreement, normal with works of this nature, is not a challenge to the author's credibility, which is not at all in doubt, but only to attest to the nature of historical events and the multiple meanings they offer to contemporary recorders. (pp. xvi–xvii)

In his review of the book at its public presentation at Abuja, the capital city of Nigeria, on 31 March 2005, Pini Jason, points to the two primary potentially contestable sites in the work: the author's stand on Biafra and his representation of Ojukwu. Contending that Efiong neither denounces Biafra nor alleges that he was either misled or forced to rebel, Jason acknowledges that Efiong nonetheless had contrary opinions on how events on both sides of the conflict had been handled; Jason completely avoids Efiong's *characterization* of Ojukwu. Yet that is part of the primary burden of his memoir.

Nigeria and Biafra: My Story is Efiong's testament to his apparently ambivalent devotion to Biafra. Even in retrospect, insistent that the war for secession (rather than one of 'rebellion') was a people's heroic response to the virtual threat of extinction, his definition of the beleaguered East includes the Igbo, Ibibio, Ijaw, Atam, Annang, Efik, Kalabari, Ogoni, Okirika, and he is passionate in his belief that the struggle was not futile. Yet with a burning zeal for a united Nigeria, Efiong's crucial project is to highlight and *account* for the prevailing circumstances that led him to fight for Biafra which he was to lead back to the Nigerian fold. His province is mainly four of the darkest years of Nigerian history and his transcription of his perception of that history is authoritative. Yet his access to truth through memory, his *staging* of the conflict itself on a primarily tragic arena and his impressive characterization of the dramatis personae give the memoir the drama and density of imaginative literature.

NOTE

1   Derek Peterson has observed that the autobiography was the most widely practised literary genre in colonial Kenya, and remarked that Christian evangelism and nationalism encouraged this form of production. Noting the general inclination to read these works for historical or ethnographic evidence, Peterson (2006), focusing on the autobiographies of the Christian Charles Muhoro and Cecilia Muthoni, contends that they be seen primarily as literature, given their 'poaching from literature composed by other people, roping testimonies of conversion, English-language biographies, and record books into their life stories'. He shows how even testimonies and confession were literary forms with recognized conventions.

WORKS CITED

Akpan, Ntieyong U. *The Struggle for Secession, 1966-1970: A Personal Account Of the Nigerian Civil War.* London: Frank Cass, 1971.

Babangida, Ibrahim, B. Foreword to Philip Efiong, *Nigeria and Biafra: My Story.* Princeton, NJ: Sungai, 2004. xii–xv.

Brink, Andre. 'Stories of History: Reimagining the Past in Post-Apartheid Narrative'. In Sarah Nuttall and Carli Coetzee (eds). *Negotiating the Past: The Making of Memory in South Africa.* Cape Town: Oxford University Press, 1998 29–42.

Efiong, Philip. *Nigeria and Biafra: My Story.* Princeton, NJ: Sungai, 2004.

Falola, Toyin. Introduction to Philip Efiong. *Nigeria and Biafra: My Story.* Princeton, NJ: Sungai, 2004: xvi–xxiii.

Jason, Pini. 'Review of *Nigeria and Biafra: My Story* by Philip Efiong' at a Public Presentation at Sheraton Hotel Abuja, Nigeria, 31 March 2005.

Madiebo, Alexander. *The Nigerian Revolution and the Biafran War.* Enugu: Fourth Dimension Publishers, 1980.

McLuckie, Craig W. 'Literary Memoirs of the Nigerian Civil War'. In Chinyere Nwahunanya (ed.), *A Harvest from Tragedy: Critical Perspectives on the Nigerian Civil War Literature.* Owerri: Springfield Publishers, 1997. 31–58.

Obasanjo, Olusegun, *My Command: An Account of the Nigerian Civil War, 1967–1970.* London: Ibadan & Nairobi: Heinemann, 1980.

Oriaku, Remy. 'Political Memoirs of the Nigerian Civil War.' In Chinyere Nwahunanya (ed.), *A Harvest from Tragedy: Critical Perspectives on the Nigerian Civil War Literature.* Owerri: Springfield Publishers, 1997: 59–85.

Peterson, Derek. 'Casting Characters: Autobiography and Political Imagination in Central Kenya'. *Research in African Literatures* 37.3, 2006: 176–92.

Of the Versification of Pain: Nigerian Civil War Poetry

Ogaga Okuyade

The idea of an extraordinary Nigerian destiny underwent a collective shock with the eruption of the Nigerian civil war. The high hopes offered by the departure of the colonialist from Nigerian's political scape were completely eroded by the crisis of the immediate post-independence era. What was initially a tribal military discord within the elitist cadre of the Nigerian military degenerated into a destructive tangle of national tragedy. Thus, after an inchoate euphoric ecstasy of self-rule, disillusion set in, resulting from what Neil Lazarus (1986) describes as Africa's 'preliminary overestimation of emancipatory potential' (p. 50).

The Nigerian civil war is about the ugliest moment in the history of post-colonial Nigeria – a moment of hatreds and sufferings. Benjamin Stora (1999) describes the war scape as a place 'where gunpowder is in the air and where the combatants' weakness and heroism are revealed' (p. 80). This period recorded a bumper harvest of artistic and imaginative creativity – most of which painted an apocalyptic vision. Numerous voices spoke of the tragedy and cruelty of the war. Commissioned and non-commissioned officers of the military cabal, Nigerian nationalists, scholars, students and politicians of all sides produced a plethora of print, ranging from autobiographies and memoirs to pamphlets, plays, poetry collections and poems, scattered across the pages of journals and anthologies. Of all these genres, the autobiographical genre is the most striking because of the realistic and diary-like character of the narration. However, the other genres make a valid contribution to the documentation and reportage of the war, especially poetry, with its emotionally charged, artistic and faithful rendering of events.

Considering the barrage of literary works on the Nigerian civil war, Chidi Amuta (1988) suggests that, 'the Nigerian Civil War could well be said to be the single most imaginatively recreated historical experience in Africa so far' (p. 85). While Funso Aiyejina (1988) contends that, 'until the civil war, Nigeria had no major public historical rallying point' (p. 112). The imaginative accounts of the Nigerian civil war demonstrate how Nigerian writing has moved into a new relationship with history. This was the war that only began on one side as an intertribal feud which was parachuted into a systematic bureaucratization of genocide and that ended, on the other side, with the use of instruments of mass destruction capable of obliterating human life across the entire Nigerian nation.

As soon as independence was ushered in, the political leaders who inherited the colonial apparatus of governance lost focus as they took over the mantle of leadership. Independence is a return to *status quo ante*, not a political transfiguration but a mere metamorphosis of human varieties. The dual criteria for ascendancy are multi-partyism and conventional elections. Both criteria became the bane of the new nation. The political crisis of the era culminated in widespread violence, bloodshed and electoral fraud, which left the political climate cloudy. The election of 1965 created the path for the military's easy entrance into governance. The military coups of 1966 were a quantum leap in the face of crisis and they catalyzed the war.

Following the concatenation of political upheavals of the early 1960s, Nigerian literature became prophetic in temper and the writers created with a sagacious temperament. This tone of foreboding and the brooding sense of historic doom recurs across this first generation of Nigerian writers, ranging from the organ-amplitudes of Wole Soyinka's apocalyptic grandiloquence to the quieter, more personal and eccentric accents of Christopher Okigbo. These writers understand the finite dimensions of Nigeria, and have been aware of the dangers represented by the escalation of political and moral degeneracy. *A Dance of the Forests*, written by Wole Soyinka and published in 1960, was staged as part of the events for the celebration of independence and smacked of the impending strife. In his *Trial of Brother Jero* (1964), Jero the artful prophet declares:

> I saw this country plunged into
> Strife. I saw the mustering of men,
> gathered in the name of peace through
> strength ... and on the door leading
> into your office, I read the words,
> minister for war ... it is a position of power. (p. 40)

Chinua Achebe's *A Man of the People* (1966) ends with a note of pessimism and inconclusiveness. The coup may just be a metaphor for the crisis that will unfold in due course. The novel sounds the death knell of a doomed project, signifying the failure of the democratic process. Achebe enunciates very clearly the usurpation of this process by the political forces of centralization and corruption. Christopher Okigbo the most promising poet of the era, cautions the nation about the 'Path of Thunder'. Okigbo's poems reveal the tyrannical spirit that will overthrow the hope of the independence and destroy the dream of the newly weaned nation. In poem after poem in 'Path of Thunder', he delivers a severe indictment of a nation's history hijacked from its basic progressivist ideals towards chaos and tyranny: 'Thunder has spoken, left no signatures broken' (p. 63). He concludes the poem with the note of the immediacy of crisis, 'Thunder can break – Earth, bind me fast / obduracy, the disease of elephants'. In 'Hurrah for Thunder' the poet prophesies his own fall 'if I don't learn to shut my mouth I'll soon go to hell I Okigbo town crier, together with my iron bell' (p. 67).

Okigbo's 'Path of Thunder' occupies a seminal and inaugural position in the criticism of Nigerian war poetry. Okigbo maps the topography of the war while the succeeding generation of poets broadened the horizon. In Okigbo's 'Path of Thunder' something melancholic looms against the background of shadows and apocalypses, a prophecy of the end of an historic epoch.

One begins to wonder whether the agony of war can be aestheticized? Chidi Amuta (1988) is of the opinion that because war 'puts the greatest pressure on human nature, relationships and institutions, it becomes also a fertile ground for the literary imagination' (p. 86). Nigerian war poetry does record with emotional clarity this bleak moment of Nigeria's history in a way that no other genre of writing has achieved. Being an expression of thoughts and feelings as well as a representation of their vision of the war, their poetry invariably responds to the 'nowness' of the situation. Furthermore, it evinces the inexhaustible possibilities of Nigerian poetry. Though much of the poetry on the Nigerian civil war is lamentatory and most of them read like a jeremiad, the poets capture the conflict and are able, as Soyinka puts it, to appropriate 'the voice of the people and the full burden of their memory' (1999: 21). Alex Johnson (1980), remarks that, 'because the proximity of the experience, the deep passions engendered by events and the personal involvement of the individual do have a direct bearing on the artistic creation' (p. 149). The poetry of the era is not bereft of artistic commitment because of the history of the time. The poets exhibit an easily discernible artistic control in their presentation of the history of the era.

By the end of the war the poets not only painted pictures of the violent raw absurdity of death in time of war, but had made a radical shift in the kind of poetry they produced. The titles and themes of this new poetry emphasize a programmatic concentration on issues of national destiny. Nsukka, a town that houses the only University of the Eastern region became the garden in which the post-Okigbo poets flowered. Chukwuma Azuonye (1972) suggests in his introductory note to *Nsukka Harvest* (a chapbook in which Nsukka alumni and undergraduates expressed their grief and disgust at the blatant waste of life and property, that this outburst of imaginative creativity was informed by an 'utter disgust over the incipient brutalization of the country' (p. 1). This callous despoliation of the collective dream of the Nigerian people continues to haunt the psyche of these writers as, '… the sadness of a generation whose life ambitions had been cut short by a sad and senseless war' (p. 2). This crisis becomes 'the burden of memory' (Soyinka 1999) that continues to haunt the nation.

The Biafran writers told not of the wanton destruction of the war but of their hopes for a wounded society. As Chinua Achebe (1977) puts it: 'Biafran writers are committed to the revolutionary struggle of their people for justice and true independence' (p. 84). The social contract of the Nigerian civil war traps the poets between the facts of history and aestheticism, giving them little room to mediate or negotiate their craft between the two extremes. But how, in the words of Foulkes (1983) 'are literary texts perceived to pass meaning and under which conditions do we attach meanings to them?' (p. 20).

Chinua Achebe who occupies a canonical position in African fiction took advantage of the contracting power of poetry at the level of language and space to capture the mournful tone of the era, he churns out dirges which are symbolic of the time. In 'The First Shot' Achebe subtly captures the 'millipedic' commencement of the war:

> That lone rifle-shot anonymous
> In the dark striding chest-high
> Through a nervous suburb at the break
> Of our season of thunders will yet
> Steep its flight and lodge
> More firmly than the greater noises
> ahead in the forehead of memory (*Beware Soul Brother*)

The above excerpt evinces both the immediate evil of the war as well as its far-reaching and remote consequences.

Gabriel Okara (1978) describes the turmoil of an air raid during the war with lyrical delicateness:

> … a thick black smoke
> rises sadly into the sky as the jets
> fly away in gruesome glee …
> Again suddenly the air cracks
> above rooftops cracking striking
> rockets guffawing bofors stuttering LMGs
> ack ack placks diving jets (*Fisherman's Invocation* p. 37)

The poetry of Pol Ndu reiterates the disillusionment over the meanings of the conflict, the progressive collapse of a dream and the strength of the possibility of new dreams. Ezenwa-Ohaeto (1988) remarks that Pol Ndu, 'loads each word with poetic meaning and he manages to achieve a great intensity' (p. 253).

The themes of misery and pain preoccupy the poems in Ndu's *Songs for Seers* (1974), and in 'Evocation' the poet portrays the sinister aura that accompanies the threat of war:

> Fire flakes
> rain with
> fire balls

the shrieking
the sleeping
the naked
the ragged
The clothed
melting
in the frenzy (*Seers*, p. 20)

Nwachukwu-Agbada suggests that this unpunctuated poem is emblematic of 'the speediness of war arsenal' (p. 146). These lines capture the ambience of uncertainty and the spate of confusion that envelop the inhabitants of a town about to be lost to war.

In a metaphorically dense and a lyrically intense poem, 'Troy', Ndu reaches back to antiquity and the destruction of a town in Eastern Nigeria, perhaps Nsukka, parallels that of Troy:

Love,
butter-flies fluttering in the lull
of plunders carnage, blunder
rape and hope raised on quicksand (*Seers* p. 20)

Most pressingly, Ndu's poems articulate an uncompromising cynicism about the war and the potential for destructive evil in even the most seemingly innocent and private of men. He calls for the replacement of the human with another species:

When the row drowns
with its characteristic hiss in tuffs of ash,
brings steel brooms
and metal bags
for chukwu may star afresh.
This time
with plastic apes (*Seers* p. 16)

In 'Biafra Revisited', Ndu affirms that memory as Soyinka puts it, 'rejects amnesia' (p. 20), the past has drifted into the plains of history yet it is indelible in the mind. Ndu evokes an ambience of awe, where man is reduced to a bestial and sinister creature whose presence foreshadows chaos. Ndu admonishes individuals who fought alongside with him during the war to:

take the past events as the repentant woman's past
always forgotten and always retold. (*Seers* p. 32).

Ndu's imagery in the poem is that of the monstrosity of violence and the consequences of the chaos is the death toll, which is unimaginable. The poem brings to bear the image of Golgotha. The personae, perhaps stares at the ruins and wreckage of war.

Chinweizu's *Energy Crisis and Other Poems* (1977) also captures the traumatic experience that the war engenders. 'The Vanished City' like Ndu's 'Troy' describes not just the evacuation of people from the city but the animus that informs the destruction of the city. The poem also evokes the anarchic state of the city, 'she drummed to her gods; her gods came not. She drummed but they stood in a circle afar'. The last stanza evokes the sense of confusion, a city in disarray:

City of the dead!
Dead city of the dead!
...
Like a goat she died with her boast and fools.
skeletons of mansions rattle the breeze
under a coverlet of stars (*Energy Crisis* p. 51)

J. P. Clark's war poetry in *Casualties* relies on descriptive details with a searing emotional evocation. The first poem in *Casualties*, 'Songs' is nostalgic in its historical descriptions and the collection as a whole is an indictment of the entire nation. The poem not only portrays the futility of war but gives Nigeria a distinctly doomed position in history – Nigeria is not just a new sanctuary for dirgic rhythm but she joins the fraternity of war torn nations, 'we are characters now other than before' ('A Decade' p. 85).

Ken Saro-Wiwa's *Songs in a Time of War* captures the unpredictability of a war situation, most especially in 'Night Encounter'. Saro-Wiwa attempts to specify the theoretical basis of propaganda in relation to art. He concludes the poem 'Were You There?' with a note of grave sincerity, directed especially at those who contemplate war from a distance: 'you would not smile at the radio account of victories and smashed battalions' (*Songs* p. 22).

For those who began to publish a decade or so after the war, this elusive and profound relationship between history and artistic creativity becomes the key to a whole poetic world. Although some traumas take time to make themselves felt in imaginative work a little surprising to note how many budding Nigerian poets of the 1980s have been obsessed by the harrowing memory of the civil war, even when the writer was too young to have taken part in the war. Harry Garuba (1988) describes Odia Ofeimun's poetic scape as never moving far away from an 'intense awareness of decadence ...' (p. 271), as in 'Where Bullets Have Spoken':

And what prayers, pray, where bullets have spoken
a plague rolled by madmen to feed the eighty millions
what smile where dark craters have blighted
a sun that we had despaired of holding (*Poet Lied* p. 21).

Ofeimun's charming, rhapsodic and evocative lines which he realizes through incantatory poetics evoke the horrifying agony of war. 'Exodus 67' captures the totality of an anarchic situation: 'the Iroko is spitting fire if you have a child strap him to your bosom' (p. 23).

Catherine Acholonu seems to be a lone female poet among the teeming masculine voices on the war. *Nigeria in the Year 1999*, published in 1985, is suffused with metaphors of loss, rape, personal and collective angst. In 'Other Forms of Slaughter' Acholonu recalls the women who suffer the worst forms of physical, psychological and sexual abuse, during wars when they are hunted down as prey. The subject of her poetry is sombre and cruel, evoking images of abductions, rape and imprisonment:

> there were other forms
> Of slaughter
>
> When rods of aggression
> Rip through the sealed valves
> Of flutes of reed
>
> When innocent virgins
> Basking in the sun
> Suddenly wake up to
> Greedy eyes
> Lecherous tongues
> And devouring breath
>
> Tear open
> The thrills of their
> Delicate legend
> Unfolding a lustful era
> Of anarchic bestiality.
>
> Yeah
> These were other forms of slaughter (*Nigeria*, p. 33)

The poem ends in an exclamatory note, 'Yeah/these were other forms of slaughter' This is not a connotation of triumph, but the sudden release from the exhaustion of the other kinds of 'deaths' individuals suffer during war. 'Harvest of War', 'The Refugee' and 'Man alone' portray the pernicious scene of war.

Soldiers who were active participants in the war have also contributed their voices to the post-war publications. *Voices from the Trench,* edited by Mamman Vatsa (1978) and Domcat Bali's *War Cries* evoke the trail destruction left by war. Vatsa's 'If We Must Die' lashes out at the inglorious acts of those engineering the war, who push him, 'To shoot to kill/Those against whom/I have no ill' (p. 128).

> Out of rage and range of the guns
> To countries strange
> Leaving me to die
> Empty – like lie. (*Trench*, p. 129)

As the crisis deteriorates, people fall in great numbers – women and children and solders who lack knowledge of the cause of the war. The engineers of the rift, 'zoom out in planes...' (p. 128).

Soldier-poets do not only articulate the harrowing and excruciating experience of war, but also the evil and illogicality of the enterprise. Major Attu's 'Advance to Contact', enunciates clearly the vulnerability of man during wartime and the volatility of the situation which changes as often as the weather from a morning victory to the agony of an evening defeat:

We moved ahead …
Every day
We died and lived
Till the end. (*Trench*, p. 43)

During war, soldiers and civilians take turns with death. Olu Akinyode's
'Sacrificial Lambs' assesses the relationship between the gods and man,
the gods in this context being the leaders who have drawn the nations into
this dance. The poem describes soldiers as sacrificial offerings to the
bloodthirsty gods, 'When the gods are annoyed with us/we roast and turn
to appease their anger' (p. 25).

In Bali's poetry there is no complete victory in war. In 'Assault Across
the Niger' the bravado of the federal troops is portrayed yet they still faced
death as they 'greedily went into town to loot' (p. 32). Bali's poetry is
descriptive in style, a kind of reportage giving a chronological account of
events:

I was gripped with fear as the
H – hour drew near,
And I began to shiver and perspire,
'you must control yourself, I thought in despair,
As I issued orders that were unclear…

Rat – tat – tat – tat – boom – boom – boom,
Rent the air as our guns released the bombs
To herald H – hour and spell doom
To whoever dared to be in the path.
('Assault Across the Niger', in *War Cries*, p. 10)

The most fascinating thing about Bali's collection is its descriptive
fidelity. The lines carry the readers into the deserted streets, the unconscious of the soldiers and their fields of fire, bringing to bear the disparity
between a simulated outward bravado and the internal psychic wrangle
of the individual, creating a cinematographic account of the situation.

The Nigerian civil war has become the watershed of Nigeria's post-
colonial geopolitical history. Cruelty and human brutality exceeded worst
expectations. When reviewing Nigeria's post-colonial history, many will
no doubt come to understand the period of the Nigerian civil war as one of
the most amazing: inspiring, at times horrifying, always fascinating, a
period of extremes, in which destruction and vice reached unfathomable
depths. Nigerian war poetry serves as a ledger for the artistic documentation of the war, but the poetry also marks the beginning of a new epoch in
the history of Nigerian poetry. It moved from the provincial and private
status it had assumed before the war, to being a vehicle for mass orientation, thus expanding its scope, and bestowing on it an entirely whole-
some new temper.

The work still dealt with the traditional themes of the integrity of the
individual or the viability of the nation's collective destiny during and

after the war, but at the level of technique, there was a great deal of experimentation. This poetry does not only speak of hope for a wounded society, but the poems become authentic documents of a nation in crisis. Poetry from the 1970s marked a paradigm shift in Nigeria – these works exhibiting a monolithic thematic thrust but a discernibly distinct tone. The civil war story will continue to be of strategic importance for Nigeria. The poetry of the era allows us to understand and to perceive the devastating blow of the war and to quote Ezra Pound's definition of art; 'it is news that stays news' (cited in Alter, p. 55).

WORKS CITED

Achebe, Chinua. *A Man of the People.* London: Heinemann, 1966.
—— *Beware Soul-Brother: Poems.* Enugu: Nwamife, 1971.
—— *Morning Yet on Creation Day.* London: Heinemann, 1977.
Acholonu, Catherine. *Nigeria in the Year 1999.* Owerri: Totan, 1985.
Aiyejina, Funso. 'Recent Nigerian Poetry in English: An Alternative Tradition'. In Yemi Ogunbiyi (ed.) *Perspectives on Nigerian Literature,* Vol. I, Lagos: Guardian Books Ltd, 1988: 112–28.
Alter, Robert. 'History and the New American Novel'. *Dialogue.* Vol. 9, No. 1, 1976.
Amuta, Chidi. 'Literature of the Nigeria Civil War'. In Yemi Ogunbiyi (ed.) *Perspectives on Nigerian Literature* Vol. 1. Lagos: Guardian Books Ltd, 1988: 85–92.
Azuonye, Chukwuma (ed.) *Nsukka Harvest.* Nsukka: Odunken Publications, 1972.
Bali, Domcat. *War Cries.* Lagos: Civilities Ltd, 1984.
Chinweizu, *Energy Crisis and other Poems.* New York: Nok, 1977.
Clark, J. P. *Casualties.* London: Longman, 1970.
—— *A Decade of Tongues.* London: Longman, 1981.
Ezenwa–Ohaeto. 'Pol Ndu'. In Yemi Ogunbiyi (ed.) *Perspectives on Nigerian Literature.* Vol. 2, Lagos: Guardian Books Ltd, 1988: 250–5.
Foulkes, A. P. *Literature and Propaganda.* London: Methuen, 1983.
Garuba, Harry. 'Odia Ofeimun and Femi Fatoba' In Yemi Ogunbiyi (ed.) *Perspectives on Nigerian Literature.* Vol. 2, Lagos: Guardian Books Ltd, 1988: 269–76.
Johnson, Alex. C. 'Sunset at Dawn: A Biafran on the Nigerian Civil War'. *African Literature Today.* Eldred Durosimi Jones (ed.) ALT 2, 1980: 149–60.
Lazarus, Neil. 'Great Expectations and After: The Politics of Postcolonialism in Africa Fiction'. *Social Text* 13 (14), 1986: 49–63.
Ndu, Pol. *Songs for Seers.* New York: Nok, 1974.
Nwachukwu-Agbada, J. O. J. 'Songs from Thunder: Nigerian War Poetry'. In Chinyere Nwahunaya (ed.), *A Harvest from Tragedy: Critical Perspectives on Nigerian Civil War Literature.* Owerri: Springfield Publishers, 1997: 141–65.
Ofeimun, Odia. *The Poet Lied,* London: Longman, 1980.
Okara, Gabriel. *The Fisherman's Invocation.* Benin City: Ethiope; London: Heinemann 1978.
Okigbo, Christopher. *Labyrinths,* with *Paths of Thunder.* London: Heinemann, 1971.
Saro-Wiwa, Ken. *Songs in a Time of War.* Port Harcourt: Saros International Publishers, 1985.
Soyinka, Wole. *The Dance of the Forests.* Oxford: Oxford University Press, 1963.
—— *The Trials of Brother Jero.* Oxford: Oxford University Press, 1964.
—— *The Burden of Memory, the Muse of Forgiveness.* Oxford: Oxford University Press, 1999.
Stora, Benjamin. 'Women's Writing between Two Algerian Wars'. *Research in African Literatures.* Abiola Irele (ed.). Vol. 30 (3), 1999: 78–94.
Vatsa, Mamman. *Voices from the Trench.* Enugu: Fourth Dimension, 1978.

```
┌─────────────────────────────────────────────┐
│                                               │
│  Reviews                                      │
│                                               │
│                                               │
│                                               │
└─────────────────────────────────────────────┘
```

Edited by James Gibbs

Aniceti Kitereza, *Mr. Myombekere & his Wife Bugonoka, their Son Ntulanalwo & Daughter Buliwhali: The Story of an Ancient African Community*. Translated by Gabriel Ruhumbika

Dar es Salaam: Mkuki na Nyota Publishers, 2003, 718 pp., £29.95; ISBN 9976686382
Distributed by African Books Collective, www.africanbookscollective.com

In early 1945, Aniceti Kitereza finished writing a great novel, *Myombekere na Bugonoka na Ntulanalwo na Buliwhali*, in Kerewe, his mother tongue, spoken on Ukerewe Island which lies on the Tanzanian side of Lake Victoria. For about a quarter-century afterwards, he could not find a publisher. In 1968, Gerard Hartwig, a sympathetic American researcher, advised Kitereza to translate his novel into Swahili to increase the chances of finding a publisher. Despite misgivings about his ability to undertake the translation, despite his anxiety about the loss in translation of the richness of the Kerewe original, and despite the poor state of his health, Kitereza set to work. The following year, the Swahili version was ready, but it was only in 1981 that the Tanzania Publishing House accepted it. By then, Kitereza was 85. Sadly, he passed away just days before copies of his book arrived in Tanzania. We read all this and much more in Gabriel Ruhumbika's very useful introduction to his English translation of the novel that was published in 2003.

Over the years, efforts were made to translate this novel into other languages, specifically French and German, with mixed results. Ruhumbika's English translation is unique in several senses. It is based on the original Kerewe version and is supplemented by copious notes. Ruhumbika is himself Kerewe and is an experienced writer, translator and literary scholar.

So great was Kitereza's commitment to recording his people's culture for posterity that no challenge would discourage him. While the history of this novel testifies to Kitereza's perseverance and his unwavering determination, the novel itself is built on the story of the trials and tribulations of Mr Myombekere and his wife Bugonoka. For many years they are childless, regarded as a tragic condition in Africa. Despite his predicament, Myombekere defies his relatives' urging that he divorce his wife and marry another one. Eventually, Myombekere's wife bears a son, Ntulanalwo, and then a girl, Buliwhali. In the fullness of time, Ntulanalwo grows up and marries; Mr. Myombekere dies, and Buliwhali marries.

The suffering that Myombekere and his wife endured due to childlessness mirrors, to a certain extent, the story of Kitereza's own life: his wife, Anna, bore four children all of whom died in infancy. To the end of his life, Kitereza remained committed to her, not taking another wife as was customary in such circumstances.

Marriage and the family are central in Kerewe culture and marriage and the family are central in *Myombekere*. Kitereza dwells on this theme in various ways, the most notable being the long tale, 'How Men and Women Came to Live Together,' which he incorporates into his narrative. In the beginning, says the tale, men lived by themselves and women lived by themselves. The men tilled the land and grew food, never eating meat, while the women ate only meat. The women had many dogs that they used for hunting. It was a time of perfect happiness. However, the animals were destroying the men's crops, and so, one day, the men borrowed the dogs from the women intending to exterminate the destructive animals. Unfortunately, the men failed to follow the rules for handling the dogs and the dogs were lost, later becoming wolves. Facing certain starvation, the women went to the land of men. In the meeting that followed, the men apologized for their conduct and the subsequent talks resulted in the men and women deciding that they needed to live together. The theme of forgiveness and compromise shines through this narrative, even as the tale conveys the message that the coming together of men and women gave rise to many problems that haunt the human race. A moving account of human fallibility, the story captures the pathos of human existence, especially the condition of women. At the same time, it dramatizes gender issues so as to expose the weaknesses of both men and women, and is unusual in presenting men as responsible for the loss of paradise.

Kitereza sought to record for posterity the culture of the Kerewe. He learned from elders and, as a result, *Myombekere* is a treasure trove of traditional knowledge and of information about Kerewe life. It describes various customs, beliefs, and taboos, and includes descriptions of activities such as cooking and eating, brewing and serving beer, healing, conflict resolution, and the protocols of proper interaction between people. Such a broad agenda might have resulted in a boring treatise, however Kitereza weaves all these elements into an engaging, substantial fictional narrative.

Kitereza is a great storyteller. The tale of how men and women came to live together exemplifies perfectly his narrative and rhetorical techniques. Defamiliarization and signifying, as well as humour, are among his favourite techniques. After telling us that the men and the women eventually found themselves in pairs, Kitereza avoids mentioning sex by saying 'you all know what happens when grass comes too near fire' (p. 256). Even though he wrote down his story, he tends to operate like an oral storyteller, freely incorporating features of performance such as repetition, digression and onomatopoeia. In his introduction, Ruhumbika notes that some of these features were among the most difficult to translate into English.

Because of the linguistic differences between Kerewe and English, Ruhumbika also confronted the challenge of mediating the tension between the literal and idiomatic form of translation. His approach manages quite well to retain the essential flavour of the original language. I can sense this since Kerewe is a Bantu language like my own Matengo. I have read Kitereza's

Swahili version of *Myombekere* which tends to deviate from Standard Swahili, exhibiting many features of mother tongue interference. These considerations aside, Kitereza's novel, now available in several languages, presents a golden opportunity not only for literary study but also translation studies.

Myombekere is a major landmark in African writing, memorable not only for its narrative technique and handling of theme but also for its quintessential humanity. A keen observer of human nature and behaviour, Kitereza revels in pointing out the foibles of humans without compromising his respect for his people and, by extension, all people. If Ruhumbika's translation had been published in the 1940s, when the original Kerewe text was completed, the world would have recognized Kitereza as a great pioneer and as a classic exemplar of the tradition which later produced such literary giants as Chinua Achebe and Mazisi Kunene.

Joseph L. Mbele
English Department, St Olaf College, Northfield, Minnesota

Ahmadou Kourouma, *Waiting for the Wild Beasts to Vote*, Translated from the French by Frank Wynne
London: William Heinemann, 2003, 440 pp., £12.95; Hb; ISBN 0434088141
Initially published in French in 1998; US translation in 2001

Corrupt politicians would seem to be the bane of Ahmadou Kourouma's life, but equally a plentiful supply of such creatures is indispensable to fire up his imagination. *Waiting for the Wild Beasts to Vote* (2003) is a story of contemporary African politics, a *tour de force* of political satire about an Africa betrayed by its political leadership. It is essentially an anatomy of power, power at its most cynical and clinical, driven by the contradictory forces of Western colonialism and Eastern European Communism. Kourouma writes about poverty and corruption in Africa in the way of a Wole Soyinka or Chinua Achebe, through complex allegories rich in anger, playfulness, whimsy and irony. This novel is one of the most acute and powerful indictments of African politics in the postcolonial moment to appear in recent years. Recent European conduct is not let off the hook, especially in its French, shamelessly neo-colonial manifestations, but at the heart of Kourouma's novel is an incisive assessment of Africa as, daily, it looks at itself in the mirror, as it were. Sadly, moreover, while a retrospective history of Africa, Kourouma's novel could easily be reinterpreted for the present day by replacing the dozens of dictators of the past on whom he bases 'Koyaga' with the Mugabes of recent years, the misery he depicts has been in rich supply in Liberia, the Sudan, Sierra Leone and Somalia.

Waiting for the Wild Beasts to Vote is the story of 'President Koyaga, General, Dictator' (p. 67), leader of a mythical country, whose achievements the narrative sets out to celebrate in detail, through the *donsomana*. 'In the Malinké tongue' the *donsomana* 'is an epic told by a *sora* with his *koroduwa* – an apprentice in the purificatory stage, the cathartic stage' (p. 2). In traditional Malinké culture, the '*donsomana* is a eulogy, a literary form whose aim is to celebrate the actions of heroic hunters and heroes of every kind' (p. 29). As his life as one of the more brutal and long-living African dictators begins to unravel, Koyaga calls for the performance of the *donsomana*, which he hopes will reinvigorate his hold on political power. The presence of 'the responder' tempers the unctuous subservience of the *sora* and the subversive irreverence of Tiécoura produces some of the most gruesomely funny lines in the text.

Structurally, the novel begins and ends with the *donsomana*. Insofar as 'the narrative structure of the *donsomana* [...] demands that we recount the hero's life from the moment the seed was implanted in the mother's womb' (p. 16), we learn of Koyaga's life story through a minute detailing of each of his main acquaintances. Koyaga allows Kourouma to depict a generic African dictator composed by drawing on the individual traits of a posse of African despots, including Mobutu Sese Seko ('he whose totem is the leopard'), Houphouët-Boigny ('he whose totem is the caiman'), and Emperor Bokassa ('he whose totem is the hyena'), for the continent, we are told, and then regularly reminded, is a land 'as rich in tyrants as it is in pachyderms' (p. 315). 'Africa', Kourouma's narrator asserts, 'is by far the continent richest in poverty and dictators' (p. 440). Written in a deceptively simple style that conveys the mesmerising structures of oral story-telling, *Waiting for the Wild Beasts to Vote* leads readers into an increasingly cacophonous world that is intrinsic to the heavily structured narrative of the *donsomana*. It combines Kourouma's weird and wicked sense of humour with the wonderful world of his imagination.

By sticking throughout the work to the rather limiting structure of the *donsomana* Kourouma sets himself a challenging task, for there is a risk that because of its repetitious nature the reader might begin to grow restless. Kourouma knows this, and in the manner of the Malinké *griot* who tells the story, Bingo, the tale is interspersed with proverbs, placed at the opening and closing of each narrative section. These, and the 'musical interludes' that we are told accompany oral story telling in this mode, invite the listener (reader) to rest a while, and allow the teller to imbibe deeply from the strength of language, for '[p]roverbs are the thoroughbreds of language; when words fail, it is through proverbs that we find them again' (p. 41). Traditional narrative devices are invoked here precisely as a lens through which the corrupt present can be analysed, understood, exorcised. Indeed, it is a measure of the writer's skill that there is never a dull moment in this voluminous novel; having been told at the outset how the narrative is to proceed, the reader is seduced by the incantatory pull of story-telling, by Koyaga's gargantuan appetite for power and by the cruelties and horrors he perpetrates to hold on to it.

Echoing Walter Benjamin's famous words, *Waiting for the Wild Beasts to Vote* becomes as much a work of fiction as a document of post-colonial history. Here, Kourouma offers one of the most provocative histories of Africa since 'independence' and of its struggle to find its feet. In that sense the character of Maclédio, 'Minister of Orientation' (p. 2), might be seen to represent Africa's quest for purpose and direction in its post-independence stage. Now Koyaga's right-hand man, Maclédio has lived his life in search of a 'true idol', each time believing himself in the presence of 'the person he had been seeking' (p. 180); the novel implies that Africa owes much of its misery to the constantly shifting alliances with outside forces, at times voluntarily entered into, mostly through force majeur. The spectres of the Cold War and of Frantz Fanon's influential reading of African power politics haunt the narrative, providing it with much of its political and imaginative impetus.

It may be tempting to describe *Waiting for the Wild Beasts to Vote* as a hopelessly cynical portrait of contemporary Africa. At one level it lacks the subtlety of Achebe's vision, sharing with Soyinka a strident view of Africa's tragedies. Yet, in the novel's carnivalesque ending, Ahmadou Kourouma, who died in Paris during December 2003, conveys an irrepressible belief in the ability of African people to rebel against the tyrants who have robbed them of the dream that decolonization allowed them to glimpse. Works such as *Waiting for the Wild Beasts to Vote* do much to examine and expose the horrific excesses of post-independence Africa, and bear witness to a reality that for too long has been overlooked.

Tony Simoes da Silva
Transcultural Studies, University of Wollongong

Daniel Mengara, *Mema*
London: Heinemann (African Writers Series), 2003, 122 pp., £5.50;
ISBN 9780435909239

Daniel Mengara's short novel, *Mema* (2003) tells the story of a strong and charismatic woman, the narrator's mother – 'Mema' in the intimate language he adopts to talk about her. *Mema* is essentially a story about the power of love and memory, of a mother's burning love for her children and of her son's recollections of his mother. Through their story Mengara reflects on how certain traditions become unquestioned and poorly understood social constraints once they lose their meaning. He also examines the impact of colonialism on a small, isolated community. The world captured here is a blend of rich and colourful village life, of intricate and at times brutal cultural practices, and of the encounter with the Fulassi (white people). This is a novel of the contact zone.

Written in clear and uncomplicated language, the novel's complexity is the result of its thematic focus rather than of narrative dexterity. For Mengara elects to structure the novel round one key narrative conceit that posits memory as a way to piece together Mema's difficult and fragmented relationship with her community and her family. In *Mema*, Mengara weaves together the personal and the political in ways that are mutually enriching. Echoing a common concern in African writing with cultural flux and social disintegration, *Mema* is at its best when it tells the story of a fiercely independent woman intent on challenging the old social forces by which her community still lives in a world now in the midst of profound and revolutionary changes.

Through repeated and often confusing moments of flashback – more or less (un)conscious acts of remembering – the narrator constructs the portrait of his mother with the love of a son and the objectivity of the biographer, shifting between loving and unsettling facets of her character. In this uncommonly frank account of a son's memory of his difficult and unpredictable mother, the narrator ponders also the limited options available to women in many societies, in a way that allows the novel to stand at once as an indisputably African work of literature and as a provocative commentary on gender relations. In a direct allusion to Chinua Achebe, moreover, Mengara uses the narrator's vow to his mother that he will not forget that 'the white man had prevailed because they made our people forget their own wisdoms' (pp. 121–2) to comment on what remains an impossible conundrum for African writers: how to use the foreign to make sense of the local.

This is a simple yet intense work of imagination, told with considerable energy and insight, supported by a cast of strong characters and a credible plot. On occasion it is also much too reliant on a tried and tested formula, for after Achebe, Ngugi wa Thiong'o and Bessie Head it is hard to write about foreign cultural hegemony, identity and self without appearing derivative and clichéd. As the story of an unusually strong-minded woman, and of her struggle to ensure a better future for her son, *Mema* is a great read; as a novel concerned with doubling up as a political document it comes across as somewhat contrived and lightweight.

Tony Simoes da Silva
Transcultural Studies, University of Wollongong

Shimmer Chinodya, *Chairman of Fools*
Harare: Weaver Press, 2005,182 pp., \$14.95 / £11.95; ISBN 1 77922 041 3

Irene Staunton (ed.), *Writing Now: More Stories from Zimbabwe*
Harare: Weaver Press, 2005, 306 pp., \$31.95 / £19.95; ISBN 1 77922 043 X
Both titles distributed by African Books Collective, www.africanbookscollective.com

Shimmer Chinodya's *Chairman of Fools* narrates the experiences of a Zimbabwean writer, Farai Chari who has returned temporarily to his family in Harare after working at a university in the United States. Chinodya acknowledges that he writes in the 'tradition' of the maverick Zimbabwean writer Dambudzo Marechera who died in 1987. Marechera became a cult figure after his death because of his refusal to conform and sing the praises of the new nationalist society. For Chinodya, though, what matters about Marechera is his innovation and courage as a writer, what he referred to in a *Guardian* interview as 'his sense of the moment and sense of words' and that 'he tells you what he thinks, unedited'. Like Marechera, Chinodya represents an urban society under pressure through the thoughts and actions of a disaffected male intellectual who is taken to the edge of madness.

Farai is not a conventional hero. The novel begins with a monologue from his wife, Veronica, condemning what she refers to as his 'phoney artsy life' (p.1) and warning him that she is changing and will not take any more of his abuse. Veronica's church-going, which has empowered her, inhibits Farai's beer drinking and womanizing lifestyle. Farai 'is a man waiting to be found; a confused being waiting to be rediscovered until restored to himself' (p. 6). Chinodya's self-reflexive conceit of the famous writer who is known by everyone in Harare is sustained throughout the novel. Both the policeman who stops Farai for drunken driving and the nurse on the psychiatric ward where he is a patient have read one of his novels for 'O' level. Farai claims a film is being made about his life and the plot he imagines for the film follows the career of the writer Shimmer Chinodya. However, this fame also elicits scorn and ridicule. The policeman asks, 'Do you have to get drunk to write your books, Mr Chari?' and the nurse is re-reading her 'O' level set text to discover whether Farai is ill because he thinks too much. This disparagement may reflect the 'ordinary' Zimbabwean's ambivalence towards the independently minded Zimbabwean writer from Marechera onwards.

Chinodya reveals a darker underside to the humour and playful banter of the novel. Farai is haunted by the ghost of his schizophrenic brother and the evangelist preacher on the radio seems to be addressing him personally. His erratic behaviour leads to his hospitalization and the diagnosis of bipolar disorder. The psychiatric ward appears to be a metonym for the country and the mood swings and depression from which Farai suffers are metaphors for the condition of many Zimbabweans. Yet, the novel also shows the resilience of Farai and the society around him. He is, as his wife says at the end of the novel, a survivor and, despite his individualism, he has drawn strength from the community of 'fools' who elected him their chairman and from reconciliation with family and friends.

Weaver Press's collection of short stories by Zimbabweans, *Writing Now* (2005) follows on from its previous anthology, *Writing Still* (2003). *Writing Still* had considerable success. The writer-musician Brian Chikwava won the Caine Prize in 2004 for his story 'Seventh Street Alchemy' and Charles Mungoshi's 'The Sins of the Fathers' was highly commended. Irene Staunton, in her introduction to *Writing Still* states that the book deals with 'the complex and challenging issues that have arisen [in Zimbabwe] in the last twenty years'. *Writing Now* has no introduction but the stories in the later anthology also deal with these issues. Chikwava and Mungoshi have again submitted stories, as has Chinodya, and the book has a similar mix of established and relatively unknown writers. None of the stories quite matches 'Seventh Street Alchemy' in its experimentation or 'The Sins of the Fathers' in its exposition of the pain wrought by quasi-nationalism. Nevertheless, there is much good writing here and even some of the less stylistically accomplished stories have ideas and emotions worth conveying.

John Eppel's 'Orthello' describes the attempt of a schoolteacher, Dillard, 'to adapt some of the lines in *Othello* to accommodate the casting of a white boy as Othello and a black girl as Desdemona. Dillard's rewriting of Shakespeare shows how language can be manipulated to fit political (and politically correct) agendas. The story also has a wider context, revealing a corrupt society in which there is a rapidly increasing gap between the Bulawayo *nouveau riche* and the poor. In one paragraph, Eppel encapsulates the economic crisis in Zimbabwe: payments to war veterans, military engagement in the DRC, land reform and the creation of 'a black market economy where black, white, and brown marketeers became shockingly rich in a shockingly short period of time, while the rest of the country grew abject' (p. 98). Christopher Mlalazi shows the effect of this economic decline on one poor family in the realist story 'Pay Day Hell'. The protagonist, Doubt, who is always in debt because of rampant inflation, cannot meet the material expectations of his family. His wife, Siphiwe, prostitutes herself for food and scavenges pieces of cloth to make ugly clothes and quilts for sale. The unremitting horror of their lives leads to Doubt's violence and his fear that his son will despise him in the same way he despised his own weak and poverty-stricken father.

In Rory Kilalea's unusual story 'Unfinished Business', the narrator is a writer who takes on an assignment to write about the forgotten people of Zimbabwe – the old – and discovers that 'Old people are not necessary nowadays. Zimbabwe ruins' (p. 152). The story takes the form of an investigative report as the writer interviews old people of different races and backgrounds who are now nearly destitute. His foreign agent tells him his article isn't 'edgy enough' (p. 166) but, ironically, 'edgy' is exactly what the story is as Kilalea uses wit and cynicism to piece together fragments of individual lives and social comment.

Another group of forgotten people in Zimbabwe are featured in Chiedza Musengezi 's 'Space'. Musengezi, who has interviewed women in prison for another Weaver Press anthology, portrays the experiences of Naomi and her pregnant friend, Monica who, after giving birth, is deserted by her child's father. The story successfully balances description of the women's subjection to the orders of a callous warden with an understanding that the system itself is at fault. Stanley Mupfudza's 'Forever Haunted by Rita's Eyes' tells the story of two childhood misfits, a sickly, bookish boy who befriends Rita, the despised daughter of a shebeen queen, and then betrays her when he participates in her gang rape. The story of the childhood betrayal and his later meeting with Rita and her child is told with a fine attention to detail and nuance.

As these stories suggest, the representation of Zimbabwe in *Writing Now* is, on the whole, bleaker than in *Chairman of Fools*. *Writing Now* raises interesting questions about readership. Given the high cost of books in Zimbabwe, is it more likely to reach an international audience and the Zimbabwean diaspora than in-country readers? Zimbabwe has produced an enviable body of literary work. With over three million Zimbabweans living outside the country at the time of writing, it will be interesting to see how Zimbabwean literature will develop. *Writing Now* and *Chairman of Fools,* in representing Zimbabwean cultural identities which can be recognized across geographical borders, are contributing to a national literature in the widest sense.

Pauline Dodgson-Katiyo
School of Social Sciences & Humanities,
Newman University College, Birmingham

Chris Abani, *Graceland*
New York: Farrar, Straus and Giroux, 2004, 322 pp., £8.99; ISBN HB 0-374-16589-0

Chris Abani made a precocious start to his literary career by publishing *Masters of the Board* when he was sixteen. His achievements were quickly recognized: a poet and playwright, he received the 2001 PEN USA Freedom to Write Award, the 2001 Prince Claus Award, and the 2003 Lannan Literary Fellowship. In 2004, the publication of *Graceland* propelled him into the literary stratosphere, and established him as, without doubt, one of the most exciting writers to emerge from Nigeria in the new millennium. The novel earned him the 2005 Hemingway/PEN award, and it will win new admirers.

In it we encounter a young Nigerian school-leaver, Elvis Oke, who is trying to survive as an Elvis Presley impersonator. He is pathetic: his dance routine is terrible and his get-up comical. In a telling scene early in the novel, he encounters a woman when stepping out of a *molue*. She looks at his running make-up and his wig, and asks brusquely, tellingly: 'Who do dis to you?' And that is the question we ask as we read about Elvis hurtling towards destruction and as we meet the motley crew of exotic characters who traipse through the pages of the book. They lead him towards pain and loss and, ultimately, towards the redemption hinted at in the title of the book that is, significantly, also the name of the Presley mansion.

The strange cast who add to the book's otherworldly ambience includes Oke's father, an alcoholic who has been traumatized by the death of his wife, Comfort, his father's live-in lover, Oye, an all-knowing grandmother with a Scottish accent, the ever-resourceful Redemption, the mysterious Colonel, the King of Beggars, Jagua Rogogo with his boa, and the always-transforming Okon. In the middle of them is Elvis, sensitive, confused and doomed to lose all the women who mean anything to him. These include his cousin Efua, who flees home to escape sexual abuse, his aunt, Felicia, who goes to America to be with her husband, and his mother and grandmother who die in their sleep.

Graceland is an extraordinary and admirable novel. It explores incest and homosexuality, redemption and loss, naked power and its wanton abuse, human and organ trafficking, lost innocence and sexual awakening. In the course of chronicling Elvis's journey we encounter a country, a city and a people teetering on the edge of a precipice. The book also offers an explicit homosexual sex scene, and provides insight into the perennial struggle between fathers and their sons. The focus, however, is the bittersweet story of Elvis Oke whose young life has been beaten horribly out of shape by the persistent blows of fate. ('Who do dis to you?') In a sense it is a journey in search of the self, but on a larger scale it is a quest for redemption and for unattainable grace. The resourceful Redemption captures the situation Abani has brought before us in bewailing the fact that 'Only prophets fit help us now, we be like de Israelites in the desert. No hope, no chance, no Moses...'

Toni Kan
Poet and Novelist

Uzodinma Iweala, *Beasts of No Nation*
London: John Murray, 2005, 177 pp., £9.99; ISBN 0 7195 6843 9

In *Beasts of No Nation*, the narrator asks: 'If army is made of soldier, and we are not army then how can we be real soldier.' It is one of many questions posed in this powerful first novel by Uzodinma Iweala, a Harvard graduate who was inspired by an encounter with a young woman who was once embroiled in a conflict. Somewhat predictably, given the wars that have ravaged Africa in recent times, the woman's involvement was as a child soldier.

The first attacker encountered in the novel is described in distinctly non-human terms. 'I am seeing yellow eye belonging to one short dark body with one big belly and leg thin like spider's own.' The reader wonders: is this a man, woman, insect or beast? Then, 'KWAPA! He is hitting me,' and we are plunged into the intensely sensorial narrative of Agu, a child soldier. The setting is an unnamed West African country; and Agu could have been caught up in any of the bloody civil wars that have been waged in the sub-region.

The would-be assailant is Strika, a traumatized boy who has been mute since he saw his parents killed. This was followed by conscription into a wretched army, utter degradation at the hands of others, and his own brutal behaviour towards those in the towns and villages along the way. Like the central character Agu, Strika is half-starved and drug-crazed. High on 'gun juice', they start 'liking to kill'. Agu and Strika are sexually abused by the villain of the piece, the leader of the pack. Known simply as Commandant, he represents those who exploit children in times of conflict. The problem is that Commandant and other characters are somewhat two-dimensional, lacking the complexity that would make it possible to understand the factors that fuel such conflicts.

In spite of their first encounter, Strika and Agu form a strong bond and support each other. And as Commandant – 'the man who is driving the enemy to madness'– sinks into paranoia, he grows increasingly dependent on the two boys. 'I am his one eye. Strika is the other,' Agu says of the man under whose tutelage their only value is in their capacity for mindless savagery. The boys hope for a peaceful future. 'One day there will be no more war and we can be living together in a house and eating all the food we are wanting to eat.' They do not ask for much but what little it is seems unattainable. This is a narrative in which hope dies, literally, in the shape of a symbolically named child soldier – one of many who expire in the course of the novel.

In the unrelenting bleakness of Agu's existence, it is quite possible to envy the dead: the only ones who have escaped and realized the wish to fight no more. People die in a variety of ways in *Beasts of No Nation*. Some commit suicide, some are killed, some are 'helped' to die. As to what hand God has in the proceedings, Agu is certain that, 'God is forgetting everybody in this country.'

Agu is part of a rebel army in the southern part of the country, contending with government forces in the North. This is all we know about the conflict, beyond the fact that leaders like Commandant operate according to maps by which they plot which portions of the country they would like to have for themselves. Their ambitions are in turn roughly schemed into the fighting which seems never ending, so that children like Agu, once sucked into the conflict, see no end in sight. 'I am seeing that the only way to stop fighting is to die. I am not wanting to die.' Even with the rise of the 'mapless' Rambo, Agu remains convinced that 'gun is more important than me'.

In the war, 'Time is passing. Time is not passing' – so Agu marks time by remembering days of innocence in his village before the war. In one of the most powerful chapters, Iweala paints a picture of peaceful times, with the slow build up of menace as war creeps up on the villagers' lives. The boy's mother and sister are evacuated by the UN while he stays behind with the men. Agu witnesses the death of his father, after bullets make the latter perform a dance of death, the Commandant takes the boy under his wing.

Killing, as Commandant tells Agu, 'is like falling in love'. Agu kills soon enough. 'I am growing hard between my legs,' he observes. In the sexualized militarism of the novel, Agu is not only aroused by acts of violence, penises are 'soldiers' standing at attention, and the abusive Commandant gives the boy special favours because, as the child says: 'I am saluting his soldier for him.'

There is a graphic *manga* quality to the novel. The horror is piled on so thick and fast that it is almost deadening. But there are constant jolts, thanks to the demonstrative effect of the language, delivering aural punches that are startling in their immediacy. Machete slashing into flesh comes with a 'KPWUDA KPWUDA' sound; the incursion of war and its arsenal into Agu's village would occasion a dreaded 'GBWEM GBWEM' sound; and laughter would naturally be a maniacal 'kehi kehi kehi' cackle.

The book's title evokes the inscription given wide currency in a record by Afrobeat music legend Fela Anikulapo-Kuti, who lampooned countries comprising the United Nations as 'beasts'. It is ironic how powerless that 'world body' often is at preventing conflicts in which all manner of terrible things happen. In his use of language and images, Iweala makes it possible to see how, given the right – or wrong – circumstances, human beings can commit the gravest acts of inhumanity. The language reflects this and the novel is replete with examples of people being described as 'this thing', 'dog', 'goat', and 'sheep'. One child soldier remembers his blown apart mother as 'meats' hanging from a tree. Even the perpetrators of atrocities cannot but acknowledge their own debased humanity. 'Now we just be looking like animal.' As the killings escalate, Agu can no longer tell a man from a goat.

Praised for its innovative use of language, *Beasts of No Nation* however shows the potential pitfalls when an American-educated author – in this case the 23-year-old Iweala – attempts to render the Pidgin English of a barely educated West African boy traumatized by war. The language of the novel has impressed many Western reviewers, but one could argue that they are not well placed to determine the success or otherwise of the use of non-standard English. One such critic noted the 'staccato-like pidgin English, mangled and bent by African inflection'. However, if the language is mangled by anything, it is the author's handling of 'African inflection', or the lack of it, that is responsible. It is tempting to think that Iweala wrote as he did as part of an experiment. A stronger proposition may be that the debut novelist has engaged in an effort to be 'true' to Agu's voice. But the language functions somewhat arbitrarily in the reading, so that short spurts of 'good' English area glaringly inconsistent with Agu's 'voice'. This is Pidgin written by someone who does not show an intimate familiarity with the form.

Language reservations notwithstanding, one recognizes that this is urgent work, and the mode of expression serves to sharpen the sharp edge of Agu's tale. The worst of what is imagined is painted very graphically for the reader. However, the incessant flow of blood produces little by way of surprise. The comic defiance of a Madam and the more decisive action of one of her girls – are among the few unexpected moments in the book. This is conflict pared down, so much so that the possibility of a wider understanding eludes the reader. Other narratives of conflict involving armies of children will be needed for a fuller appreciation of the variations and nuances not allowed by Agu's perspective.

Beasts of No Nation offers a convincing portrait of the psychology of a child soldier. In the natural order of life in his village, Agu would have become a man. Instead, he is caught in a twilight existence where, neither a man nor a real soldier, he represents a grotesque perversion of childhood. Turned into a merciless killing machine, he develops the instincts of an animal, the keenest of which is the instinct for survival. Terrifyingly, it is ultimately through this survival instinct that he reaffirms his humanity.

Molara Wood
Writer and Critic

Woeli A. Dekutsey & John Sackey (eds), *An Anthology of Contemporary Ghanaian Poems*
Accra: Woeli Publishing Services, 2004, 144 pp., pbk. £ 14.95; ISBN 9964978863
Marketed outside Ghana by African Books Collective,
www.africanbookscollective.com

Demanding reviewers often expect a poetry anthology to be a longed for treasure chest holding jewels capable of opening one's senses to the lyrical wonders neglected in our absent-minded daily encounters with literature. Ama Ata Aidoo performs this function with a startling image embedded in 'In Memoriam: The Ghana Drama Studio', where she writes of the building as a

> white gazelle
> which slept under the city nims,
> away from the tropical morning glare,
> but
> poised,
> always,
> for a cue
> to spring into swift precise action.

The expectation is true of this anthology from Ghana, a country where, as the editors point out in their Preface, 'poets have been singing lustily' for decades, 'but in the wilderness'. The fervent *performance* of poetry in Ghana has rarely gone hand in hand with similarly enthusiastic *publication*.

This is badly-needed anthology, then. And other Ghanaian literary genres (drama, for instance) would certainly benefit from the kind of initiative Dekutsey and Sackey have taken. They have assembled a good number of verses by well-known authors, so that we get solemn intonation from Kofi Awoonor, bittersweet irony from Ama Ata Aidoo, raw indictments by Abena Busia, and, from the pen of Kobena Eyi Acquah, ethical thrusts. These last include the following lines from his 'In the Navel of the Soul':

> In the navel of the soul
> the midwives of the spirit say
> they can hear a heart-throb
> The experts, of course,
> disagree

I was particularly struck by Dannabang Kuwabong's sombre lament, 'The Exile's Return', part of which reads:

> I the anonymous exile
> Stole down the coast
> Bordering my nativity grove
> To wake up to no dreams
> But to contentment of being
> concealing disillusion.
> No special rites awaited my homecoming.

Kwabena Osei-Boahene provides compelling lines on immigrant life in Europe in 'The Running Man' including the following which move well until let down by the tired image in the last line:

> I am forever on the run with not a soul
> in sight I am the running man
> The mouse flees from the cat
> The chick from the merciless hawk
> and I from mortal man
> I am forever on the run from
> the long arm of the law

The restrictions of the anthology format inevitably meant the strict selection of poets and of poems from each author. In some cases the result will leave both reviewers and readers unsatisfied. For example, I was puzzled by the absence of some of the pillars of Ghanaian verse: one looks in vain for the aural somersaults of Atukwei Okai and the elegiac moods of Kofi Anyidoho.

This volume was assembled following a nationwide invitation, issued through various newspapers, to poets to submit work for publication. Such an initiative cannot but further enrich the final product, even though it is hard to overlook some drawbacks with the approach. These include the fact that the poems are simply listed in alphabetical order. Though there are notes at the back, there is no biographical information about the authors or bibliographical notes on the works.

Many of the lines by the 'new' poets selected by the panel of judges betray a penchant for heart-on-sleeve expression of feelings and rhetorical tones. These sometimes dominate over the ineffable ambiguity that constitutes the marrow of poetry as a genre. The posturing is evident in the several religious poems that may resonate with the evangelical congregations found in contemporary Ghana. The worrying lack of spiritual tension informs G. Dake's 'Evangelism' that provides the following:

> But, Oh! who would carry the message
> to the deaf ears of the sinking travellers?
> who would be an eye to the blind ...
> Send me, send me, Lord
> Here I come.

Somewhat similar posturing is encountered in the following hollow lines from a love poem, 'To His Fair Lady' by Peter D. Aniagye:

> If I were a wealthy king,
> I would build you a beautiful castle,
> Where you would live forever as my queen.

Suspect notes can also be found in poems bewailing the corrupting influences of Western ways and the loss of traditional roots.

On the other hand, there are distinctive, promising, new, controlled voices in this volume, and these include Doris Adabasu Kuwornu and Damasus Tuurosong. The later succeeds with his sorrowful depiction of Africa as 'The Mourning Continent' in which we read:

> The white fly's belch of satisfaction
> The sad victory song of the black victor,
> Ring out loud in my ears.
> The flapping wings of owl
> Disturb the silent, solemn song
> Of the mourning continent

Annotations on each poem are included in an appendix and are yet another praiseworthy aspect of the volume. However, on occasions the commentary suffers, like some of the new poets, from oversimplifying poetical nuances. This is certainly true when faced with baffling images such as those used by Kojo Laing in 'Africa Sky':

> Once in the storm,
>   Africa is handled in a dance by lost girls,
> who meet to make my thoughts wander
> into places where roots are suddenly
>   fewer than the threads that bind them.

As the publisher's Preface states, such detailed analyses of the poems as are provided are to be viewed in the context of the use of the book in schools. One could add, they will also recommend this publication to school and college librarians.

Pietro Deandrea
Facoltà di Lingue e Letterature Straniere, University of Torino, Italy

---

Tayo Olafioye, *A Stroke of Hope*
Lagos: Malthouse Press, 2000, xxxviii + 82 pp. $8.95 / £4.95 pbk
ISBN 9780231242.
Tayo Olafioye, *Arrowheads to My Heart*
Lagos: Malthouse Press, 1999, 83 pp. $8.95 / £4.95 pbk; ISBN 9780230521
Tayo Olafioye, *Ubangiji: The Conscience of Eternity*
Lagos: Malthouse Press, 2000, 101 pp. $8.95 / £4.95 pbk; ISBN 9780231226

All volumes in Malthouse African Poetry series, distributed by the African Books Collective, www.africanbookscollective.com

Let's start with the wholly good.

One ought not dismiss the sensual pleasures of books: thus I note how appealing I find the shape and size of these volumes from Malthouse; almost like pamphlets, though weightier; tall and narrow, inviting you to slide them in your back pocket; suggesting, even, in their feel, folded maps (the critic in me begins to wonder what sort of terrain does Olafioye chart?). I have always been a sucker for maps, poring over them, isolating cities, tracing out routes between cities, towns and hamlets, imagining what lies between.

Imagine too, someone pinching a book of poetry. Just imagine. These three books, long and narrow and just thin enough to be able to slip comfortably into back pants pocket, almost beg to be nicked by some pickpocket, be it on the streets of New York, a Lagos market or the Paris Metro. If only all the world's vices were so deliciously edifying.

Yet the question before us is whether the poetry lives up to the promise of the books' form. In part the answer might be found in the fact that as I delight in the shape and feel of the books we must acknowledge the unfortunate deficiencies of form in some books published on the continent: the thin, almost transparent paper, the occasionally splotchy ink, and the folded, mis-trimmed or mis-bound pages.

As for the poetry itself, there is an earnestness to many of the poems which is ... what? Disconcerting? Cloying? Well, just a bit too earnest. In this cynical age it is perhaps far too easy to dismiss and take potshots at such earnestness. But in this or any age earnestness cannot and should not be used as cover for sloppy or banal or just plain bad versifying. Perhaps that's a bit too strong, but when you encounter poems such as 'O.J. — the hound dog' and 'Celine Dion' (both collected in *Ubangiji: The Conscience of Eternity*), where the earnestness is the very thing about the poem that makes you cringe, it is difficult to be forgiving: 'She wonders what / heavenly voice seems, / if Celine Dion sings / the ethereal tunes of angels. / The world legend of peace and harmony.' ('Celine Dion' p. 73); 'Nicole, not only earthly / Babiari, white too - / if their honey-pots / cement his psycho-shells / The ghost of Marcus / in the shadow. This hound of blemish.' ('O.J. — the hound dog' p. 40).

These are minor poetic travesties.

Now it is not for the chosen topic that the poems suffer, but the treatment. Consider the brief poem 'Euro Disney' collected in *Arrowheads to my Heart*. The ideological position staked out in this 8-line poem is a familiar one:

> An American colonization of your folly
> An idiotic universal celebration
> Of pleasant stupidities.
> Perhaps a needed anti-dote
> To a world gone bunker
> Disneyland: the American magic land
> An eternal happiness for a second
> After all: life itself is Empty. (p. 69)

We are well used to the notion of American culture as neocolonialism, and the commonplace that closes the poem – of fleeting 'eternal happiness' and the emptiness of life – are, well, commonplace. But there is both a nuance and a properly poetic quality to the 'pleasant stupidities' and 'needed anti-dote / To a world gone bunker' that gives a depth to the poem that too many others are lacking.

In many ways, Olafioye's is an attempt at crafting a 'popular' poetry – perhaps of the Osundare style, though using a very different frame of reference and register. This by no means is meant to minimize the creative effort behind the works in question. However, too often it seems as if the desire to connect with the concerns of the day in verse leads to a disconnect from poetic underpinnings and the reader is left wondering 'Why?' It is a question that is asked of many poets and much of the poetry published today.

Olafioye is perhaps most appropriately self-reflective, if unintentionally so, in the note he appends to the poem titled, 'The *Matterhorn* of Kindness' (*Ubangiji*, p. 72): in it he writes that the Matterhorn is 'A gorgeous mountain in Switzerland, and also a replica in Disneyland, California.' It is such an unintentionally appropriate diagnosis of the trickiness of Olafioye's work that one wonders why someone in the editorial process could not have picked up on the hint and sent the works back for some more editing, or perhaps reselection. Olafioye is very much trying to straddle a series of paired worlds: Nigeria and America, literature and popular culture, poet and scholar, poet and memoirist, success and failure.

Poetry is such a personal art and form that one hesitates to judge too harshly; although, I might add, such intimacy does not seem to dissuade those given over to effusively praising poets. The best poetry is that which rings true to the reader, in which she hears echoes of her own cries and joys, and sees bits of her own world reflected back; warped a bit, perhaps, fragmented, but recognizable nonetheless. Too unlike, too fragmented, and the image is unpleasant, and the picture nonsensical or cartoonish. Yet too similar, too unmediated by a poetic voice, style, sensibility, or form and we feel ourselves (and the poet) to be superficial and vapid. Poetry cannot bring us the Matterhorn, only a sense of its majesty or a poor replica.

Too often Olafioye falls back on the banal, on cliché. And the self-congratulatory wisdom paraded before us in his verse makes the earnest clichés grate that much more; clichés don't need emphasis, and when given point the reader feels doubly abused. In the poem, 'Sexual Harassment in the Land', we come across the following:

> The male specie, the Criminal,
> And the guillotine:
> His moral disinfectant
> Gender oppressor as charged.
> Soul-brother-original,
> Beware
> However innocent you may be.
> Not all men on the haunt
> Even when affable. (*Arrowheads to my Heart p. 78*)

It's an easy sentiment in an easy (that is, almost non-existent) poetic line. There is nothing really challenging, thematically or formally, in these lines. There is a visceral, almost audible appeal to 'Soul-brother-original, / Beware' – and the nod to Achebe is pleasantly understated – but the jokey defensiveness and seething rhetoric of the piece ('But what plaintiffs puke / Is self righteousness / .... Very laughable') tell us more of Olafioye's anger than lend any insight or poetic pleasure.

Too often I am asking myself, *where is the poetry in this?* The verse here is really driving me to ask what makes a poem; perhaps a worthy and important question, but it does not bode well for my appraisal of these particular collections. In *Ubangiji: The Conscience of Eternity*, there are a number of poems betraying a fondness for list making – 'The brain', 'Sometimes' and 'The Catechism of Nature' for instance – lists which I guess Olafioye assumes can provide form. But apart from the far too easy final lines of 'Sometimes' – 'Sometimes I do not know / Who I am' (p. 46) – there is no coherence to these poems outside of that implicit in this rather vapid linear ordering. I have struggled with the grammatical clunkiness of 'The Catechism of Nature' (p. 50), trying to find some meaning or purpose to it: 'Someone's humane to someone's beastliness' opens the poem and it's a pattern that continues for six five-line stanzas. We are led to the first quality (the good quality) by contraction, and its counterpoint (the bad quality) through the possessive. I stumble over the reading of it; the first reading of that first line causing me to pull up short – something sounds funny – and then read through the rest of the poem breaking the contractions though still it lumbers along: 'Someone is humane to someone's beastliness...' Yet *Ubangiji* has one of Olafioye's strongest poems, 'Song of the Sage (For Basic Nigerians)'. Its stripped down stylistics and tight, almost curt lines give it a pointedness lacking elsewhere: 'don't trust a buddy-buddy / their mattan smiles' (p. 99).

The collection, *A Stroke of Hope*, is organized, at least in the beginning, around his hospitalization and recovery from a series of life-threatening illnesses. The 'Gratitude' section, in the thanks offered and the fears expressed, brings to the reader the sense that herein lies a poetic last will and testament. It also forces one to ask the rather creepy question: I wonder if he survived his illness - am I reading the last words he wrote? It's a delicate question for the critic to pose himself. So I scramble to the computer to see if Olafioye survived. He did.

Unlike the other two collections, this one includes substantial prefatory material which, after a while, tends towards the tiresome. One wonders about the purpose of including these pieces – a rehashing of the course of his illness in prose, praise for the doctors, praise for Olafioye's poetry – they shed little light on the poetry itself. Are these the first faltering steps towards autobiography, memoir, 'life writing'? Though they avoid the worst excesses of self-pitying rooted in such self-reflection in dangerous times, one wishes that the verse would just begin.

And once it does? As with the other two collections there are striking lines but few poems that stand out as a whole. 'I will be history / after a season' (p. 15) gives poignancy to a poem of rather commonplace reflections on mortality. And there is a rhythm, a real music to the lines of 'They start again':

> They start again, politicians
> Who gorge to fill
> Their bowels to expand,
> Despite the dry bleedings
> Of ordinary Nigerians. (p. 41)

In fact, the poem totters on the brink of song. It is, unfortunately, song that is too much absent from the rest of the collection.

For those who are at all familiar with 'mainstream' contemporary African verse, there's not much new here, nothing to really excite the passions. Which is unfortunate. And there's no telling. These collections might very well ignite

the interest of folks who are new to African poetry. If the pickpocket who
pinches them finds something that speaks to him, then he is right to pay no
attention to this.

Mark L. Lilleleht
Global Studies,
University of Wisconsin-Madison

Lola Shoneyin, *So All the Time I Was Sitting on an Egg*
Ibadan: Ovalonian House, 2001, 72 pp., £7.95; ISBN 978-027-026-4
Lola Shoneyin, *Song of a River Bird*
Ibadan: Ovalonian House, 2002, 72 pp., np; ISBN 978-36581-0-7

> Before you Mama Opoto
> naked I want to stand
> This price for my innocence?
> Astronomical! (*Riverbird*, p. 62)

Rewritings of Christopher Okigbo have been tried before and will be again, but
rarely has the parody been exercised with such mischievous delight. Lola
Shoneyin transforms 'Heaven's Gate' into 'Heathen's Gate' and goes on to
establish a link between this gate and 'Asas Gate', glossed as 'a brothel in
Ibadan that was prominent in the 80s'. Is this parody of a Nigerian classic bold
or outrageous, impious or honest, affectionate or self-serving? Shoneyin, who
is a performer, editor and arts administrator as well as a poet, clearly enjoys
setting herself against the staid and stuffy. Not even the sainted Christopher
Okigbo of blessed memory is immune from attack. This is what she does to
him – and lives with *Labyrinths*. It is, we are told, one of her 'constant travel
companions'.

Another reference to the Nigerian literary heritage may be present in the
very title of the collection from which the lines are taken. *Song of a River Bird*
recalls J. P. Clark's 'Streamside exchange' that begins 'River bird, river bird'. In
these intertextual ways Shoneyin, a graduate in English from Ogun State
University, announces her arrival *vis-à-vis* an earlier generation of (mostly
male) Nigerian poets. The daughters, daughters-in-law or grand-daughters of
the Sixties generation are here having their say in a distinctive, confident
voice. They are borrowing from their 'forefathers', transforming, changing,
using parody and pastiche with a swagger that claims a right to being 'post-
Sixties' writers.

Shoneyin's emergence has not been easy. Those birth attendants and
teachers from OUP and CUP, Heinemann and Longmans who stalked the
maternity wards, the primary school-rooms and the senior common rooms in
those now far off Sixties have long since retired. Several, indeed, have
departed for the great editorial office in the sky and their by-lines are not of
this world. Now young women are doing it for themselves. In this case self-
help includes establishing Ovalonian House, an independent outfit that
announces its concern with high production standards through high production values in the volumes being reviewed.

It is significant that Asas Gate is described as 'prominent in the 80s' for these volumes bring together poems that are the harvest of some years of growth, observation, experience and writing. This is work that reaches back and then moves on through the Nineties into the new millennium. There are poems here for the victims of the thugs who brutalized Nigeria during Abacha's reign, both those who did not survive, such as Ken Saro-Wiwa (presented in an unreflective, messianic manner, *Egg*, p. 41), and those who did, including Ogaga Ifowodo to whom Shoneyin sends a 'ballad of rusty hinges' (*Egg*, p. 48).

The fact that pain has not been banished with Abacha's demise and that there is 'unfinished business' for the new era is indicated by the poem for 'Bola Ige that can profitably be read in conjunction with Shoneyin's contribution to Bookcraft's volume marking 'the Passage of a Modern Cicero'. It is also present in her barbed 'Epitaph' for a nation:

Here lie the vestiges of a national disaster
devised by soldiers in fits of laughter.
But wouldn't you be jolly and merry too
If Swiss banks couldn't thrive if it wasn't for you? (*Riverbird*, p. 35)

A wider, continental concern is shown in a poem for Rwandan Refugees who are sharply 'snapped' in a couple of lines: 'Shirtless ribs press through/ the Cyclops lane of misery'. (*Egg*, p. 37).

Tuning in to the voices in which Shoneyin speaks, one occasionally catches the expected legacies of British influence: nursery rhymes, and the Bible make their presence felt. There are also distinctive 'trans-Atlantic usages', possibly encouraged by the period Shoneyin spent on the writers' programme at the University of Iowa in 1999. Sometimes these are incorporated in a self-conscious manipulation of convention, as in 'Jesse Blues' ('to the memory of those who perished when pipelines exploded in Jesse', *Riverbird*, p. 40), sometimes they are slipped into the flowing, dancing verse through a reference to 'candy' or a command to 'listen good'. Despite these usages, and the assured command of English, one can detect an occasional West African trick of speech. It is present in the use of 'parlour' and pervasive in the frames of reference that include Asas Gate! The voice is, thus, 'Cosmopolitan Nigerian'; the address of the publishing house, appropriately, '*New* Bodija Estate, Ibadan'.

The two volumes named above are divided into sections and the sometimes playful sub-headings indicate some of the poet's gender-specific concerns. Sub-headings include *Clitoranguish, Matriscope, Brooding, With Flustered Feathers* and *Clucking*. These provide a context for the effervescent verses in which a variety of forms are confidently handled. These are a quite naturally a young woman's poems, and reflect her concerns, relationships and experiences, the pressures on her, the attitudes she has encountered and those she has adopted to survive. Shoneyin expresses herself with an abundance of wit and sharp observation, and, not surprisingly given the context in which she makes her presence felt, she has provoked antagonism and name-calling. In an on-line interview she says she has 'been called everything from a man-eater to a lesbian to a feminist'. Certainly she adopts many roles and imagines herself speaking, as a dramatist might, for many different people in an abundance of voices. It is to her credit that she encompasses a range of emotions and that she touches pain without becoming maudlin. She hints at anguish without sentimentality.

Shoneyin is acutely aware of the expectations of what was once patronizingly dubbed a 'female pen'. The following complete poem, entitled 'To be Truly Lady-like in Speech', is something of a literary manifesto:

> To be truly lady-like in speech is easy.
> First you strip lusty words
> of their public connotation,
> then you dress them up in fancy frills
> and pretend that your eyes have never beheld a man,
> beautiful and bare (*Egg*, p. 31)

Though some will find the tone occasionally strident, I think that from this, and from the other lines I have purloined for this review, it can be appreciated that Titilola Alexandrah Shoneyin is 'just' a strong individual. She is frank, decisive, direct and has sensibly rejected the insincerity of the historic concept of the 'truly lady-like'. She has dropped the 'Alexandrah' that she was lumbered with at her naming ceremony, and, as 'Lola Shoneyin, is a very welcome addition to the voices from Nigeria currently making themselves heard.

James Gibbs
Bristol

Es'kia Mphahlele, *Down Second Avenue*
Johannesburg: Picador Africa, 2004, 211 pp., R. 95.00; ISBN: 1 7701000-7-5

Childhood can be full of magic and wonder because as the years pass even the most difficult and painful memories fade, losing their edges as nostalgia eats away at them like water wearing away a rock. In Es'kia Mphahlele's *Down Second Avenue*, first published in 1959 and re-issued by Picador Africa in a potentially important new series, childhood retains that wonder and magic, but nostalgia can only cover so much. Like a petticoat peeping out from beneath a skirt, this memoir by the doyen of South African literature allows glimpses that speak not just of magic and wonder but of something insidious.

Mphahlele leads us into the world of a young man trying to come to terms with an existence that becomes stranger and stranger with every passing day. The narrative unravels in a series of gradual progressions: from the provincial to the cosmopolitan, from innocence to experience, from naïve ignorance to growing consciousness. There is magic and wonder aplenty in Maupaneng where the narrator's life begins, but it is a motherless childhood lived in the shadow of poverty and of a miserly grandmother. Nature looms large too, sinister, menacing and dangerous in the hulking mountains and the roaring River Leshoana. However, the real danger does not manifest until the narrator reaches the city, until he arrives at Second Avenue. That is not just a spatio-temporal locale, but also a metaphor for all the places where the poor and oppressed are confined against their will. There, the sinister, the menacing and the dangerous are embodied in the police, the Malaita, as well as in the pervasive poverty and sickness.

Mphahlele's ability to evoke the scenes of childhood in a no-frills, matter-of-fact narrative style imbues this book with beauty. He tells his story with a detached tone which makes the issues he addresses all the more immediate and the pain he evokes all the more intense. For example, we read:

> In a split second I felt a large hand take me by the scruff of the neck and push me out. Another hand from nowhere reached out for me. Another slapped me a few times on the cheek ... I don't know how I was eventually thrust out of the crowd, but I stumbled down the curb. Only then did I feel that someone had kicked me in the back as well.

When he speaks of the incident that finally drove a wedge between his parents, you find it hard to believe that he is speaking about his own parents. 'He limped over to the pot on the stove. In no time it was done. My mother screamed with a voice I have never forgotten till this day. Hot gravy and meat and potatoes had got into her blouse and she was trying to shake them out.' This narrative style also works beautifully in intensifying the movement from smug acceptance to political awakening. Indeed, Mphahlele's realization of his place in the scheme of things as the Apartheid system evolved is at once shocking and poignant. As awareness grows, his mother's advice assumes clarity and gravity. She had said: 'Beware of the white man, he's very, very strong.' Young Es'kia is determined to test that strength and, in doing so, he loses his job, causes his family to suffer and, finally, goes into exile.

Down Second Avenue, a book about a young man born in 1919 coming of age in an oppressive society, speaks of a specific period, but the echoes still reverberate. Its republication in Picador Africa is warmly welcomed.

Toni Kan
Poet and Novelist

Véronique Tadjo, *The Shadow of Imana: Travels in the Heart of Rwanda*. Translated from French by Véronique Wakerley.
Oxford: Heinemann, African Writers Series, 2000, 118pp., £7.75 PB;
ISBN 0435910159

The shocking images of death and suffering from the 1994 massacre in Rwanda left all who saw them reeling at the capacity of human beings for cruelty. They showed the world how ethnic differences can be the cause of immense hatred. Véronique Tadjo's travelogue *Shadow of Imana* makes an important contribution to our understanding of the situation because it illustrates a side of Rwandans not conveyed by the televised images. By recounting what she learned when she visited sites of the genocide in 1998, Tadjo shows that Rwandans are exorcising their horrific past and starting to live again.

A part of a project initiated by the Arts and Media Association in France and aimed at reflecting on the memory of the Rwandan massacre, *The Shadow of Imana* is a detailed account of the author's journey into the heart of

Rwanda. From Mary Kingsley's *Travels in West Africa* (1897) to Catherine Oddie's *Enkop Ai: My Life with the Maasai* (1994) we have been exposed to travelogues written by white women, but this book breaks new ground by recording the travel experiences of a black woman. As far as I know, Tadjo is the first black woman to record her travel experience in Africa in book form.

Through descriptions of the sites of the massacres, by recording the numbers of those who died, by detailing the methods used to kill, as well as through personal stories of the survivors, Tadjo takes us with her on her journey. She lays bare the chaos that engulfed the Rwandan nation in 1994, and forces us to confront what happened. Portraits of victims and narratives of survivors not only convey the enormity of the crimes committed but also provide an opportunity for reflection on larger issues. These include the exercise of political and economic power, ethnic differences and divisions, gender relations, and the attitude of the world community to unity, peace and stability within and among nations.

Tadjo's book goes beyond illustrations of the horrors of the genocide. The narratives of the survivors indicate the resolve of Rwandans to rebuild their lives and their nation. Their stories also demonstrate the gradual but steady process of healing. The narratives show the people's determination to forgive the past in order to create a future for their children, a future in which the experiences of the past are not erased but are used to provide an archive from which lessons can be learnt.

The pain of the 1994 genocide will long haunt Rwanda and the world, but we should also recognize the determination of the people to start again. We must acknowledge their belief in the importance of peace, because, in my view, this makes possible the process of forgiveness. The mingling of the more distant and more recent past is demonstrated in the very structure of the book since Tadjo interlaces horrific accounts of the massacre with poetic passages and traditional folk tales. This pattern indicates not only the hopes and determination of the survivors to live again but also portrays the beauty of their landscape and illustrates everyday Rwandan practices. In daily life a link is established between the people and the spirits of those who have died. Of course, the dead include those who were cut down in 1994 when chaos engulfed a small state and the world watched, shocked, horrified, but inactive.

Elinettie Chabwera
School of English, University of Leeds

Phanuel Akubueze Egejuru, *Chinua Achebe: Pure and Simple, An Oral Biography*
Lagos: Malthouse, 2001, xi + 205 pp., $27.95; ISBN 978 023 148 X

I grew up in the small, serene university town of Nsukka in Eastern Nigeria and the year I turned six, we had new neighbours on the tree-shaded Marguerite Cartwright Avenue. My earliest memories of them are of the twin silver American cars, larger than anything we were used to, which came to reside in the garages next door. Soon, I made friends with the children, particularly the youngest daughter, Nwando, who was my age and in the same class at the University School. Nwando's father, a quiet, kindly gentleman who seemed to speak very little, was the writer, Chinua Achebe. His fame had preceded him and yet, when they came to live next door, he seemed too ordinary, too simple. We found it difficult to believe that this was the author of *Things Fall Apart*, which I had by then, precociously read. Phanuel Egejuru's 2003 oral biography, recreates the essence of this writer who was once called by *The Irish Times* (even as he disclaimed it) 'the man who invented African literature'.

Using words from interviews with over seventy subjects, Achebe's family, friends, colleagues and staff, Egejuru paints an engaging picture of the writer's childhood, upbringing, education, and subsequent career. She explores themes that are reflected in Achebe's work, but is keen to produce a portrait of the man behind the works. Hers is not a critical biography, but an attempt to present to the world a picture of the man, Chinua Achebe.

She is largely successful and in fairly simple, easy to read language captures the simplicity, depth and humanity of the writer. It is apparent from the number of people interviewed, the travelling she has engaged in and the depth of her questioning that Egejuru has devoted a lot of time and effort to this project. She has dug deep for her information. The rooting out must have been a complex process for, as Achebe tells her in speaking about his family, 'I think there is something about our relationships which is difficult to put into words.' From personal experience, I suggest that his statement applies to Igbos generally, and perhaps all Nigerians.

There are moments of humour in the book, especially in the accounts of Achebe's childhood, and some of these are heard through the voices of his older siblings. Surprisingly though the chapter titled 'A Delicate Sense of Humour' contains very few convincing examples of the author's wit.

Egejuru's account shows how her subject has sought to engage with his society to bring about positive change. Through the voices of some of those who worked with him, she provides an insight into Achebe's involvement in politics during the Nigerian Civil War and as Vice-Chairman of the Peoples' Redemption Party from 1982 to 1983. Achebe has not just been cocooned in an abstracted writer's world,

In an important footnote Egejuru declares that when embarking on the project, she 'had no idea that Ezenwa-Ohaeto had already started his mammoth biography' (*Chinua Achebe: A Biography,* James Currey: Oxford 1997). In her Acknowledgements, she thanks Ohaeto (or 'Ezenwa-Ohaeto' as the late scholar, inscrutably, preferred to be known) whose book, she says, was a reference point for comparing information or checking the correct names of individuals. From this it appears that both projects were going forward simultaneously, with the cooperation of the shared subject. Inevitably, one wonders at what point the biographers became aware of this. This matter is relevant since Egejuru, whose book has emerged several years after Ezenwa-Ohaeto's, gives the absence of any scholarly biography of Achebe as one of her main reasons for embarking on her project. Egejuru's study explores Achebe's human relationships in far greater detail than the Ohaeto biography. It provides a view of the writer as a human being, separated from the artist; a separation which Egejuru confesses Achebe is uncomfortable with.

Egejuru compares her role to that of a 'court recorder' merely taking down what her interviewees tell her and reproducing it for the public, but this is disingenuous. Beginning from the Preface, it is clear that Egejuru is not a disinterested stenographer. Her respect for Achebe (which she attempts to justify) permeates the entire book.

Perhaps out of reverence for her subject, she has, like Ohaeto, steered clear of controversy. For instance, Egejuru vigorously defends Achebe on the charge of micro-nationalism that was levelled against him for opposing a state burial for the Yoruba politician, Obafemi Awolowo. But she does not explore Achebe's justification for an incident that occurred while he was a student at Ibadan, one that was grist to the mill of those who claimed Achebe was a tribalist. In the incident, narrated by Chukwuemeka Ike and Mabel Segun, Achebe and others smashed a glass-fronted notice-board and tore down an article that maligned four female undergraduates from Achebe's home region. Egejuru quotes Segun as saying 'I was shocked because I really liked Chinua and I didn't expect him to do that kind of thing. I was a bit hurt because I had been the butt of most of these articles, but Chinua didn't take an axe to defend me. Why should he defend these girls? So I wasn't happy.' Mabel Segun was from what became the Mid-Western Region.

Another issue which Egejuru appears not to have explored sufficiently is Achebe's relationship with Christianity. She cites his brother-in-law as suggesting that Achebe's 'concept of the white man' had negatively affected his Christian faith. In contrast, Achebe's sons recount how their Christian faith helped the family cope after the motor accident in 1990 that left the novelist wheelchair-bound. It would have been enlightening to hear Achebe himself on this issue, particularly in the light of a recent comment by Chimamanda Adichie. Adichie, an Igbo writer who has been compared to Achebe and who grew up in the house in Nsukka in which he used to live, commented as follows on the dilemma facing contemporary Igbo Christians: 'I am also interested in colonized religion, how people like me can profess and preach a respect of their indigenous culture and yet cling so tenaciously to a religion that considers most of that indigenous culture evil.' (www.nigeriansinamerica.com in October 2003) In his autobiographical essay, 'Named for Victoria' (1965, repr. in *Morning Yet on Creation Day*, 1975), Achebe himself has alluded to his position as a child born at the 'crossroads of cultures'.

The packaging of Egejuru's book is unattractive, the print is dense and difficult to read, and there are occasional typographic errors, perhaps the results of the vicissitudes facing the Nigerian publishing industry. Malthouse Publishers have continued to produce titles against the odds, but this book indicates that more attention ought to be paid to presentation. Despite these and other shortcomings, *Chinua Achebe: Pure and Simple An Oral Biography* is an important addition to the ranks of Achebe scholarship. It will be a reference for readers seeking insight to the human Chinua Achebe for many years to come.

Ike Anya
Specialist Registrar, Public Health. Bristol North Primary Care Trust

Pietro Deandrea, *Fertile Crossings: Metamorphoses of Genre in Anglophone West African Literature*
Amsterdam and New York: Rodopi, 2002, xix + 293pp., Hb €70; Pb €30;
PB ISBN 90-420-1478-4

Pietro Deandrea's ambitious monograph is the first of its kind, offering insights into West African prose, poetry and drama, and breaking the generic and thematic boundaries which have contained most literary scholars to date. The book is written in three equal parts – one for each genre – and organized into short, impeccably researched chapters which focus on individual writers. Deandrea analyses the 'cross-contaminations' and metamorphoses of genre to occur in his selected texts: thus the theatricality of West African poetry is assessed, alongside the poetic and lyrical qualities of Anglophone prose and drama. The rationale for this pan-generic enterprise is contained in the opening pages, where Deandrea explains that 'a high degree of incorporativeness' characterizes West African poetry, prose and drama, troubling Western genre classifications (p. xi).

Focusing primarily upon Ghanaian literature, with cross-references to Nigerian writers and to one Sierra Leonean author, Deandrea selects writers whose work appears to 'contaminate' the purity of their chosen genre. His central argument revolves around the notion that Anglophone West African literature is open and malleable, adaptive and transgressive. In part, this transgressiveness occurs as a result of the 'syncretistic' relationship between authors and oral traditions, especially when the folktale trickster or the griot appear on the printed page (pp. 94–7; 168–80). Similarly, West African 'magical realist' authors and their successors fuse genres and styles in a manner that transcends existing categories.

While convincing, this argument reveals the central problem of *Fertile Crossings*, acknowledged by Deandrea in his Introduction: is it not a little ironic, he asks, to divide up an entire book according to the very Eurocentric genre categories which are, in his view, challenged by West African writers (p. xiii)? The open acknowledgement of this paradox does not resolve it: whilst Deandrea occasionally proposes more localized aesthetic criteria for the classification of West African material, the tendency in his book is towards the textual analysis of individual works rather than towards the synthesizing of ideas or the development of a theoretical framework. As a consequence, the unsatisfactory genre divisions remain in place throughout the book to be permanently 'transgressed' by individual West African authors. While his material is handled with great subtlety and sensitivity, this model risks reproducing the very 'empire writes back' concept of postcolonial literature from which the book is keen to distance itself.

In the interests of cultural contextualization, Deandrea rejects postcolonial theory, referring dismissively to a 'Holy Trinity' composed of Homi Bhabha, Edward Said and Gayatri Spivak, each of whom is influenced by French poststructuralist thought (p. xv). Towards the end of the book, however, a curious footnote exempts Spivak from criticism (p. 271); similarly, Said makes no further appearances in the text. The main target emerges as Bhabha, whose supposed lack of sociocultural sensitivity to *any* location is seen to reproduce Eurocentric ideas which erase the meanings conferred in local cultural contexts. In place of these 'high' theorists, Deandrea makes excellent use of the critical work of West African author-intellectuals such as Femi Osofisan and Isidore Okpewho who focus upon local aesthetics, oral traditions, social contexts and histories.

Deandrea's reaction against the 'Holy Trinity' raises ethical questions concerning the uses and misuses of postcolonial theory in West African literary studies. Does postcolonial theory come *at the cost of* indigenous intellectual production and local contexts, necessitating an 'either-or' choice between the two? Why has postcolonial theory failed to 'catch on' with West African intellectuals and literary scholars in the last two decades? Is postcolonial theory to be *defined* by the work of Spivak, Said and Bhabha, or, in a similar manner to Deandrea's privileging of neglected West African writers, can one make use of less prominent theorists and models to develop an understanding of the cross-fertilizations and patterns in West African literature?

Deandrea's skilful, persuasive textual analyses demonstrate his talent and passion for West African literatures, and *Fertile Crossings* is impressive for its refusal to reiterate established debates about canonical West African writers and texts. Many hitherto neglected writers are included alongside the international favourites, and several international favourites are ignored altogether. Thus, unpublished Ghanaian plays are analysed alongside the work of Efua Sutherland; the poetry of Kofi Anyidoho and Kobena Eyi Acquah is discussed at length in preference to the better-known Nigerian poets; Kojo Laing and Syl Cheney-Coker are discussed alongside Ben Okri; and Chinua Achebe's work is not analysed at all. In this manner, Deandrea's selection provides a refreshing alternative to the standard surveys of African literature, and his many interviews with West African authors supplement his analyses with intriguing reflections on writing and reception.

Given the wealth of primary and secondary references in *Fertile Crossings*, the lack of an index is frustrating. Similarly, the publisher has failed to notice one entirely blank page where page 81 ought to be, and a host of minor typos. Nevertheless, the book conveys a strong sense of contemporary literary production in Ghana and Nigeria. Helpful summaries of texts are provided as well as many pages of detailed textual analysis, making the book a useful resource for newcomers to West African literature as well as for specialist researchers. Above all, Deandrea's encyclopaedic approach reinforces a sense of the diversity of literature that is produced in contemporary West Africa and, in so doing, he challenges scholars to think beyond the canon.

Stephanie Newell
English Department, University of Sussex, Brighton, UK

Alain Ricard, *The Languages & Literatures of Africa*
Oxford: James Currey; Trenton, NJ: Africa World Press; Cape Town: David Philip, 2004, 230 pp., £15.95; PB ISBN 0-85255-581-4, HB 0-85255-582-2

This is a fascinating book for Anglophone readers concerned with African languages and literatures primarily because it has been written by a Francophone author, and was indeed published ten years ago in a first version in French. Alain Ricard is an unusual Francophone writer given his longstanding interests in the work of such as Wole Soyinka and the Tanzanian playwright, Ebrahim Hussein, as well as in African language literary production, and one feels a significant subtext to this book is his urgent desire to promote an exchange of dialogue between the Francophone and Anglophone literary worlds – not forgetting Lusophone interests which are also touched on. Whilst I would by no means wish to denigrate the excellent work of a small group of Anglophone scholars in promoting interest in the Francophone African literary world, it is not often that those of us whose French is not as good as it might be have the opportunity to see so clearly into the mindset of African literature as viewed from France.

Ricard is also engaging because he is a great enthusiast, both for African writing and for exploring the role of African languages in literary production – the latter an area that has received little interest traditionally in Francophone literary studies. However I do find his habit of handing down emphatic judgements – Soyinka is the pre-eminent African playwright, and Senghor the supreme African poet – a little irritating, especially as the grounds for such judgements are not explored with great complexity. Indeed complexity of debate is on a number of occasions a casualty in this book, and this is understandable given that in less than three hundred pages Ricard is trying to cover Africa's entire literary production over the period of the twentieth century.

The Languages and Literatures of Africa can be seen as a book of two halves. The first six chapters concern themselves primarily with African oral, manuscript and published production in African languages or in translation from African languages. In this section Ricard gives a concise and eminently readable history of a number of African language literatures. He freely acknowledges his debt to such as the great African linguistic scholar Albert Gérard, and builds on this work with insights drawn from his own considerable travels round Africa. The second part of the book moves closer to the present in its study of the three genres, poetry, theatre and the novel, as written in French or English.

I say Ricard moves closer to the present because it seems to me that the most glaring problem for this text is that, though recently published, and though Ricard says he has updated the 1995 French version, it is quite dated. He discusses the Yoruba travelling theatre, for example, as a vibrant phenomenon; yet that theatre has for many years now been in eclipse, largely superseded by video making, which is never mentioned. While he is enormously interested in examples of how languages are interwoven in literary production Ricard never appears to have heard of such experiments as that carried out by leading Zimbabwean playwright, Cont Mhlanga, in the 1980s and '90s in writing his plays in what he dubbed 'Ndenglish', a conscious mixture of English and Ndebele chosen to maximize audience accessibility. While Ricard celebrates early Amharic literary production in Ethiopia no post-1970 texts are mentioned, and the burgeoning Tigrinya literature of Eritrea, a country that only came into nationhood in 1991, is utterly ignored. Basically Alan Ricard is an unreliable witness for literary production after the 1980s and it would have been much better for his book if this time limitation had been acknowledged.

Ricard's agenda to this book becomes increasingly clear in the reading. He believes that great writing will emerge when the sensibilities of Europe and Africa mutually fertilize African writing, and he argues that 'The fundamental question is one of exchange, of *métissage*, of mutual appropriation' (p. 197). It is on the grounds of lack of interest in African cultural and linguistic forms that Ricard criticizes much Francophone literature, seeing it as suffering from an elitist cultural strait-jacket that believes only French-educated African intellectuals can produce significant literature. Wole Soyinka is heaped with praise at every mention precisely because he is seen as embodying 'mutual appropriation' of European and Yoruba language and cultural forms in his drama. Yet surely Ricard's approach remains significantly, if not imperialist, at least post-imperialist. Why must African writers learn from Europe in order to be great? And who is to judge of this greatness? Europeans? European-educated Africans? Maybe African writers would like to learn from each other. When European writers are required to learn from African literature – as indeed many world musicians have learnt, even if indirectly, from African music, then Ricard may make his demands for *métissage*, until then he should perhaps continue to seek to decolonize his mind.

Jane Plastow
Theatre Studies, Workshop Theatre, and Centre for African Studies,
University of Leeds

Ola Rotimi, ed. *Issues in African Theatre*
Ibadan: Humanities Publishers, 2001, 125pp., £14.95 / $24.95; ISBN 978-36266-5-5
Distributed by African Books Collective, www.africanbookscollective.com

A new publication with the name of the once boundlessly energetic 'Ola Rotimi' on the cover and dated 2001 comes as more than a surprise. An explanation for this voice from beyond the grave is provided by Uko Atai's Preface that concludes

> Professor Ola Rotimi started work as the 'Guest Editor' on what is now, three years after, this book. We, the so-called 'younger generation', are deeply honoured to complete the work and place this book in your hands, and hopefully in your minds.

Readers have in their hands a volume that, as Rotimi, might have put it, spans the 'giddy gamut of debates and issues raised in and around the Nigerian theatre'. The volume contains eight papers, notes on contributors and an index. The papers include tightly focused essays on particular writers or individual works (Rotimi on Efua Sutherland, Charles Uji on Bode Sowande, Oluwalomoloye Bateye on an Adam Fiberesima operetta), down-to-earth accounts of 'theatre matters' (Olalere Oladitan on performers and copyright, Olu Akomolafe on building an audience on a university campus) and more general studies of form and ideology. In the last category, I place S.E.T. Gbilekaa on radical poetics, Atai on language issues and Foluke Ogunleye on Nigerian television drama.

Despite the fact that the book appeared at the dawn of the twenty-first century there is a sense that it has been held up in the understreams waiting to be born. This is partly because several of the papers visit the quite distant past and rely on 'yesterday's' resources. Bateye examines an operetta written in 1971 and Akomolafe describes a marketing drive undertaken in 1986. The musty smell would not matter so much if one felt that the authors of other papers had been able to keep up with the critical debates. However, again and again one glances down the sources quoted for recent publications, and one looks almost in vain for references dating from the 1990s. I think that only Oladitan, who refers to a Copyright (Amendment) Decree of 1992, and Uji, who lists an Osofisan play published in 1995 and an essay of his own that appeared in 1996, respond to work done in the decade prior to the publication.

I suspect the problem is that university libraries in Nigeria have simply not been able to keep up with purchasing new titles. The contributors don't complain but their anguish at their inability to engage with basic texts is felt. It can be sensed in Ogunleye's comment that 'the script (of Soyinka's TV play *My Father's Burden*) [was] not available' (p. 74). Her lack of contact with this landmark text in Nigerian television drama reduces the value of her account of television drama in Nigeria, particularly since it is not clear what she bases her remarks about the play on. In the absence of library holdings of ephemeral and, possibly, of Lindfors' magisterial series, *Black African Literature in English*, it is apparent that some researchers have to depend on the support, good will and files of their colleagues. For example Atai writes that Abiola Irele's paper on 'The Achievement of Wole Soyinka' was made available to him by Kole Omotoso. In fact, this should have been in any decent Nigerian library of 'Af. Lit. Crit.' since it was reprinted, as 'The Significance of Wole Soyinka', in *Perspectives on Nigerian Literature: 1700 to the Present, Volume One*, edited by Yemi Ogunbiyi and published by Guardian Books, Lagos (1988).

A cry of a different sort is heard in Uji's first note where he cites his own University of Ibadan thesis and adds:

> For the purpose of keeping the records straight I must bring to the readers' notice the fact that a substantial part of this particular work has been ignominiously and mercilessly plagiarised for a BA project [.... submitted] to an artistic department in one of Nigeria's universities in the 1988/89 session.

He adds 'It is needless to name the plagiarist and the department concerned' (p. 62).

Plagiarism is an ever-increasing problem in universities world-wide, but I don't think academics have to worry about 'keeping the records straight' by listing plagiarized undergraduate work. I suggest that, perversely, a scrap of hope can be snatched from this story since it seems to involve a student who consulted an unpublished thesis. The use to which that privilege was put is despicable, but it is good news that there was a library with an accessible thesis.

While some of the contributions to *Issues in African Theatre* are written with admirable clarity, I find that lucidity is sometimes lost and I must, in closing, signal my concern. It may seem churlish to draw attention to Rotimi in this regard, but his paper does stand at the front of the collection and it does introduce a manner that others follow, with variations. When Rotimi turned his attention to Sutherland's *Foriwa* and wrote that it 'visualizes the ideal of a new nation, highlighting such patriotic motifs as inter-ethnic mutuality and a positive cleavage with the insularity and petty prejudices of the past', I wish he had expressed himself more simply. I wish he had aimed for clarity rather than resonance, precision rather than alliteration. On the stage such rhetoric may impress, on the page, and this is a book of sentences about not for the stage, it confuses.

James Gibbs
Bristol

Flora Veit-Wild & Dirk Naguschewski (eds)
Body, Sexuality, and Gender: Versions and Subversions in African Literatures 1, Matatu 29-30
Amsterdam/New York: Rodopi, 2005, xix + 274 pp., €65 / $ 81;
ISBN 90-420-1626-4

This *Matatu* volume presents thought-provoking readings of body, sexuality and gender in contemporary African literature. The essays collected by Flora Veit-Wild and Dirk Naguschewski demonstrate that African literature has undergone a significant revolution: cultural shifts in African societies have paved the way for an environment in which issues of gender and sexuality are no longer submerged. Now some authors discuss sex more openly. The diversity of this volume supports the editors' premise that African literature, with its many versions and subversions, is not monolithic and cannot be subjected to a single uniform truth of theoretical discourse. Their volume delves into the critical examination of body, sexuality and gender in Africa, uncovers the secrecy of the past, challenges the superiority of some theoretical arguments, and explores taboo subjects such as homosexuality and lesbianism.

'Gendered Bodies', the first of four main sections, explores the manifold gifts of the female body. Chikwenye Okonjo Ogunyemi discussing Bessie Head's *Maru* demonstrates that women who are gifted with supernatural power can invade male spaces and participate in the (re)negotiation of global power relations. Robert Muponde takes up Yvonne Vera's *Butterfly is Burning* and examines how women negotiate their positions using their bodies and sexual pleasure to gain power over men. The issue is complicated, however, because just as woman's body is a gift that may arouse pleasure and passion, it can also be invaded, violated and injured. *Tu t'appelleras Tanga* by Calixthe Beyala is the text for Sigrid G. Köhler's essay. Köhler explains how the woman-to-woman relationship between black and the white female prisoners can develop a logic of its own. Focusing on feminist fiction by men, Monica Bungaro discloses how male authors, such as Nuruddin Farah, Abdulrazak Gurnah, André Brink, and Ben Okri, have come to see the need for shifting gender relations.

'Queered Bodies', the second section of the book, confronts the topics of homosexuality and bisexuality in literature and cinema. Using Queer Theory to analyse South African literature, Cheryl Stobie identifies the strategies that successfully subvert dominant binaries. Drew Shaw draws on Dambudzo Marechera's works to reconstruct the argument about homosexuality in Africa that has been fuelled by President Mugabe's hate speeches and shows how the male body is used as a site for contested masculinity. Marechera's writings are distinctive in pointing to what some have regarded as taboo subjects. Vera's *Butterfly is Burning* and Tsitsi Dangaremba's *Nervous Conditions* provide the background for Elleke Boehmer's discussion of lesbianism as an 'un-realized' form of self-expression. Unoma N. Azuah identifies a number of Nigerian female writers who explicitly deal with lesbianism in their works. The recently established voices of 'Lola Shoneyin, Promise Okekwe, Temilola Abioye, and Azuah herself radically confront men's dominant position and also challenge the positions of well-known Nigerian feminist writers. Alexie Tcheuyap discusses the representation of nudity and homosexuality in African films and concludes that the representation falls between the genres of eroticism and pornography.

The third section of the substantial collection of essays, 'Tainted Bodies', concentrates on pigmentation and examines the meanings attached to skin colour. Susan Arndt points out that non-Western cultures have received comparatively little attention in Western gender studies and that, while whiteness is 'unmarked' among Western feminists, blackness is a 'marked' category. She questions the approach of white feminists delineating a universal 'womanness' in not taking into consideration the cultural differences between African and Western cultures. Jessica Hemmings draws attention to the dangers of skin-bleaching creams and the way skin bleaching projects two selves into the public world: the fabricated and the natural. Sarah Nuttall, in presenting a textual analysis of poems by Arthur Nortje, identifies the notions of anatomy and flesh and discusses the relationship between the body and the composition of poetry. Alioune Sow concludes the section on 'Tainted Bodies' with remarks about the ways in which African writers use physical disabilities to illustrate both variations and alterations in society. Disabled bodies are integrated into society to show the contrast these bodies offer and the new literary spaces they open up.

The final section, 'Violated Bodies', explores the traumatic effects of war and rape on women. Akachi Adimora-Ezeigbo and Marion Pape examine Nigerian war literature written by female authors. Works in this category invade male spaces and challenge dominant paradigms projected by male authors. Female writers have embarked on constructing and reconstructing women's experiences during the Nigerian Civil War, focusing on the role of women in keeping families together. Women are envisioned as holding the key to peace in war-torn communities. The writings of Flora Nwapa, Buchi Emecheta, Leslie Ofoegbu and Rose Njoku are used to show that, while women have been involved in war, they have remained invisible in the representation of war, gaining visibility only by providing their own accounts. Martina Kopf discusses Yvonne Vera's *Under the Tongue* and Lucy Graham uses J.M Coetzee's *Disgrace* to explore women and children's traumatic experience of sexual abuse.

Body, Sexuality, and Gender questions the supremacy of certain theoretical discussions, unravelling the canonical order of literary texts in the process. It is a groundbreaking volume that will undoubtedly appeal to many readers of African literature. However, it should be pointed out that it privileges some forms of African creativity over others by largely neglecting African drama. Furthermore, there is imbalance in the gender representation of the authors and issues: most of the authors are women, and female issues dominate the discussions. As a book breaking into new spaces, it is important to give equal representation to the sexes. It must be said that African men have received very little critical examination in gender studies. I would add that some of the essays attempt to cover too many works, making it impossible to offer detailed discussions of individual titles, and, some are more concerned with discussing Western literary theories than African literature.

Despite these shortcomings, *Body, Sexuality, and Gender* contains impressive, insightful readings of bodies, sexuality and gender in Africa literature. The examination of specific works from specific African societies – North, South, East, and West African authors – means the book avoids the common error of generalization. Flora Veit-Wild and Dirk Naguschewski have achieved their goal of laying out new paths for African literature as a means of escaping archaic inscriptions and debates.

Wisdom Agorde
Department of English and Film Studies, University of Alberta,
Edmonton, AB

Short Notices from the Editor of the Reviews Section

Ekasa Scribes, *Face to Face: Poems and Short Stories About a Virus*
Accra: Woeli, 2004, 101 p., £14.95; ISBN 9988626088

This publication brings together the work of competition prize-winners who took part in a workshop led by German novelist Norman Ohler and funded by the Goethe Institute, Accra. The competition, that attracted more than 170 submissions, was for writing on the topic of AIDS, and AIDS was also the focus of the workshop.

Ohler observes in his Introduction that 'None of [the participants] had any desire to write about AIDS prior to the workshop'. Alarm bells should have started ringing at this point, and, although interest was engaged and work was produced, there are only a few moments when the contributors to *Face to Face* hint at genuine engagement with the topic.

Publication of these stories and poems is premature, and I fear that I cannot recommend this volume. Librarians who do order it will encounter problems with cataloguing since 'Ekasa Scribes' is the name chosen by the members of the workshop as a communal identity. I suggest that they regard the volume as by 'Asabea Acquah and others'. Acquah's contribution, a story entitled 'Yaw', opens strongly and has some well-observed details, that, I am confident, would generate lively discussion. By encouraging rigorous attention to writing skills and to the handling of the issues raised, group contributions might propel the author towards moulding her narrative into publishable shape.

While the prose pieces in this collection are generally stronger than the verse, all the submissions require attention on the two fundamental points just referred to: writing skills and handling issues. In view of these comments, there are clearly fundamental questions to be asked about the process by which this material leapt into print.

African Visions 2003, Women of Africa Voices from the Motherland, a celebration of contemporary African writing organized by the Africa Centre, 38 King Street, Covent Garden, London WC2E 8JT
arts@africacentre.org.uk/www.africacentre.org/africanvisions2003.htm
VHS and c.d.

During 2003, the staff of the Africa Centre organized a tour of the UK by Tsitsi Dangarembga, Assia Djebar and Lila Momple. In sessions chaired by Yasmin Alibhai Brown, Fay Weldon, Sue MacGregor, Beverley Naidoo, Patrick Neate and Aminatta Forna, they visited, usually in full strength, the Ilkley Literature Festival, the British Empire and Commonwealth Museum (Bristol), the Cheltenham Festival of Literature, the Royal Festival Hall (London), the Birmingham Book Festival and Leicester Libraries.

The ambitious programme brought together writers who work in different languages and this meant the proceedings were slowed down by translations. From my experience in Bristol, and from the edited versions, this was only a minor problem and always a useful reminder of the issues of transmission that we all face all the time. Such literary events are usually entirely ephemeral, but on this occasion 65-minute compact disc and VHS recordings of the presentations and exchanges were produced. The edited version gives an immediate sense of exchange and encounter that will be of value to teachers and students.

James Gibbs

Index

Veit-Wild, Flora (ed.), *Body,
    Sexuality & Gender,* 166-8
Vera, Yvonne, 3, 7, 9, 87-102, 166-7
    Butterfly Burning, 3
    Stone Virgins, xiv, 3-6, 9, 87-
        102
    Under the Tongue, 3, 167

Wood, Molara, Uzodinma Iweala:
    Beasts of No Nation, 145-8

Zambia, 3, 103-4
Zeleeza, Robert, *Exile,* 3
Zimbabwe, xiv, 2-3, 5-7, 11-2, 87-
    102, 103-5, 107, 109-11, 142-4,
    163; civil war, 95-7, 99
    ZANLA, 87, 89, 91-3, 95-6, 100
    ZANU, 87, 90-4, 97-100
    ZAPU, 87, 92-3, 95-7
    ZIPRA, 87, 95, 97, 101